THE CONSTITUTIONAL STATUS
OF ACADEMIC TENURE

This is a volume in the Arno Press collection

THE ACADEMIC PROFESSION

Advisory Editor
Walter P. Metzger

Editorial Board
Dietrich Goldschmidt
A. H. Halsey
Martin Trow

See last pages of this volume
for a complete list of titles.

THE CONSTITUTIONAL STATUS
OF ACADEMIC TENURE

Edited by
Walter P. Metzger

ARNO PRESS

A New York Times Company

New York / 1977

Editorial Supervision: MARIE STARECK

———◆———

Reprint Edition 1977 by Arno Press Inc.

Copyright © 1977 by Arno Press Inc.

THE ACADEMIC PROFESSION
ISBN for complete set: 0-405-10000-0
See last pages of this volume for titles.

Manufactured in the United States of America

———◆———

Library of Congress Cataloging in Publication Data

Main entry under title:

The Constitutional status of academic tenure.

    (The Academic profession)
    Reprint of 12 pamphlets published between 1879-1974 by
various publishers.
    CONTENTS: Byse, C. Academic freedom, tenure, and the
law.--Pettigrew, H. W. Constitutional tenure.--Finkin,
M. W. Toward a law of academic status. [etc.]
    1. College teachers--Legal status, laws, etc.--
United States--Addresses, essays, lectures. 2. College
teachers--Legal status, laws, etc.--United States--Cases.
3. College teachers--Tenure--United States--Addresses,
essays, lectures. I. Metzger, Walter P. II. Series.
KF4240.A75C65   344'.73'078   76-52627
ISBN 0-405-09982-7

ACKNOWLEDGMENTS

"Academic Freedom, Tenure, and the Law: A Comment on *Worzella* v. *Board of Regents* by Clark Byse from *Harvard Law Review,* Volume 73, 1959-1960, Copyright © 1959, 1960 by The Harvard Law Review Association, was reprinted by permission of the *Harvard Law Review* and the author.

" 'Constitutional Tenure': Toward a Realization of Academic Freedom" by Harry W. Pettigrew from *Case Western Reserve Law Review,* Volume 22, Number 3, April 1971, Copyright © 1971 by Case Western Reserve University was reprinted by permission of *Case Western Reserve Law Review.*

"Toward a Law of Academic Status" by Matthew W. Finkin from *Buffalo Law Review,* Volume XXII, 1972-1973, Copyright 1973, *Buffalo Law Review* was reprinted by permission of the *Buffalo Law Review.*

"The Supreme Court Speaks to the Untenured: A Comment on *Board of Regents* v. *Roth* and *Perry* v. *Sindermann*" by William Van Alstyne from *AAUP Bulletin,* Volume 58, Number 3, September 1972, © 1972, American Association of University Professors was reprinted by permission of the American Association of University Professors.

Permission to reprint "Employment of Nontenured Faculty: Some Implications of *Roth* and *Sindermann*" written by Carol Herrnstadt Shulman has been obtained from *Denver Law Journal,* University of Denver, (Colorado Seminary), College of Law. This article appeared in Volume 51 of the *Denver Law Journal* at pages 215 through 233. Copyright © 1974 by the *Denver Law Journal,* University of Denver, (Colorado Seminary), College of Law.

CONTENTS

Byse, Clark
ACADEMIC FREEDOM, TENURE, AND THE LAW: A Comment on
Worzella v. *Board of Regents* (Reprinted from *Harvard Law Review,*
Volume 73), Cambridge, 1959

Pettigrew, Harry W.
"CONSTITUTIONAL TENURE:" Toward a Realization of Academic
Freedom (Reprinted from *Case Western Reserve Law Review,*
Volume 22), Cleveland, 1971

Finkin, Matthew W.
TOWARD A LAW OF ACADEMIC STATUS (Reprinted from *Buffalo
Law Review,* Volume XXII), Buffalo, New York, 1972

Van Alstyne, William
THE SUPREME COURT SPEAKS TO THE UNTENURED: A Comment
on *Board of Regents* v. *Roth* and *Perry* v. *Sindermann* (Reprinted from
AAUP Bulletin, Volume 58), Washington, D. C., 1972

Shulman, Carol Herrnstadt
EMPLOYMENT OF NONTENURED FACULTY: Some Implications of
Roth and *Sindermann* (Reprinted from *Denver Law Journal,* Volume 51),
Denver, 1974

*THE BOARD OF REGENTS OF THE KANSAS STATE
AGRICULTURAL COLLEGE* v. *B. F. MUDGE* (1878)

PEOPLE ex rel. KELSEY v. *NEW YORK POSTGRADUATE MEDICAL
SCHOOL AND HOSPITAL* (1898)

COBB v. *HOWARD UNIVERSITY* (1939)

W. W. WORZELLA, Plaintiff and Appellant, v. *THE BOARD OF
REGENTS OF EDUCATION OF THE STATE* of South Dakota, and
Harry J. Eggen, Frank Gellerman, Eric Heidepriem, Byron Helgerson,
Lem Overpeck, Maylou Amunson, Dona S. Brown, as Members of said
Board, and H. M. Crothers, Acting President of South Dakota State
College, Defendants and Respondents (1958)

BOARD OF REGENTS OF STATE COLLEGES et al v. *ROTH* (1972)

PERRY et al. v. *SINDERMANN* (1972)

*ARNETT, DIRECTOR, OFFICE OF ECONOMIC OPPORTUNITY,
et al.* v. *KENNEDY et al.* (1974)

ACADEMIC FREEDOM, TENURE AND THE LAW

A Comment on *Worzella* v.
Board of Regents

Clark Byse

$\boxed{C\ O\ M\ M\ E\ N\ T\ S}$

ACADEMIC FREEDOM, TENURE, AND THE LAW: A COMMENT ON WORZELLA v. BOARD OF REGENTS †

Clark Byse *

THE unique responsibilities of colleges and universities in the United States are to extend the frontiers of knowledge, to make available to students the wisdom and knowledge of the past, and to help them to develop their capacities for critical, independent thought. If these vital tasks are to be performed with any degree of success, teachers in institutions of higher learning in this country must be as free as possible from restraints and pressures which inhibit independent thought and action. They must, to use a customary phrase, be free to pursue truth wherever it may lead.

This justification of freedom for teachers is essentially the same as that which accounts for the inclusion in state and federal constitutions of prohibitions against governmental interference with freedom of expression. Free trade in ideas is indispensable to enlightened community decision and action.[1] But there is more to academic freedom. As Professor Machlup has written:

> Professors need more than this absence of governmental sanctions, more than a guarantee that they will not be jailed for the expressions of their thoughts. If they are to be encouraged to pursue the truth wherever it may lead . . . they need protection from all more material sanctions, especially from dismissal. . . .
> . . . . More than in most other occupations, the dismissal of a

---

† 93 N.W.2d 411 (S.D. 1958).

* Professor of Law, Harvard Law School. B.E., Wisconsin State Teachers College, 1935; LL.B., Wisconsin, 1938; LL.M., Columbia, 1939, J.S.D., 1952.

[1] Mill's classic expression is worth repeating:

[T]he peculiar evil of silencing the expression of an opinion is, that it is robbing the human race; posterity as well as the existing generation; those who dissent from the opinion, still more than those who hold it. If the opinion is right, they are deprived of the opportunity of exchanging error for truth: if wrong, they lose, what is almost as great a benefit, the clearer perception and livelier impression of truth, produced by its collision with error.

MILL, *On Liberty*, in UTILITARIANISM, LIBERTY AND REPRESENTATIVE GOVERNMENT 81, 104 (Everyman's ed. 1951).

professor jeopardizes or destroys his eligibility for another position in his occupation. The occupational work of the vast majority of people is largely independent of their thought and speech. The professor's work *consists* of his thought and speech.[2] If he loses his position for what he writes or says, he will, as a rule, have to leave his profession, and may no longer be able effectively to question and challenge accepted doctrines or effectively to defend challenged doctrines. And if *some* professors lose their positions for what they write or say, the effect on many other professors will be such that their usefulness to their students and to society will be gravely reduced.[3]

The principal means for protecting faculty members from unjustified dismissals is tenure.[4] The most widely accepted statement of academic tenure, formulated by the Association of American Colleges and the American Association of University Professors, provides: "After the expiration of a probationary period, teachers or investigators should have permanent or continuous tenure, and their services should be terminated only for adequate cause, except in the case of retirement for age or, under extraordinary circumstances, because of financial exigencies."[5] There are many variations and modifications of this basic idea in the tenure plans of American colleges and universities. But the essential characteristic of tenure is continuity of service, in that the institu-

---

[2] See CHAFEE, THE BLESSINGS OF LIBERTY 250 (1956): "Professors are different from the general run of people. They ought to be different. Most people think in order to take action. Professors ought to think for the sake of thinking." (Footnote not in the original.)

[3] Machlup, *On Some Misconceptions Concerning Academic Freedom*, 41 AMERICAN ASS'N OF UNIVERSITY PROFESSORS BULL. 753, 755-56 (1955).

[4] For a discussion of other justifications of academic tenure, see Stene, *Bases of Academic ·Tenure*, 41 AMERICAN ASS'N OF UNIVERSITY PROFESSORS BULL. 584 (1955).

It must be recognized that tenure can become an instrument to perpetuate incompetence and mediocrity rather than to advance scholarship and talent. But the fact that tenure can be debased does not mean that it is less valuable. It means only that other processes must not be neglected — including careful selection of those to whom tenure is awarded and courageous action by administrators and faculty to weed out those who thereafter become professionally unfit.

[5] 1940 Statement of Principles on Academic Freedom and Tenure, in 44 AMERICAN ASS'N OF UNIVERSITY PROFESSORS BULL. 290, 291-92 (1958). The statement was originally formulated and endorsed by the Association of American Colleges and the American Association of University Professors, and was later adopted by the following organizations: American Library Association; Association of American Law Schools; American Political Science Association; American Association of Colleges for Teacher Education; Association for Higher Education, National Educational Association; American Philosophical Association; Southern Society for Philosophy and Psychology. *Id.* at 290.

tion in which the teacher serves has in some manner relinquished the freedom or power it otherwise would possess to terminate the teacher's services.[6]

A helpful analogy to academic freedom and tenure may be found in what may be termed "judicial freedom and tenure." The Constitution provides: "The Judges, both of the supreme and inferior Courts, shall hold their Offices during good Behaviour, and shall, at stated Times, receive for their Services a Compensation which shall not be diminished during their Continuance in Office." [7] The standard of "good behavior" for the continuance in office, Hamilton wrote, "is the best expedient which can be devised in any government, to secure a steady, upright, and impartial administration of the laws." [8] Such a standard for continued employment of faculty members who have proved their competence during a probationary period similarly provides a safeguard from restraints and pressures which otherwise might deter a "steady, upright, and impartial" performance of the teacher's indispensable task of critical thought and analysis.[9]

The principle of academic tenure is almost universally recognized in American higher education.[10] But it is not so widely understood by practitioners in other professions, including the bar and the judiciary. It is this lack of understanding which probably accounts for the decision of the Supreme Court of South Dakota in *Worzella v. Board of Regents of Educ.*,[11] in which the court — in sustaining Dr. Worzella's dismissal by the board — held that the tenure plan of the South Dakota State College of Agriculture and Mechanics Arts violated the state constitution.

---

[6] Security against dismissal may be for a fixed term, or for the professional life of the teacher; in the former case the tenure is "limited," in the latter it is "indefinite," "continuous," or "permanent."

[7] U.S. CONST. art. III, § 1.

[8] THE FEDERALIST No. 78, at 483 (Gideon ed. 1818) (Hamilton). In *id.* No. 79, at 491, Hamilton stressed that *"a power over a man's subsistence amounts to a power over his will."*

[9] See CHAFEE, *op. cit. supra* note 2, at 241: "The government pays judges, but it does not tell them how to decide. An independent . . . university is as essential to the community as an independent judiciary."

[10] For a dissenting view, see Post, *On Relinquishing Tenure*, Vassar Alumnae Magazine, March 1959, p. 13. See also Podell, *Assault from Within*, 65 COMMONWEAL 427, 429 (1957), which states that academic freedom is rarely infringed by the "dramatic dismissal of a professor. Often, less noticed but more effective limitations are accomplished through the altering of employment practices, standards, budgets, salaries and curricula . . . ."

[11] 93 N.W.2d 411 (S.D. 1958).

The purpose of this Comment is to appraise the court's handling of this important academic-freedom and tenure case. The merits of Dr. Worzella's discharge will not be discussed, for I am not here concerned with the propriety either of his actions or of those of the Board of Regents. The primary objective is to invite attention to the very serious shortcomings in the court's reasoning, so that other judges, who may in the future be faced with a similar problem, will not lightly follow the *Worzella* case. It is hoped also that the discussion might contribute to a better understanding by the bar and judiciary of the role of the law in maintaining and protecting academic freedom and tenure in American higher education.[12]

FACTS, HOLDING, AND OPINION

The Board of Regents of Education of the State of South Dakota approved a Statement of Tenure Policy of the South Dakota State College of Agriculture and Mechanic Arts in 1952.[13] The statement provided that after service of a probationary period faculty members should have "permanent tenure," and that tenure could be terminated by a reduction of staff due to "financial circumstances," or by "dismissal for cause." The president was given power to bring charges which were to be heard by an elected faculty committee. The hearing before the committee was to be "conducted according to such rules of procedure as the committee may establish," but the statement specifically provided that the accused teacher should be "entitled to representation" by a person of his choice, should be confronted with the witnesses against him, and should have the right to present witnesses and documentary evidence on his behalf and to cross-examine opposing witnesses. A full stenographic record was to be kept, and the hearing committee was to make findings and recommendations. The recommendations and transcript of the record were to be filed with the president. The president was to "make the decision whether to recom-

---

[12] For a more complete discussion of the role of the law in tenure cases, see BYSE & JOUGHIN, TENURE IN AMERICAN HIGHER EDUCATION: PLANS, PRACTICES, AND THE LAW (1959). Chapter III, "Tenure and the Law," discusses various legal problems presented by tenure plans and practices of American colleges and universities. I have drawn heavily on this volume in preparing this comment.

[13] [1951–52] 32 S.D. REGENTS OF EDUC. BIENNIAL REP. 365 (1953). The statement of tenure policy, which is printed in *id.* at 365–69, is reproduced in the appendix to this Comment. For the text of a tenure-policy statement which preceded submission and approval of the State College statement, see *id.* at 300–01.

mend dismissal" to the Board of Regents. A faculty member whose dismissal was recommended by the president had the right to "appeal for a hearing before the Regents."

At the time the tenure statement was approved, Dr. W. W. Worzella was a member of the faculty of South Dakota State College. He had been appointed Professor of Agronomy in 1943 and had served continuously until his discharge by the Board of Regents on January 11, 1958, at which time he was head of the Department of Agronomy. The circumstances of his dismissal are thus summarized in the opinion of the Supreme Court of South Dakota:

> He [Dr. Worzella] was dismissed after an extensive investigation into the personnel and administrative affairs of State College by the Board. After the investigation the Board prepared a written report. With reference to Dr. Worzella the Board found he " . . . wittingly or unwittingly, permitted himself and his name to become involved in serious personal disputes and activities in the many years above referred to, and has . . . been guilty of insubordination; that by virtue of the controversial character he has become, it would not be to the best interests of South Dakota State College for him to be retained." The Board concluded "the retention of Dr. W. W. Worzella as head of the Department of Agronomy is incompatible to the best interest and welfare of State College. its students, and the State of South Dakota as a whole, and that he should be summarily dismissed and relieved from all further duties under his current contract; his compensation, however, to continue as therein provided during the remainder of this fiscal year." His summary dismissal followed.[14]

Dr. Worzella sought a writ of mandamus to compel the board to reinstate him. It was conceded that he held "permanent tenure" under the statement of tenure policy approved in 1952 and that the procedure outlined in the statement had not been observed in his dismissal. The trial court refused relief,[15] and he appealed.

The Supreme Court of South Dakota affirmed. The court's opinion is not entirely clear but the rationale of the decision appears to be that the statement of tenure policy was invalid because it conflicted with the provision in the state constitution that the college

---

[14] 93 N.W.2d at 412.
[15] Worzella v. Board of Regents, S.D. Cir. Ct., March 10, 1958.

should be "under the control of" the board.[16] The court said: "Without the right to employ, and power to discharge, its employees the Board loses its constitutional right of control."[17] Under the terms of the statement of tenure policy "apparently the Board could not discharge or remove a faculty member with tenure for any reason if the President failed or refused to file a complaint, or if the Tenure Committee and the President failed or refused to recommend dismissal."[18] Such a limitation is an "unlawful encroachment upon the Board of Regents' . . . power of control over such college."[19]

---

[16] S.D. Const. art. XIV, § 3 provides: "The state university, the agricultural college, the normal schools and all other [state-supported] educational institutions . . . shall be under the control of a board of five members appointed by the governor and confirmed by the senate under such rules and restrictions as the legislature shall provide." Pursuant to this authority the legislature provided for the appointment of a Board of Regents and gave the board broad powers of governance. The court quoted the following South Dakota statutory provisions:

> The Board of Regents is authorized to employ and dismiss all officers, instructors. and employees of such institutions, necessary to the proper management thereof, to determine their number, qualifications, and duties, fix the term of their employment, and rate and manner of their compensation, and provide for sabbatical leave on part pay; provided, that no person shall be employed or dismissed by reason of any sectarian or political opinions held.

S.D. Code § 15.0709 (1939);

> The Board of Regents shall have power to enact and enforce all rules and regulations, not in conflict with any law, and deemed necessary by it for the wise and successful management of the institutions under its control and for the government of students and employees therein.
> The Board may delegate provisionally to the president, dean, principal, or faculty of any school under its control, so much of the authority conferred by this section as in its judgment seems proper and in accordance with the usual custom in such cases.

S.D. Code § 15.0714 (1939).

The court stated that these code provisions "merely confirm and clarify the Board of Regents' constitutional power to employ and dismiss all officers, instructors and employees at all institutions under its control. These provisions become a part of every contract of employment entered into by the Board. Gillan v. Board of Regents of Normal Schools, 88 Wis. 7, 58 N.W. 1042, 24 L.R.A. 336 [1894]. It cannot be restricted, surrendered, or delegated away." 93 N.W.2d at 413.

The court did not quote S.D. Code § 15.0708 (1939) which provides in part, "Except as otherwise expressly provided in this Code, the Board of Regents shall have power to govern and regulate each institution under its control in such manner as it shall deem best calculated to promote the purpose for which the same is maintained . . . ."

[17] 93 N.W.2d at 413.

[18] *Ibid.*

[19] *Id.* at 414. It is worthy of note that whereas the supreme court based its conclusion on the constitutional power of control, the trial court reasoned that the statutory power contained in S.D. Code § 15.0709 (1939) to "dismiss" officers and instructors was unlimited and could not be bargained away. This problem is discussed in Note, *Contract Rights of Teacher Discharged from Educational*

Analysis

Unfortunately, the court's opinion does not tell us why the constitutional provision placing the college "under the control of" the board incapacitates the board from delegating a portion of its powers to the faculty and the president.[20] The opinion does not, for example, discuss the history of the constitutional provision in an effort to determine whether there was a common understanding to that effect at the time the constitution was adopted. Nor is there any discussion of the purpose to be attributed to the provision. Nor is there an evaluation of the importance of academic freedom in the life of the college, or of the relationship of tenure to the maintenance and protection of that freedom.[21]

Instead, the opinion states: "The exact meaning and intent of this so-called tenure policy eludes us. Its vaporous objectives, purposes, and procedures are lost in a fog of nebulous verbiage."[22]

Institution Incorporated Under Special Statute, 35 ILL. L. REV. 225 (1940); BYSE & JOUGHIN, *op. cit. supra* note 12, at 79–82. See also Cobb v. Howard Univ., 106 F.2d 860 (D.C. Cir.), *cert. denied*, 308 U.S. 611 (1939), in which the dismissed teacher sought a mandatory injunction directing the university to reinstate him. The court, in a carefully reasoned opinion which contrasts sharply with that in the *Worzella* case, held that the board of trustees' statutory power to remove a professor " 'when, in their judgment, the interests of the university shall require it,' " 106 F.2d at 863, precluded the court from issuing an order of reinstatement. The court left open the question whether the statutory power disabled the board from making a contract which, although it could not be specifically enforced, might be the basis of a judgment for damages.

[20] The court cited the North Dakota decision of Posin v. State Board of Higher Educ., 86 N.W.2d 31 (N.D. 1957), in which the Supreme Court of North Dakota stated that because of the provision of the North Dakota constitution that the board "shall have full authority over the institutions under its control," a board regulation that a teacher would only be removed for cause after a hearing did not limit the board's "right to discharge . . . without assigning cause for . . . removal and without a hearing, if it saw fit to do so." *Id.* at 36. The *Posin* case thus is on a par with the *Worzella* decision, and is subject to the same criticism. It is not as bad on its facts, however, for unlike the South Dakota Board in *Worzella*, the North Dakota Board in *Posin* did give the teacher a hearing as provided in the tenure plan: "It is clear from the record before us that . . . appellants [were] allowed all of the rights to which they were entitled under the College constitution . . . ." *Ibid.*

The *Posin* and *Worzella* opinions are alike in that neither contains any indication that the court understood the importance of academic freedom and tenure in American higher education.

[21] Quite the contrary. The court stated, "The advisability of establishing and the merits of academic tenure are not involved. We are concerned only with the validity and enforceability of the tenure policy approved for State College by the Board of Regents." 93 N.W.2d at 412.

[22] *Ibid.*

The statement of tenure policy is set forth in the appendix to this comment so that the reader may judge the accuracy of this assertion. My own judgment is that although it contains a few ambiguities, the statement is a reasonably well-drafted and conventional tenure plan. More important, the purpose of the tenure statement is clear beyond doubt. It is unfortunately true that the court failed to understand the purpose of the statement and that it misread a particular provision. But this failure and misreading were not the fault of the draftsmen of the statement.

The clear purpose of the statement was to provide assurance to teachers at State College that after they had served a probationary period they would not be discharged except for cause and after a hearing before a committee of their peers conducted under a procedure which complied with the principles of academic due process. In seeking concrete assurance concerning these three objectives — limitation of the power to discharge, participation of members of the faculty in the decisional process, and procedural due process — the teachers at State College were simply endeavoring to secure the explicit agreement of the governing board to principles which many, if not most, teachers in higher education believe are important and which have been widely endorsed.[23] Further, the plan they proposed was in almost every respect completely conventional. The three aspects of the plan which in light of the court's opinion require analysis are: (1) the role of the president in initiating dismissal proceedings; (2) the role of the faculty in the decisional process, and (3) the role of the president in determining whether to recommend dismissal to the Board of Regents.

The plan provided that "charges against a faculty member shall be filed with the Committee [of faculty members elected by the faculty] by the President, who shall designate a person to present

---

[23] See the 1940 Statement of Principles on Academic Freedom and Tenure, *supra* note 5; BYSE & JOUGHIN, *op. cit. supra* note 12 *passim*.

In Laba v. Board of Educ., 23 N.J. 364, 393, 129 A.2d 273, 290 (1957), Justice Jacobs stated: "The greatness of the United States has in no small measure been due to the basic freedoms of inquiry and expression which educational institutions at all levels have nurtured and defended so faithfully. The traditions of academic freedom and tenure have been twin bulwarks in the maintenance of strong and independent faculty staffs . . . ." See also Cobb v. Howard Univ., 106 F.2d 860, 865 n.21 (D.C. Cir.), *cert. denied*, 308 U.S. 611 (1939) ("It is common knowledge that teachers, in seeking academic connections at the collegiate level, lay increasingly greater emphasis upon provisions for tenure . . . .").

the charges before the Committee." [24] Vesting the power to initiate dismissal proceedings in the president or other high administrative officer of the institution conforms to accepted practice.[25] Although in one sense a university president constitutes a mediating third force between faculty and governing board, in another and very real sense the president represents the governing board vis-à-vis the faculty. Thus, it was entirely reasonable for the draftsmen of the tenure statement to designate the chief administrative officer of the college as the person who should initiate the charges. It is difficult to believe that the constitutional provision putting the college "under the control of" the board disables the board from utilizing the services of the chief administrative officer of the college in such a conventional fashion. But even if it is assumed that the constitutional "control" provision means that the board must have power to initiate proceedings directly, rather than through its representative, the president, the appropriate judicial resolution of the problem would have been to construe the plan also to authorize direct initiation of proceedings by the board, rather than to invalidate the entire plan because of an understandable failure on the part of its draftsmen to include a specific provision for direct board institution of dismissal proceedings.

Far more important than the question of who should bring the charges is the problem of what should be the role of the faculty in dismissal proceedings. There are some who would give the faculty the primary responsibility.[26] They urge that since the president is the one who institutes the proceedings, he should be disqualified from adjudicating the case. They would also assert that senior faculty members with tenure do more than anyone to determine the quality, character, and strength of the institution and that this faculty group — rather than busy lay trustees — has the independence, ability, and experience to reach fair and informed judgments concerning professional fitness. Those holding to this view take seriously the dictum of President Paul Ansel Chadbourne of Williams College, "Professors are sometimes spoken of as working for the college. They are the college." [27]

Although faculties are better able than governing boards to determine questions of professional fitness, existing tenure plans

---

[24] Statement of Tenure Policy of South Dakota State College, para. IV(2)a(1), p. 320 *infra.*

[25] BYSE & JOUGHIN, *op. cit. supra* note 12, at 146.

[26] *E.g., id.* at 146–49.

[27] Quoted in HOFSTADTER & METZGER, THE DEVELOPMENT OF ACADEMIC FREEDOM IN THE UNITED STATES 274 (1955).

in American higher education rarely vest final authority in tenure-termination cases in the faculty or its representatives.[28] Instead, there usually is a compromise arrangement which recognizes both the importance of faculty judgment and the formal legal responsibility of the governing board. Thus the 1940 Statement of Principles of the Association of American Colleges and the American Association of University Professors provides, "Termination for cause of a continuous appointment . . . should, if possible, be considered by both a faculty committee and the governing board of the institution." [29] The 1958 Statement on Procedural Standards in Faculty Dismissal Proceedings, adopted by the same two organizations, is particularly instructive.[30] The introduction to that statement reads in part: "A necessary precondition of a strong faculty is that it have first-hand concern with its own membership. This is properly reflected both in appointments to and in separations from the faculty body. . . . It seems clear on the American college scene that a close positive relationship exists between the excellence of colleges, the strength of their faculties, and the extent of the faculty responsibility in determining faculty membership." [31] In other words, the faculty should decide. But it is also emphasized that modern college faculties are "part of the complex and extensive structure requiring legal incorporation, with stewards and managers specifically appointed to discharge certain functions," [32] and reference is made to "faculty awareness of institutional factors with which governing boards must be primarily concerned." [33] In other words, the governing board also has a role.

The specific reconciliation of these two interests proposed by the 1958 Statement is that after a faculty committee has heard the case in accordance with the principles of academic due process, "the president should transmit to the governing board the full report of the hearing committee. . . . [A]cceptance of the committee's decision would normally be expected. If the governing board chooses to review the case . . . . the decision of the

---

[28] BYSE & JOUGHIN, *op. cit. supra* note 12, at 124.

[29] 1940 Statement of Principles on Academic Freedom and Tenure, para. a(4), *supra* note 5, at 292.

[30] 44 AMERICAN ASS'N OF UNIVERSITY PROFESSORS BULL. 270 (1958). Both the 1940 and the 1958 Statements are reproduced in the appendices of BYSE & JOUGHIN, *op. cit. supra* note 12.

[31] 44 AMERICAN ASS'N OF UNIVERSITY PROFESSORS BULL. 270, 271 (1958).

[32] *Id.* at 270.

[33] *Id.* at 271.

hearing committee should either be sustained or the proceeding be returned to the committee with objections specified." [34] If the proceeding is so returned, the committee is to reconsider the case, taking into consideration the governing board's objections and receiving new evidence if necessary. The committee's report then goes to the governing board again, and "only after study of the committee's reconsideration should the governing [board] . . . make a final decision overruling the committee." [35] In other words, the faculty judgment should be given great weight but, in the end, it may be overruled if the governing board so decides.

The relevance of all this to the matter at hand is that the State College statement of tenure policy did not break new ground in this respect. In fact, it said nothing at all concerning the effect to be given to the Tenure Committee's determination. The committee's sole responsibility was to "make recommendations to the President . . . . [who] will make the decision whether to recommend dismissal of the person concerned to" the Board of Regents.[36] There is nothing in the tenure statement which requires the president to agree with the committee's recommendations. The tenure statement made a hearing by the committee a condition precedent to action by the board, but a committee recommendation of dismissal was not made a condition precedent to board action, or to action by the president.

The court thus errs in several places in its opinion when it asserts that the board could not dismiss a faculty member unless the committee first recommended dismissal.[37] There is, of course, no

---

[34] *Id.* at 274.

[35] *Ibid.*

[36] Statement of Tenure Policy of South Dakota State College, para. IV(3)b (7)–(8), p. 322 *infra.*

See also [1951–52] 32 S.D. REGENTS OF EDUC. BIENNIAL REP. 300 (1953) (minutes of the meeting of the State Board of Regents of April 25 and 26, 1952). At this meeting, held one month before the State College tenure statement was approved, the board adopted a general statement of tenure policy submitted by the presidents of the institutions of higher learning under the board's jurisdiction. Paragraph III of that statement, which set the framework for the State College statement, also makes it clear that the faculty's role is solely advisory:

The procedures to be provided in case of releasing a staff member having tenure shall be determined by the institution; except that a standing faculty committee shall be elected which shall not include administrators; such committee shall be empowered to arrange and hold hearings if requested by the party whose release is sought, and advise with the president of the institution concerning proposed releases of members of the staff.

Such a plan shall be adopted by each institution and recommended to the Board of Regents.

[37] See 93 N.W.2d at 413–14: "Apparently the Board could not . . .

way of knowing whether this erroneous reading of the provisions
of the tenure statement affected the court's decision. But error
on so obvious and important a point does not inspire confidence
in the court's decisional process. And it is an additional indication that the court failed to give this important case the careful
consideration it deserved.[38]

This brings us to the final feature of the tenure statement which
the court found objectionable: the power of the president to determine whether or not to recommend dismissal. It will be recalled that the plan provided that if the president did recommend
dismissal, the teacher involved might "appeal for a hearing" before the board. The fair inference is that on appeal the board
might approve or disapprove the president's recommendation.
The prerogatives of the board thus were safeguarded in event of
a presidential recommendation to dismiss. The only limitation
on the board's power would occur if the president did not recommend dismissal and if the board disagreed with that decision.

In giving the president this limited power, the tenure statement
of State College did not conform to the standards recommended
in the 1940 and 1958 Statements of the Association of American
Colleges and the American Association of University Professors,
for it will be recalled that both of those statements authorized
consideration by the governing board.[39] It was here that the
State College draftsmen made their "mistake" (if that is the correct term to describe their failure to anticipate the court's sur-
prising reaction in this case). For had the statement provided
that the president should transmit his recommendation to the
board for its action, the court could not have decided the case in
the manner it did. The question, of course, is whether the draftsmen's "mistake" warranted imposition of the extreme sanction of
invalidating the entire plan.

Writing some time before the *Worzella* case, I appraised a
group of tenure plans which gave the president final authority

remove a faculty member with tenure for any reason . . . if the Tenure Committee and President failed or refused to recommend dismissal. . . . Without the
prior action and approval of the President and Tenure Committee the Board is
powerless to act. The President and Tenure Committee do not serve in an advisory capacity only. Their action and approval are conditions precedent to any
dismissal of college personnel by the Board." In distinguishing a Montana case,
the court says, "In Montana the recommendation of the faculty service committee is advisory only." *Id.* at 414.

[38] See p. 310 *supra*.
[39] See p. 314 *supra*.

in tenure-termination cases. Although the appraisal was in terms of the protection which the plans gave to tenure, the discussion and conclusion are applicable to the State College tenure statement:

> A few tenure plans, instead of making the governing board the final decisional authority, vest that power in the president.[40] Giving the president, rather than the trustees, final authority may appear to provide greater protection to the tenure relationship, because college and university presidents usually have risen from the teaching or research ranks and therefore may be presumed to have a more sympathetic understanding of the values of academic freedom and tenure than lay trustees. To be weighed against this presumed superior insight are the following considerations: (a) lay trustees who elect presidents do not always require that their choices be devoted adherents to academic freedom; (b) presidents sometimes appear to be unduly sensitive to public opinion, and too frequently public opinion is found in strident statements of pressure groups rather than in the sober second thought of the community; and (c) judged on the basis of past cases, it may be anticipated that there will be no basic differences between the president and the trustees in most discharge cases. These factors suggest that although giving the president rather than the trustees final authority is a break with the American tradition of trustee control, the change is not one of substance.[41]

If this reasoning is correct — and there is nothing in the court's opinion to suggest the contrary — the shift from regental to presidential decision at State College was more a matter of form than of substance; so basic an interest as academic freedom and tenure should not founder on a mere matter of form.

It should be noted also that the provision for presidential recommendation was embodied in a plan adopted by the Board of Regents. Plainly, a governing board which has promulgated a tenure plan has authority to make reasonable changes in the plan.[42] An amendment providing that the recommendations of the Tenure Committee and those of the president should be transmitted to the Board of Regents for final decision probably

---

[40] "E.g., Carnegie Institute of Technology. Cf. Bryn Mawr College: A teacher with tenure may be removed 'only by the recommendation of the President and the affirmative vote of not less than four members of the Committee on Appointments. . . .' Temple University: '[T]he President or Board of Trustees shall . . . issue such order as seems fair and just . . . [which] order shall be final and conclusive.'" (Footnote renumbered.)

[41] BYSE & JOUGHIN, op. cit. supra note 12, at 127–28.

[42] See id. at 115–16.

would be upheld.[43] This means, then, that the board had not ir-revocably transferred this power to the president, but that the president was to exercise it until the plan was properly amended to restore the power to the Board of Regents. This temporary quality of the president's authority is an additional reason why the tenure statement did not unconstitutionally deprive the board of its power of "control."

Finally, even if it be assumed that this degree of presidential participation in the dismissal process was constitutionally ob-jectionable, it is not at all self-evident that the entire tenure plan had to be invalidated. The last sentence of the introductory para-graph of the statement of tenure policy reads, "Thus no faculty member shall be dismissed in violation of commonly accepted standards of academic freedom." This is the key sentence of the statement. What follows is an implementation of that basic ob-jective. Anyone cognizant with the principles of academic free-dom and tenure in American higher education would readily per-ceive that the clear purpose of the statement, and the expecta-tion of the teachers who were subject to its provisions, was that (a) after service of a probationary period, (b) a teacher should not be dismissed except for cause or because of a financial exi-gency, (c) after a hearing before his peers, (d) conducted in ac-cordance with the principles of academic due process. There is no apparent reason why a court, which recognized that the state-ment should be construed so as to give effect to its basic purpose, could not have severed the "unconstitutional" provision and held the rest of the statement valid. But there is nothing in the court's opinion which suggests it gave any consideration to this possibil-ity.

CONCLUSION

The result in the *Worzella* case may conceivably be sustained on some basis other than the one expounded in the opinion of the Supreme Court of South Dakota.[44] But the opinion itself is so seriously defective that any other court faced with a similar

---

[43] *Cf.* Schulz v. Supreme Tent, Knights of Maccabees, 236 S.W. 903 (Mo. App. 1922) (method of expulsion from a fraternal benefit association, resulting in the member's loss of insurance benefits, can validly be changed from trial by the local lodge to trial by the national board of trustees).

[44] For example, it is arguable that under the statute, the board could not limit its power to dismiss and that, therefore, a writ of mandamus should not have issued. See note 16 *supra*. It might also be argued that the tenure statement

problem should recognize its responsibility to give the matter independent analysis rather than to follow lightly the *Worzella* approach.[45]

Maintenance of sound conditions of creative scholarship in American higher education is primarily the responsibility of governing boards, administrators, and faculty members. But judges and lawyers have an important role when a tenure case is brought to court. Dean Erwin N. Griswold has well said, "It is the highest function of the lawyer to contribute to the resolution of controversies between man and man in the light of reason and the mind . . . ."[46] Had "reason and the mind" been applied in the *Worzella* case there would have been no careless assertion that "the merits of academic tenure are not involved."[47] There would have been no talk about "vaporous objectives" and "fog of nebulous verbiage."[48] There would have been, instead, a rational endeavor to construe the constitution, statute, and statement of tenure policy so as to promote rather than impede "that free play of the spirit" which is the essence of academic freedom.[49] There would have been a conscientious effort to understand the importance of academic freedom and the relationship of tenure to the maintenance and protection of that freedom. Anything less is unworthy of a responsible judiciary in a free society.[50]

---

was only the board's expression of policy or intention and did not create a legally enforceable obligation. See BYSE & JOUGHIN, *op. cit. supra* note 12, at 84.

In my opinion, on the basis of the facts reported in the case, the court should have ordered the board either to reinstate Dr. Worzella or accord him the procedural safeguards guaranteed by the statement of tenure policy.

[45] For a recent tenure case reflecting quite a different approach from that exemplified in *Worzella* and *Posin,* see State *ex rel.* Ball v. McPhee, 94 N.W.2d 711 (Wis. 1959).

[46] [1955–56] HARVARD LAW SCHOOL DEAN'S REPORT 7.

[47] 93 N.W.2d at 412.

[48] *Ibid.*

[49] The quoted phrase is that of Mr. Justice Frankfurter, concurring in Wieman v. Updegraff, 344 U.S. 183, 195 (1952).

[50] The fact that the judges who decided the *Worzella* and *Posin* cases failed to appreciate the importance of academic freedom and tenure suggests that professional organizations such as the American Association of University Professors might assume a more active role in providing the needed enlightenment. Filing an amicus brief in court cases involving academic freedom and tenure is an obvious proposal. For discussion of this suggestion, see Carr, *Academic Freedom, the American Association of University Professors, and the United States Supreme Court,* 45 AMERICAN ASS'N OF UNIVERSITY PROFESSORS BULL. 5, 19–20 (1959). See also Ingraham, *Academic Freedom — The Role of Professional Societies,* 101 PROCEEDINGS OF THE AMERICAN PHILOSOPHICAL SOC'Y 441 (1957); BYSE & JOUGHIN, *op. cit. supra* note 12, at 133.

APPENDIX

Statement of Tenure Policy of South Dakota State College

Tenure is a means to certain ends; specifically: (1) Freedom of teaching and research and of extra-mural activities, and (2) a sufficient degree of economic security to make the profession attractive to men and women of ability. Academic freedom and economic security, hence, tenure, are indispensable to the success of an institution in fulfilling its obligations to [i]ts students and to society. Thus no faculty member shall be dismissed in violation of commonly accepted standards of academic freedom.

I. Eligibility for Tenure.

1. Any faculty member on staff appointment* at South Dakota State College of Agriculture and Mechanic Arts who, in the opinion of the President and other appropriate administrators, has performed his duties and served for a period of three years and has been tendered his fourth contract shall be considered to hold permanent tenure. By mutual consent the period of probation may be a contract year, either nine or twelve months.

2. Any professionally or technically qualified faculty member already on staff appointment who has been employed three or more years and has received his fourth contract, shall be considered to hold permanent tenure.

II. Reasons for Termination of Tenure.

1. Reduction of staff forced by financial circumstances.

2. Dismissal for cause, which shall include:

   a. Gross misconduct.

   b. Permanently incapacitating mental and physical disability.

   c. Willful neglect of duty which would impair good teaching, research or services, or endanger the health of students.

   d. Failure without justifiable cause to perform the terms of his employment.

III. Suspension.

In case the stated cause for dismissal is a flagrant act, such as immorality or dishonesty, or in the case of mental or physical impairment, suspension by the college president may take place at once, pending action by the Tenure Committee and the Regents of Education.

IV. Tenure Committee and Its Function.

1. Committee

   a. To provide the machinery necessary for appropriate pro-

---

* Faculty member on staff appointment is defined as any teacher, research worker, extension worker or professional worker whose appointment is made by the Regents of Education through the office of the President. If classification of an employee is in doubt, his classification shall be determined by the President.

cedure in case of dismissal, there shall be established a standing committee on Tenure and Academic Freedom (hereinafter called the Tenure Committee), consisting of seven faculty members holding tenure, none of whom shall be an administrative officer. A department head shall not be regarded as an administrator within the meaning of this section.

b. The Committee shall be elected by the faculty from its membership. A nominating committee elected by the faculty will select a slate of candidates as follows: Two from each of the divisions (Pharmacy, Engineering, General Science, Agriculture, Home Economics, and Extension Service) and two at large. The nominating committee will consist of one member from each division and one from the Extension Service. In addition to the slate presented by the nominating committee, nominations may be made from the floor.

c. The first election is to be held before October 30, 1952.

d. Terms of office of members of the Committee shall be three years, except that in the original constitution of the Committee, two members shall be elected for one year, two members shall be elected for two years, and three members shall be elected for a three-year term. The Committee shall elect annually a chairman from its own membership. The chairman cannot succeed himself.

2. Notification
  a. Complaint
    (1) Except in cases of resignation or voluntary acceptance of change in employment status, charges against a faculty member shall be filed with the Committee by the President, who shall designate a person to present the charges before the Committee.
    (2) Upon receipt of the complaint, it shall be the duty of the Committee to cause the same to be served promptly upon the faculty member, by delivering to and leaving with him, personally, a copy of the complaint, or by mailing it to him at his last known place of residence. This letter should be sent by registered mail, with return receipt requested.
  b. Answer to charges
    The faculty member accused shall have twenty (20) days from the date of such notification in which to file an answer in writing with the Committee. The Chairman of the Committee, on written application filed with him, may grant an extension of ten (10) days for the filing of an answer.
  c. Notice of Hearing
    Upon receipt of such answer the Committee shall fix

a date for a hearing of the charges, and the accused shall be given at least ten (10) days' notice of the time and place of the hearing by registered mail, return receipt requested. Upon default of the faculty member to file an answer, the Chairman of the Committee shall so notify the President, and terminate the proceedings.

3. Hearing
   a. At the time and place fixed, the Committee shall conduct the hearing.
   b. The following rules shall apply in connection with the hearing:
      (1) Five members of the Committee shall constitute a quorum.
      (2) The individual whose dismissal is sought and the individual presenting the charges shall have the right to challenges [*sic*] peremptorily the members of the committee. Such challenges shall not exceed two (2) for each party. The right of challenge shall not be extended to substitute members of the Committee. In circumstances in which the exercise of this right would result in reducing the sitting membership of the committee below the number heretofore established as constituting a quorum, the members of the Committee shall elect from the eligible faculty personnel such number of temporary Committee members as will constitute a quorum.
      (3) The hearing shall be conducted according to such rules of procedure as the Committee may establish. The Committee shall be guided, but not necessarily bound, by the rules of evidence observed in courts of law.
      (4) The person whose dismissal is sought shall be entitled to representation during his hearing by any person of his choice. He shall be confronted with witnesses against him, shall be entitled to be present at all sessions of the Committee when testimony is being presented, and shall have the right to call and examine witnesses and to produce relevant documents in his behalf, and to cross-examine witnesses produced against him. Likewise, the person prosecuting the charges shall be entitled to be present during the progress of the hearing, call and examine witnesses, to produce relevant documents in support of the charges, and to cross-examine witnesses produced in behalf of the individual whose dismissal is sought.
      (5) A full stenographic record of the hearing shall be made and shall be available to all parties concerned.

(6) Since the final decision must be made by the President of the institution, it is desirable that the President sit with the Committee during the formal hearing as an auditor. He shall not be present during the deliberations of the Committee.

(7) At the conclusion of the hearing the Committee shall deliberate upon its findings and make recommendations to the President. The recommendations together with the transcript of the testimony at the hearing shall be filed with the President. Copies of the findings and recommendations shall be transmitted to the accused and to the person prosecuting the charges.

(8) The President will make the decision whether to recommend the dismissal of the person concerned to the Regents of Education.

(9) The hearings and records of the hearings will be restricted to use by the parties immediately concerned.

V. Appeal to Board of Regents

The faculty member whose dismissal is recommended to the Regents of Education by the President of the institution may appeal for a hearing before the Regents of Education.

VI. Demotions

The procedure outlined in the preceding sections shall apply also in the case of demotions, involving reductions in academic rank or reductions in salary which are not general in application. It is not to be construed as a demotion when an administrative officer ceases to hold his administrative position. Such employee may be assigned academic duties with a downward adjustment in salary to a level customarily paid for academic services of the nature or extent he is expected to render. Furthermore, the assignment of personnel to limited employment with reduced compensation by reason of infirmity or age, in accordance with policies of the Regents of Education, shall not be regarded as a demotion or violation of Tenure.

VII. In return for the security provided in this tenure statement the institution may expect and demand continued professional growth which may be consistent with the position a faculty member may occupy. It is also expected that notification of resignation by a faculty member on permanent tenure will be early enough to obviate serious embarrassment to the institution.

VIII. The foregoing items of this resolution are based upon good faith between the college administration and the individual faculty member.

"CONSTITUTIONAL TENURE"
Toward a Realization
of Academic Freedom

Harry W. Pettigrew

"Constitutional Tenure:" Toward a Realization of Academic Freedom

Harry W. Pettigrew

I. INTRODUCTION

A LOOK at the philosophical basis for academic tenure reveals an attempt to advance academic freedom through the protection of capable educators.[1] As succinctly stated by an Arizona court:

> [T]he broad purpose of teacher tenure is to protect worthy instructors from enforced yielding to political preferences and to guarantee to such teachers employment after a long period of satisfactory service regardless of the vicissitudes of politics or the likes or dislikes of those charged with the administration of school affairs.[2]

THE AUTHOR: HARRY W. PETTIGREW (B.S., University of Toledo; J.D., Ohio State University) is an Assistant Professor of Business Law at Ohio University and a member of the Ohio Bar.

This philosophy, however, has become lost in a morass of pragmatic attitudes.[3] Rather than serving solely to achieve the greater end of academic freedom, the concept of tenure has become a vehicle by which diverse interest groups may further their individual aims: To the novice

---

[1] For the evolution of the concept of academic freedom as the basis for academic tenure, see R. HAFSTADTER & W. METZGER, THE DEVELOPMENT OF ACADEMIC FREEDOM IN THE UNITED STATES (1969).

In 1940, representatives of the Association of American Colleges and the American Association of University Professors formulated the following definition of academic freedom:

(a) The teacher is entitled to full freedom in research and in the publication of the results, subject to the adequate performance of his other academic duties; but research for pecuniary return should be based upon an understanding with the authorities of the institution.

(b) The teacher is entitled to freedom in the classroom in discussing his subject, but he should be careful not to introduce into his teaching controversial matter which has no relation to his subject. Limitations of academic freedom because of religious or other aims of the institution should be clearly stated in writing at the time of the appointment.

(c) The college or university teacher is a citizen, a member of a learned profession, and an officer of an educational institution. When he speaks or writes as a citizen, he should be free from institutional censorship or discipline, but his special position in the community imposes special obligations. As a man of learning and an educational officer, he should remember that the public may judge his profession and his institution by his utterances. Hence he should at all times be accurate, should exercise appropriate restraint, should show respect for the opinions of others, and should make every effort to indicate that he is not an institutional spokesman. *Academic Freedom and Ten-*

teacher who has just been baptized by the waters of the meandering stream of standards for professorial success, the bestowing of tenure may serve as a means to gain recognition of tutorial excellence from his peers. To the academic administrator, tenure may serve as a carrot to extract from the nontenured faculty member further performance toward the nebulous perimeter of pedagogical accomplishment.[4] To a state legislator, the tenure system of state-supported institutions may serve as a political issue which he uses to exhort his wage-earning constituents into believing that this sanctuary for incompetents, social misfits, and subversives must be statutorily expunged from the educational system.[5]

Furthermore, even when viewed as a means by which to achieve academic freedom, the scope of academic tenure is severely delimited. Since academic freedom does not rest on a theory of special privilege or individual right (but rather on the hope for social progress through the unfettered spirit of inquiry), only those who have been granted tenure will carry the shield enabling them to better exercise academic freedom. The nontenured faculty member who choses to exercise such freedom remains virtually unprotected. Having invoked the displeasure of the university administrator, he may find his relations with the institution seriously impaired or his employment contract not renewed. In short, academic tenure is no more than an artificial line of demarcation which, until reached, leaves the novice faculty member insecure in his exercise of academic freedom.

A survey of recent case law, however, reveals that the problem has not gone unrecognized. With an increasing willingness of the courts to apply certain constitutional protections — hereinafter referred to as "constitutional tenure" — the nontenured staff member need no longer refrain from exercising academic freedom. Nontenured faculty dismissals or nonretentions that in the past would

---

ure: *Basic Statements*, in ACADEMIC FREEDOM AND TENURE 33, 35-36 (L. Joughin ed. 1969).

[2] School Dist. v. Superior Court, 102 Ariz. 478, 480, 433 P.2d 28, 30 (1967).

[3] *See generally* R. HAFSTADTER & W. METZGER, *supra* note 1.

[4] Tenure is essentially the application of civil service to the teaching profession. *See* McSherry v. City of St. Paul, 202 Minn. 102, 277 N.W. 541 (1938).

[5] The plenary power of state legislatures over education applies also to teacher tenure unless limited by constitutional provisions. Taylor v. Board of Educ., 31 Cal. App. 2d 734, 89 P.2d 148 (Dist. Ct. App. 1939). Even where constitutional provisions seemingly control teacher employment, courts have construed tenure statutes so as not to be in conflict with those constitutional provisions. *See, e.g.,* State *ex rel.* Glover v. Holbrook, 129 Fla. 241, 176 So. 99 (1937); McQuaid v. State *ex rel.* Sigler, 211 Ind. 595, 6 N.E.2d 547 (1937); State *ex rel.* Bishop v. Board of Educ., 139 Ohio St. 427, 40 N.E.2d 913 (1942); Malone v. Hayden, 329 Pa. 213, 197 A. 344 (1938).

have been upheld as consistent with the tenure system might be found to be unconstitutional today. The concept of "constitutional tenure" and the protection it affords the nontenured teacher will be discussed below; however, before doing so, brief consideration will be given to tenure systems in general.

II. TENURE SYSTEMS

Generally speaking, formal tenure systems are employment security devices. Upon an academic administrator's determination that a particular teacher has sufficiently developed himself during a prescribed probationary period, the reward of tenure may be granted. Once tenured, the faculty member's continuation of satisfactory service limits and qualifies the power which the governing body of the institution would ordinarily possess to terminate employment.[6] Only upon satisfaction of certain procedural safeguards[7] and a showing of good cause will a tenured teacher suffer dismissal.[8] The prescribed requirements for attaining tenure and the protections afforded thereby may be derived from either statute or contract.

A. Statutory Tenure

The vast majority of states have tenure statutes.[9] The provisions, however, may vary from state to state in accordance with the parti-

---

[6] Such a system of protection has negative as well as the obvious positive aspects. To the young, aggressive teacher, tenure is often a secondary substitute for promotion and salary. For the administration, such bureaucratic security may attract teachers who are seeking permanent employment with minimum performance demands. In addition, the administration, at the risk of invoking publicity, expense, and the hostility of professional teachers' groups, may be reluctant to effect the procedures required under the tenure system to dismiss a tenured teacher. Furthermore, in the relatively short period allowed for the decision of whether to grant tenure, the teacher has only recently adjusted to his position and the administration has not yet been able to evaluate his now stabilizing performance. Nevertheless, "[w]hatever its shortcomings, it is generally agreed that tenure does achieve two desirable objectives: it protects good teachers from unjust dismissal and it provides an orderly procedure to be followed in the dismissal of incompetent members of a professional staff. These are objectives of major dimensions in the administration of staff personnel." L. PETERSON, R. ROSSMILLER & M. VOLZ, THE LAW AND PUBLIC SCHOOL OPERATION 530 (1969). Moreover, the main purpose of a tenure system — to help create and maintain an atmosphere conducive to the development of academic freedom — is generally viewed as outweighing its disadvantages. See Byse & Merry, *Tenure and Academic Freedom*, in CHALLENGE AND CHANGE IN AMERICAN EDUCATION 313-28 (S. Harris ed. 1965); Machlup, *In Defense of Academic Tenure*, in ACADEMIC FREEDOM AND TENURE 306, 312-28 (L. Joughin ed. 1969).

[7] See notes 18-26 *infra* & accompanying text.

[8] See text accompanying notes 12-17 *infra*.

[9] See NATIONAL EDUCATION ASS'N OF THE UNITED STATES, RESEARCH DIV., TENURE AND CONTRACTS 33-38 (1969).

cular type and level of institution at which a person teaches.[10] Primarily, the tenure statutes are applicable to teachers at the public elementary and high school levels.[11] The public university teacher is usually not covered, or if he is, he is treated under separate statutory provisions. The educators of private insititutions never fall under the protective umbrella of tenure statutes.

Under the state tenure statutes a teacher may be required to complete a probationary period of anywhere from 2 to 5 years. If after that time the school wishes to continue the teacher's employment, he will be given a contract, nonterminable until retirement. Unless the faculty must be reduced or good cause is shown, the faculty member will retain his position.[12]

Where termination of an employment contract is sought on the basis of good cause, the reasons most commonly given are "incompetency,"[13] "immorality,"[14] "insubordination,"[15] "physical or mental unfitness,"[16] and "neglect of duty."[17] These substantive standards, although somewhat broad and vague, provide a form of protection from arbitrary dismissal by defining legal standards which are subject to judicial review. In addition, to insure that the judicial review is more than a posthumous inquest, the typical statute allows for procedural safeguards in the form of (1) written notice of the intended sanction,[18] (2) a formal written statement of the charges,[19] and (3) a right to request an open or closed hearing before the board

---

[10] "The general rule is that only those positions enumerated in the tenure statute are encompassed by its provisions. Thus locally-created positions with titles not set out in the statute are not covered. Which positions are to be covered is within the prerogative of the legislature." E. REUTTER & R. HAMILTON, THE LAW OF PUBLIC EDUCATION 448 (1970).

[11] See generally NATIONAL EDUCATION ASS'N OF THE UNITED STATES, supra note 9.

[12] See, e.g., ALASKA STAT. § 14.20.150 (1970); IDAHO CODE ANN. § 33-1212 (1963); IND. ANN. STAT. § 28-4307 (1948); KAN. STAT. ANN. §§ 72-5403,-5406,-5410 (Supp. 1965); OHIO REV. CODE ANN. §§ 3319.08-.081 (Page Supp. 1970).

[13] See, e.g., Horosko v. School Dist., 335 Pa. 369, 6 A.2d 866, cert. denied, 308 U.S. 553 (1939).

[14] See, e.g., Jarvella v. Willoughby-Eastlake City School Dist., 12 Ohio Misc. 288, 233 N.E.2d 143 (Lake County C.P. 1967).

[15] See, e.g., Johnson v. United School Dist., 201 Pa. Super. 375, 191 A.2d 897 (1963).

[16] See, e.g., Appeal of School Dist., 347 Pa. 418, 32 A.2d 565, cert. denied, 320 U.S. 782 (1943).

[17] See, e.g., Hamberlin v. Tangipahoa Parish School Bd., 210 La. 483, 27 So. 2d 307 (1946).

[18] See, e.g., LA. REV. STAT. ANN. § 17:443 (West 1963).

[19] See, e.g., State ex rel. Charbonnet v. Jefferson Parish School Bd., 188 So. 2d 143 (La. Ct. App.), cert. denied, 249 La. 727, 190 So. 2d 238 (1966).

of education.[20]   Where the teacher requests a hearing, he should have a right to legal counsel,[21] to present[22] and subpoena evidence and witnesses,[23] and to confront and cross-examine opposing witnesses.[24]   The board has the burden of proof in establishing the cause for the teacher's discharge.[25]   A full stenographic record should be made and a written decision — which may include findings of fact and conclusions of law — should be provided.[26] Tenure statutes have been construed liberally to effect the general purpose of the legislation: that is, the courts have given major emphasis to promoting the fundamental public policy of obtaining better education for the children of the state.[27]

Although the teacher is generally required to exhaust his administrative remedies,[28] the aforementioned statutory requirements afford him a means by which he may seek review in the state courts. Such judicial review is founded upon complete development and a full record of the facts presented at the hearing. The remedies most commonly sought are reinstatement and damages for breach of contract.[29] The most common issue presented is misapplication of the "good cause" standard. If the school administration was not remiss in following prescribed statutory procedures, the reviewing court

[20] See Developments in the Law — Academic Freedom, 81 HARV. L. REV. 1045, 1086 (1968).

[21] See id.

[22] See, e.g., Rehberg v. Board of Educ., 345 Mich. 731, 77 N.W.2d 131 (1956).

[23] See Developments in the Law — Academic Freedom, supra note 20, at 1086.

[24] Additional evidence is not to be presented at an executive session following the adjournment of the hearing. Moffett v. Calcasieu Parish School Bd., 179 So. 2d 537 (La. Ct. App. 1965).

[25] See, e.g., CAL. EDUC. CODE § 13412 (West 1969), which requires that upon a teacher's demand for a hearing, the school board must either rescind its action or file a complaint in a superior court setting forth the charges against the employee and allowing the court to determine if the charges are true and if they constitute sufficient grounds for dismissal.

[26] See, e.g., Morey v. School Bd., 268 Minn. 110, 128 N.W.2d 302 (1964), rehearing denied, 271 Minn. 445, 136 N.W.2d 105 (1965); cf. Agner v. Smith, 167 So. 2d 86 (Fla. Dist. Ct. App. 1964), appeal dismissed mem., 172 So. 2d 598 (Fla. 1965).

[27] E.g., Swick v. School Dist., 141 Pa. Super. 246, 251, 14 A.2d 898, 900 (1940). But see Anderson v. Board of Educ., 390 Ill. 412, 61 N.E.2d 562 (1945), and Eveland v. Board of Educ., 340 Ill. App. 308, 92 N.E.2d 182 (1950) (tenure statutes construed strictly in favor of boards of education on the grounds that such statutes create a new liability on the part of boards, and that the statutes are in derogation of certain common law rights of the school boards); Andrews v. Union Parish School Bd., 191 La. 90, 184 So. 552 (1938) (tenure statute construed liberally in favor of teachers as the primary beneficiaries of such legislation).

[28] See, e.g., Moore v. Starkey, 185 Kan. 26, 340 P.2d 905 (1959).

[29] In addition, school boards and individual members may be held personally liable under the tenure laws when they wrongfully exercise ministerial functions. Babb v. Moore, 374 S.W.2d 516 (Ky. Ct. App. 1964).

will uphold the administrative decision as long as it was based on
"substantial evidence"[30] or was not "arbitrary and capricious,"[31]

Tenure statutes generally afford little if any protection to the
nontenured teacher. Since the authority to grant tenure falls within
the broad discretion of the school board, a refusal to grant tenure
is ordinarily not reviewable by the courts.[32] In addition, the nontenured teacher generally has no right to notice of cause or a hearing for renewal, unless, as in some states, they are specifically provided for by statute.[33]

B. *Contractual Tenure*

Contractual tenure becomes most important in private and higher
education since these areas are generally devoid of statutory protection.[34] The private institutions and public universities, therefore,

---

[30] *See* Last v. Board of Educ., 37 Ill. App. 2d 159, 185 N.E.2d 282 (1962); Haus-
wald v. Board of Educ., 20 Ill. App. 2d 49, 155 N.E.2d 319 (1958); Swisher v. Darden,
59 N.M. 511, 287 P.2d 73 (1955).

[31] *See* Board of Educ. v. Allen, 6 N.Y.2d 127, 160 N.E.2d 60, 188 N.Y.S.2d 515
(1959). A trial de novo before the court is normally not permitted. Parker v. Board
of Trustees, 242 Cal. App. 2d 614, 51 Cal. Rptr. 653 (Dist. Ct. App. 1966).

[32] *Cf.* Application of Lombardo, 18 App. Div. 2d 444, 240 N.Y.S.2d 119, *aff'd
mem.*, 13 N.Y.2d 1097, 196 N.E.2d 266, 246 N.Y.S.2d 631 (1963). *But see* Albaum
v. Carey, 283 F. Supp. 3 (E.D.N.Y. 1968), where a high school teacher alleged that
he was denied tenure status for his union activities and that the state tenure laws gave
unconstitutionally broad discretion to school administrators. The district court recognized
that "[t]enure decisions present delicate and difficult questions in any educational system." *Id.* at 11. The court further stated that "[i]t may be that precise standards cannot
be formulated for determining who shall be appointed to tenure. . . . [But as] one commentator has put it . . . 'the impossibility of defining with precision the scope of the employer's appropriate control over the employee is insufficient reason for treating that
control as boundless.'" *Id.* at 12, *quoting* Blades, *Employment At Will vs. Individual
Freedom: On Limiting the Abusive Exercise of Employer Power*, 67 COLUM. L. REV.
1404, 1407 (1967). In addition, an attempted denial of tenure is ineffective where it
is coupled with the hiring of the previously probationary teacher for 1 more year.
See, e.g., La Shells v. Hench, 98 Cal. App. 6, 276 P. 377 (Dist. Ct. App. 1929). And a
teacher may be found to have gained tenure by estoppel. Eulalie M. Sanders, 72 N.Y.
Dep't R. 39 (Educ. Dep't 1951).
—A few tenure statutes do, however, set forth minimal requirements for the dismissal
of nontenured personnel. If nonretention after the probationary period does not comply
with these requirements, the court may order the administration to grant professional
tenure to the discharged employee. *See* Elias v. Board of School Directors, 421 Pa.
260, 218 A.2d 738 (1966), where the court ordered that permanent professional status
be granted to two school nurses who were certified and had served the appropriate probationary period. The tenure statute provided that temporary professional employees
had to be rated twice a year and could not be dismissed unless rated "unsatisfactory."
Neither of the nurses had ever been so rated. *See also* Mannix v. Board of Educ., 21
N.Y.2d 455, 235 N.E.2d 892, 288 N.Y.S.2d 881 (1968).

[33] *See, e.g.*, ALASKA STAT. § 14.20.140 (1970); ARK. STAT. ANN. § 80-1304(b)
(Supp. 1969); CONN. GEN. STAT. ANN. § 10-151 (Supp. 1971); N.M. STAT. ANN.
§ 77-8-9 (1953); R.I. GEN. LAWS ANN. § 16-13-2 (Supp. 1970).

[34] "The prime need is not for extramural intervention, but for each institution of

will often embody in their by-laws or regulations rights similar to those found in the tenure statutes. These rights are in turn incorporated by reference into the teacher's contract of employment.[85] Should the administration not honor the provisions, the contractually tenured teacher often has the leverage of influential, teacher pressure groups which may adopt sanctions against the university for noncompliance.[36] Along with the usual remedies available for breach of contract, there is authority for reinstatement via a prerogative writ.[37]

C. *Absence of Tenure*

Where there is no tenure system[38] or where the system lacks either substantive or procedural safeguards, the teacher is relegated to the state law respecting employment contracts. Assuming that the employment contract does not contain provisions analogous to the tenure statutes, the teacher has no right to renewal at the end of the contract period.[39] Under such circumstances, the employer, in the person of the board of education or the board of trustees, has vast discretion as to the teacher's contract renewal. The board also has the ability to discharge the teacher during the term of the contract. Al-

---

higher learning to engage in systematic discussion and analysis and to take appropriate action to make tenure as positive a force as possible for the good of education." Byse & Joughin, *Tenure in American Higher Education*: "*Specific Conclusions and Recommendations*", in ACADEMIC FREEDOM AND TENURE 210 (L. Joughin ed. 1969).

[85] *See* State *ex rel.* Keeney v. Ayers, 108 Mont. 547, 92 P.2d 306 (1939).

[36] For an analysis of the various contemporary pressures supporting academic freedom, see S. HOOK, ACADEMIC FREEDOM AND ACADEMIC ANARCHY (1969); DeBardeleben, *The University's External Constituency*, in DIMENSIONS OF ACADEMIC FREEDOM 69 (1969). *See also* AMERICAN CIVIL LIBERTIES UNION, ACADEMIC FREEDOM, ACADEMIC DUE PROCESS (1966); Joughin, *Academic Due Process*, in ACADEMIC FREEDOM AND TENURE 264 (L. Joughin ed. 1969).

[37] *See* State *ex rel.* Keeney v. Ayers, 108 Mont. 547, 92 P.2d 306 (1939) (mandamus action against state university officials); State *ex rel.* Richardson v. Board of Regents, 70 Nev. 144, 261 P.2d 515 (1953) (writ of certiorari issued to review actions of state university officials on theory that their action was quasi-judicial in nature). *But see* Davis, *Enforcing Academic Tenure: Reflections and Suggestions*, 1961 WIS. L. REV. 200, 216-18.

Where tenure regulations are promulgated by a university or a board of regents, a number of courts have refused to bind the board to contractual tenure because of the derogation of the board's statutory power to dismiss arbitrarily and without cause. *See* Posin v. State Bd. of Higher Educ., 86 N.W.2d 31 (N.D. 1957); Worzella v. Board of Regents of Educ., 77 S.D. 447, 93 N.W.2d 411 (1958); State *ex rel.* Hunsicker v. Board of Regents, 209 Wis. 83, 244 N.W. 618 (1932).

[38] Although a majority of the states have tenure statutes, a significant number do not. *See* NATIONAL EDUCATION ASS'N OF THE UNITED STATES, *supra* note 9.

[39] *Cf.* Parker v. Board of Educ., 237 F. Supp. 222 (D. Md.), *aff'd per curiam*, 348 F.2d 464 (4th Cir. 1965), *cert. denied*, 382 U.S. 1030 (1966) (arbitrary nonrenewal of probationary teacher's contract was upheld).

though such a dismissal may entitle the teacher to damages for breach of contract, the employer will escape liability upon a showing of cause.[40] Moreover — assuming that the common law doctrine of sovereign immunity is not already a bar to the suit under the particular state's law[41] — such a damage action by the aggrieved teacher is often unsatisfactory. If he prevails, he no longer has a position;[42] if he seeks and procures another position, the principle of mitigation of damages will substantially reduce the amount of his recovery.[43] Should the teacher choose injunctive relief instead, he will find that such a remedy is not generally available for breach of an employment contract.[44] The prerogative writ, where the employer is a public institution, would also fail since the continued employment of the nontenured teacher is generally not a mandatory duty of a public official.[45]

In summary, where tenure systems exist, the protections afforded by statute or contract allow for the exercise of academic freedom by those who have been granted tenure. The teacher who has not been granted statutory or contractual tenure, as well as the teacher where

---

[40] *See* Millar v. Joint School Dist., 2 Wis. 2d 303, 312, 86 N.W.2d 455, 460 (1957) (dictum).

[41] The threshold problem in a suit brought under state substantive law is that in many states the doctrine of sovereign immunity disallows suits brought against the state, except in such courts and in such manner as may be provided by statute. And suits against state institutions and officials where the state is the real party in interest are of course considered suits against the state. *See, e.g.,* State *ex rel.* Williams v. Glander, 148 Ohio St. 188, 74 N.E.2d 82, *cert. denied,* 332 U.S. 817 (1947).

At least 9 states have consented by statute to suit on their contracts: ILL. ANN. STAT. ch. 37, § 439.8(B) (Smith-Hurd Supp. 1971); MASS. ANN. LAWS ch. 258, § 1 (1956); MICH. STAT. ANN. § 27A.6419 (1962); MONT. REV. CODE ANN. § 83.601 (1966); NEB. REV. STAT. § 24-324 (1964); N.H. REV. STAT. ANN. § 491.8 (1955); N.Y. CT. CL. ACT § 9 (1963); N.D. CENT. CODE § 32-12-03 (1960); WASH. REV. CODE ANN. § 4.92.010 (Supp. 1970).

Such statutes, however, are narrowly construed. For example, in Wolf v. Ohio State Univ. Hosp., 170 Ohio St. 49, 162 N.E.2d 475 (1959), a tort action against a state-supported hospital, the court refused to find that the state had consented to suit, even though OHIO REV. CODE ANN. § 3335.03 (Page 1953) provided that the Board of Trustees of the Ohio State University could "sue and be sued." The court reasoned that since this section did not designate in what courts and in what manner suit could be brought against the Board, it was not the intention of the legislature to consent to suits against the Board.

[42] *Cf.* Independent Dist. v. Deibert, 60 S.D. 424, 244 N.W. 656 (1932).

[43] *See, e.g.,* Miller v. South Bend Special School Dist., 124 N.W.2d 475 (N.D. 1963); Coble v. School Dist., 178 Pa. Super. 301, 116 A.2d 113 (1955).

[44] *See, e.g.,* Greene v. Howard Univ., 271 F. Supp. 609, 615 (D.D.C. 1967), *rev'd and remanded on other grounds,* 412 F.2d 1128 (D.C. Cir. 1969); Felch v. Findlay College, 119 Ohio App. 357, 200 N.E.2d 353 (Hancock County Ct. App. 1963).

[45] *See, e.g.,* Posin v. State Bd. of Higher Educ., 86 N.W.2d 31 (N.D. 1957); State *ex rel.* Hunsicker v. Board of Regents, 209 Wis. 83, 244 N.W. 618 (1932).

there is no tenure system or where that system is inadequate, must rely on the limited protection afforded by a particular state's law respecting employment contracts. With such limited protection, these nontenured teachers are able to exercise academic freedom only at the risk of nonrenewal of their contracts or dismissal for unprescribed cause. In view of these risks accompanying the nontenured teacher's exercise of academic freedom, the concept of constitutional tenure becomes relevant. Constitutional tenure, however, is not significant for the nontenured teacher alone; it may be equally significant for the tenured teacher whose dismissal for cause hinges upon constitutional freedoms. Thus, although the following discussion will be directed primarily toward the constitutional protections afforded the nontenured teacher, it must be kept in mind that the applicability of constitutional tenure is not so limited.

III. THE TREND

As James Madison once stated: "If men were angels, no government would be necessary."[46] It may be added that if those who govern were even demiangels no due process requirements would be necessary. It has long been recognized, however, that arbitrariness, even deliberate arbitrariness, "is not unknown in the most elite intellectual circles,"[47] and university administrators are not necessarily among those best known as paragons of fair play. Nevertheless, until recently, in court actions brought by teachers confronted with dismissal or nonretention, the alleged arbitrary and capricious acts of the administration were generally vindicated. The courts, honoring the doctrine of judicial restraint, gave great deference to the administrator's expertise in evaluating the myriad of variables and interpersonal relationships necessary to maintain the academic homeostasis within the educational institution. But the increasingly evident impersonal bureaucracy and errant decisions of educational administrators has led the courts to more readily enter the academic environs. Whereas previously the protections afforded by the due process clause of the 14th amendment were not deemed applicable to teachers against whom the school administration had applied arbitrary sanctions,[48] today, such teachers are beginning to receive substantial

---

46 THE FEDERALIST NO. 51, at 337 (Nat'l Home Library Found. ed. 1938) (A. Hamilton, J. Jay & J. Madison).

47 Byse, *The University and Due Process: A Somewhat Different View*, 54 A.A.U.P. BULL. 143 (1968).

48 *See, e.g.*, Scopes v. State, 154 Tenn. 105, 111-12, 289 S.W. 363, 364-65 (1927) (the "monkey trial"), where the court stated:

constitutional protection. No longer need the teacher rely solely upon the conceptualisms that inhere in the state's contract or tenure laws. The hypostasis of the past that public employment is a privilege to which the state may attach conditions restricting the employee's positive constitutional freedoms — subject only to the ill-defined limitations that the conditions be reasonable[49] — has been explicitly discredited by the Supreme Court.[50] In doing so, the Court presaged a trend in the lower courts which have recognized a general due process right against arbitrary, capricious, and unreasonable action by tax-supported institutions against their teachers.[51]

To the university administrator, the spectre of federal court decisions challenging areas that were once considered the educational world's peculiar province may well be viewed with alarm. The administrator has probably just revamped, at a considerable expense in time and money, the student disciplinary system to accommodate burgeoning procedural and substantive due process requirements. Is he now faced with a similar burden respecting his faculty employment policies? Is this previously sacrosanct area of "academic process" also being overlaid with an insensitive gloss of "judicial process" which has such a degree of complexity that it leaves the administrator constantly vulnerable to the summons server? Has the clear legislative intent of the tenure statutes been controverted by a nontenured faculty member's absolute right to employment at a public institution — this right supposedly being derived from the United States Constitution? Although the answer to these questions is a qualified no, the administrator might well anticipate changes in policy which will necessarily accompany the new constitutional protections afforded the nontenured teacher. "The Fourteenth Amendment, as now applied to the States, protects the citizen against the

---

The plaintiff in error was a teacher in the public schools of Rhea county. He was an employee of the state of Tennessee or of a municipal agency of the state. He was under contract with the state to work in an institution of the state. He had no right or privilege to serve the state except upon such terms as the state prescribed. . . .

The statute before us . . . . is an act of the state as a corporation, a proprietor, an employer. It is a declaration of a master as to the character of work the master's servant shall, or rather shall not, perform. In dealing with its own employees engaged upon its own work, the state is not hampered by the limitations of . . . the Tennessee Constitution, nor of the Fourteenth Amendment to the Constitution of the United States.

[49] See, e.g., Adler v. Board of Educ., 342 U.S. 485, 492 (1952).

[50] Keyishian v. Board of Regents, 385 U.S. 589, 605-06 (1967). See also Note, Unconstitutional Conditions, 73 HARV. L. REV. 1595 (1960).

[51] See, e.g., Roth v. Board of Regents of State Colleges, 310 F. Supp. 972 (W.D. Wis. 1970); Gouge v. Joint School Dist., 310 F. Supp. 984 (W.D. Wis. 1970).

State itself and all of its creatures — Boards of Education [and Boards of Trustees] not excepted. These have, of course, important, delicate, and highly discretionary functions, but none that they may not perform within the limits of the Bill of Rights."[52] To this end, "[i]t can hardly be argued that either students or teachers shed their constitutional rights to freedom of speech or expression at the schoolhouse gate."[53] Although the courts have often stated the principle that teachers deserve special protection because of society's interest in the preservation of academic freedom,[54] the protection that is promised them under the doctrine of "unconstitutional conditions"[55] — and promised, as a general matter, to all public employees[56] — is just beginning to be realized.

IV. THE CONCEPT OF CONSTITUTIONAL TENURE

A. *Threshold Problems*

Before the substantive and procedural due process contours of constitutional tenure are considered, it is necessary to discuss the questions of jurisdiction and sovereign immunity as they pertain to constitutional tenure.

1. *Jurisdiction.*— A teacher alleging a deprivation of his constitutional rights can assert a federal cause of action under section 1983 of the Civil Rights Act of 1871.[57] Federal district courts have

---

[52] West Virginia State Bd. of Educ. v. Barnett, 319 U.S. 624, 637 (1943).

[53] Tinker v. Des Moines Indep. Community School Dist., 393 U.S. 503, 506 (1969).

[54] "Our Nation is deeply committed to safeguarding academic freedom, which is of transcendent value to all of us and not merely to the teachers concerned." Keyishian v. Board of Regents, 385 U.S. 589, 603 (1967). "The vigilant protection of constitutional freedoms is nowhere more vital than in the community of American schools." Shelton v. Tucker, 364 U.S. 479, 487 (1960). *See also* Sweezy v. New Hampshire, 354 U.S. 234, 250 (1957).

[55] "Generally the doctrine states that while a government, state or federal, may not be obligated to provide its citizens with a certain benefit or privilege, it may not grant the benefit or privilege on conditions requiring the recipient in some manner to relinquish his constitutional rights." Comment, *Another Look at Unconstitutional Conditions*, 117 U. PA. L. REV. 144 (1968). *See also* Note, *supra* note 50.

[56] *See* Comment, *supra* note 55.

[57] 42 U.S.C. § 1983 (1964). The statute provides:
> Every person who, under color of any statute, ordinance, regulation, custom or usage, of any State or Territory, subjects, or causes to be subjected, any citizen of the United States or other person within the jurisdiction thereof to the deprivation of any rights, privileges, or immunities secured by the Constitution and laws, shall be liable to the party injured in an action at law, suit in equity, or other proper proceeding for redress.

A somewhat similar federal remedy exists under section 1985(3) of the Civil Rights Act of 1871, 42 U.S.C. § 1985(3) (1964), which provides a federal cause of action for the deprivation of equal protection of the law or equal privileges and immunities under the law. Actions under section 1985(3), however, are restricted to instances where the

original jurisdiction to hear such a complaint,[58] and because the remedy available under section 1983 has been declared supplementary to any state remedies, the complainant need not seek redress in the state courts before the federal remedy may be invoked.[59]   To sustain an action under section 1983,[60] the complainant must clearly show (1) that the defendant's (university's) conduct deprived the complainant of rights, privileges, or immunities secured by the United States Constitution and laws,[61] and (2) that the conduct complained of was engaged in under color of state law.[62]

In view of the latter requirement as it is construed under the doctrine of state action, section 1983 becomes especially significant to the nontenured teacher in the state-supported institution.   As early as 1947 the Court of Appeals for the Second Circuit stated that the dismissal of a nontenured teacher from a state-supported institution under a statute providing for dismissal of a probationary teacher for any reason or no reason was " 'under color' of a state statute," and, therefore, the court had jurisdiction.[63]   It is not always necessary that such a state statute exist; indeed, state action is generally found whenever the conduct of a state agency infringes upon a person's rights.[64]   Whether jurisdiction is granted to a teacher in a state-supported university will thus depend, for the most part, upon the finding of a constitutionally protected interest.[65]

---

defendant's conduct infringes upon the rights of several persons or a class of persons. See Birnbaum v. Trussell, 371 F.2d 672 (2d Cir. 1966) (a white doctor discharged without a hearing as a result of allegations that he was biased against Negroes stated a valid claim under section 1983 and not under section 1985(3)).

[58] 28 U.S.C. § 1343(3) (1964) (granting original jurisdiction to federal district courts to hear, among others, actions asserting a deprivation of constitutional rights, privileges, or immunities under color of state law).

[59] Monroe v. Pape, 365 U.S. 167, 183 (1961); Lucia v. Duggan, 303 F. Supp. 112, 117 (D. Mass. 1969).

[60] Cf. Rutherford v. American Medical Ass'n, 379 F.2d 641 (7th Cir. 1967), cert. denied, 389 U.S. 1043 (1968); Colon v. Grieco, 226 F. Supp. 414 (D.N.J. 1964).

[61] Cf. Flemming v. Adams, 377 F.2d 975 (10th Cir.), cert. denied, 389 U.S. 898 (1967); Stringer v. Dilger, 313 F.2d 536 (10th Cir. 1963).

[62] See Powe v. Miles, 407 F.2d 73, 79-80 (2d Cir. 1968).

[63] Bomar v. Keyes, 162 F.2d 136, 139 (2d Cir.), cert. denied, 332 U.S. 825 (1947).

[64] The Supreme Court has pointed out that in a section 1983 action, "under color of law" refers to an action taken by an agent of the state whose power is derived from state law and that the action itself need not be "pursuant" to a state statute or regulation.   Monroe v. Pape, 365 U.S. 167, 187 (1961). See also United States v. Classic, 313 U.S. 299, 326 (1941).

[65] See Freeman v. Gould Special School Dist., 405 F.2d 1153, 1159 (8th Cir.), cert. denied, 396 U.S. 843 (1969); Roth v. Board of Regents of State Colleges, 310 F. Supp. 972, 974 (W.D. Wis. 1970); Gouge v. Joint School Dist., 310 F. Supp. 984, 988-89 (W.D. Wis. 1970); Parker v. Board of Educ., 237 F. Supp. 222, 226 (D. Md.), aff'd

The state action doctrine, as presently developed, does not extend so far as to bring private institutions under color of state law in all of their activities. However, institutions which are otherwise "private" have been found involved in sufficient state action to subject themselves to suits under the 14th amendment, where there exists any one or a combination of the following: (1) state control — either financial, constitutional, legislative, judicial, or administrative;[66] (2) a public function;[67] or (3) state contacts.[68] Where the doctrine has been extended to the private school, however, it has generally been limited to those institutions with a policy of racial discrimination.[69] "The courts have seemingly been reluctant to extend the doctrine to eliminate other kinds of activities that would be deemed unconstitutional if performed solely by the state."[70] Thus, until the state action doctrine has been sufficiently developed to subject private institutions, in all instances, to the due process clause, the cases involving the state-supported institutions cannot be deemed determinative of the substantive and procedural standards required of private schools.

2. *Sovereign Immunity.*— The established rule of immunity of the states from suit in the federal courts does not preclude an equity action to enjoin the acts of state officers or state agencies which allegedly deprive a person of rights granted under the Constitution

---

per curiam, 348 F.2d 464 (4th Cir. 1965), *cert. denied*, 382 U.S. 1030 (1966).

Contra, Jones v. Hopper, 410 F.2d 1323 (10th Cir. 1969), *cert. denied*, 397 U.S. 991 (1970). This court dismissed the action of a discharged teacher despite the allegation that the discharge was in violation of his first amendment rights. The court, focusing on Colorado statutes giving the board of trustees complete discretion in its employment practices, concluded that Jones had not been denied his constitutional rights because the board was under no duty to reemploy him.

[66] The Supreme Court has noted that the 14th amendment "governs any action of a State, 'whether through its legislature, through its courts, or through its executive or administrative officers.'" Mooney v. Holohan, 294 U.S. 103, 113 (1935) (per curiam), *quoting* Carter v. Texas, 177 U.S. 442, 447 (1900).

[67] *See* Marsh v. Alabama, 326 U.S. 501 (1946). *See also* Ethridge v. Rhodes, 268 F. Supp. 83 (S.D. Ohio 1967).

[68] *See* Burton v. Wilmington Parking Authority, 365 U.S. 715 (1961).

[69] *See* Comment, *Student Due Process in the Private University: The State Action Doctrine*, 20 SYRACUSE L. REV. 911, 914-19 (1969); Comment, *Judicial Intervention in Expulsions or Suspensions by Private Universities*, 5 WILLAMETTE L.J. 277 (1969). *Contra*, Van Alstyne, *The Judicial Trend Toward Academic Freedom*, 20 FLA. L. REV. 290 (1968). "[T]he presence of government has so far penetrated, that few colleges are today wholly 'private' in the sense of being altogether immune to the fourteenth amendment and the Bill of Rights." *Id.* at 291.

[70] Comment, *Student Due Process in the Private University: The State Action Doctrine*, 20 SYRACUSE L. REV. 911, 919 (1969). *See* Powe v. Miles, 407 F.2d 73, 79-80 (2d Cir. 1968); Grossner v. Trustees of Columbia Univ., 287 F. Supp. 535 (S.D.N.Y. 1968).

of the United States. In the recent case of *Roth v. Board of Regents of State Colleges*,[71] a nontenured professor whose employment contract had not been renewed brought an action under section 1983 of the Civil Rights Act of 1871[72] for declaratory and injunctive relief. Defendants raised as one of their defenses the doctrine of sovereign immunity. The court, rejecting the defendants' argument, made it clear that when a state agency or board violates federally protected constitutional rights, "[n]either the Eleventh Amendment nor the doctrine of Hans v. Louisiana, [134 U.S. 1 (1890)], affords these defendants the shield of sovereign immunity . . . ."[73] Because the proceeding is regarded as one against individuals whose action — by virtue of the Constitution — is unlawful, state agents may not claim for themselves the benefit of the state's immunity from suit.[74]

B. *Substantive Due Process*

The Supreme Court has held that the personal and professional rights of teachers, as protected under the due process clause of the 14th amendment, cannot be disregarded by the states in the operation of their educational institutions: "[E]ven though the governmental purpose be legitimate and substantial, that purpose cannot be pursued by means that broadly stifle fundamental personal liberties when the end can be more narrowly achieved."[75] Due process of law therefore requires that the interests of the state and its educational institutions be balanced against the interests of the teachers therein. The concept of "constitutional tenure" is primarily based upon the teachers' substantive rights and protections, as set forth below, that have recently emerged from the balancing of these interests.

1. *The employment of a teacher in a public school cannot be terminated because he has exercised a freedom secured to him by the Constitution of the United States.* This proposition, as related to

---

71 310 F. Supp. 972 (W.D. Wis. 1970)

72 42 U.S.C. § 1983.

73 310 F. Supp. at 974. *See Ex parte* Young, 209 U.S. 123, 149-59 (1908); Orleans Parish School Bd. v. Bush, 242 F.2d 156, 160-51 (5th Cir.), *cert. denied*, 354 U.S. 921 (1957).

74 Louisiana State Bd. of Educ. v. Baker, 339 F.2d 911 (5th Cir. 1964); *accord*, School Bd. v. Allen, 240 F.2d 59, 63 (4th Cir. 1956), *cert. denied*, 353 U.S. 910 (1957): "A state can act only through agents; and whether the agent be an individual officer or corporate agency, it ceases to represent the state when it attempts to use state power in violation of the Constitution and may be enjoined from such unconstitutional action."

75 Shelton v. Tucker, 364 U.S. 479, 488 (1960).

the broader problem of whether public employment in general can be conditioned upon waiver of a constitutional right, is of relatively recent vintage.   In the past, there was little doubt that public employment could be so conditioned.   The oft-quoted dictum of Justice Holmes, in the seminal case of *McAuliffe v. City of New Bedford*,[76] that one "has no constitutional right to be a policeman"[77] was clearly taken to uphold the arbitrary denial of government employment.[78] The Supreme Court twice held that public employment could be conditioned upon a waiver of constitutional rights.   In *United Public Workers v. Mitchell*,[79] the Court said: "Congress may regulate the political conduct of government employees 'within reasonable limits,' even though the regulation trenches to some extent upon unfettered polititcal action."[80]   And in *Adler v. Board of Education*,[81] the Court said:

---

[76] 155 Mass. 216, 29 N.E. 517 (1892).

[77] *Id.* at 220, 29 N.E. at 517.   In a more complete form, the passage from which the quoted statement was taken reads as follows:

> The petitioner may have a constitutional right to talk politics, but he has no constitutional right to be a policeman.   There are few employments for hire in which the servant does not agree to suspend his constitutional rights of free speech as well as of idleness by the implied terms of his contract.   The servant cannot complain, as he takes the employment on the terms which are offered him.   *Id.* at 220, 29 N.E. at 517-18.

[78] Such were the judicial attitudes toward public employees in the late 19th and early 20th centuries.   *See* Devol v. Board of Regents, 6 Ariz. 259, 56 P. 737 (1899); Hartigan v. Board of Regents, 49 W. Va. 14, 38 S.E. 698 (1901).   *See also* Murphy, *Academic Freedom — An Emerging Constitutional Right*, 28 LAW AND CONTEMP. PROB. 447, 457 (1963).

However, if one looks at the sentence that follows the passage quoted in note 77, *supra*, it is clear that Justice Holmes was prescribing a test of "reasonableness," not capriciousness.   Justice Holmes added: "On the same principle the city may impose any reasonable condition upon holding offices within its control."   McAuliffe v. City of New Bedford, 155 Mass. 216, 220, 29 N.E. 517, 518 (1892).

[79] 330 U.S. 75 (1947).   In *Mitchell* the Court upheld government interference in activities within the scope of the first amendment under two sections of the Hatch Act [5 U.S.C. §§ 7324-25 (1964)] which impose restrictions on federal employees engaging in political activity.

[80] 330 U.S. at 102.

[81] 342 U.S. 485 (1962).   The *Adler* Court upheld as constitutional section 3022 of the New York Education Law, N.Y. EDUC. LAW § 3022 (McKinney 1949), *as amended*, N.Y. EDUC. LAW § 3022 (McKinney 1970), which provides for the disqualification and removal from the public school system of teachers who advocate the overthrow of the government by unlawful means or who belong to organizations that have such a purpose.   Mr. Justice Minton, writing for the majority, stated:

> A teacher works in a sensitive area in a schoolroom.   There he shapes the attitude of young minds towards the society in which they live.   In this, the state has a vital concern.   It must preserve the integrity of the schools.   That the school authorities have the right and the duty to screen the officials, teachers, and employees as to their fitness to maintain the integrity of the schools as a part of ordered society, cannot be doubted.   342 U.S. at 493.

The Supreme Court subsequently found section 3022 to be unconstitutionally over-

> It is clear that [New York public school employees] have the right under our law to assemble, speak, think and believe as they will. It is equally clear that they have no right to work for the State in the school system on their own terms. . . . [T]hey are at liberty to retain their beliefs and associations and go elsewhere.[82]

But the forwarning of a change in attitude was apparent from the dissenting opinions in both of these cases. Mr. Justice Black, dissenting in *Mitchell*, stated:

> There is nothing about federal and state employees as a class which justifies depriving them or society of the benefits of their participation in public affairs. . . . I think the Constitution guarantees to them the same rights that other groups of good citizens have to engage in activities which decide who their elected representatives shall be.[83]

And Mr. Justice Douglas, dissenting in *Adler*, vigorously attacked the proposition that public employees may be relegated to the position of "second-class citizens."[84] He asserted that a person entering public service does not and cannot be forced to sacrifice his civil rights. "The Constitution guarantees freedom of thought and expression to everyone in our society. All are entitled to it; and none needs it more than the teacher."[85]

The line of cases that followed the *Adler* and *Mitchell* decisions eroded the privilege doctrine to the point that the position espoused therein could be more accurately restated as follows: Although one has no constitutional right to public employment, one does have a constitutional interest in not being denied admittance to, or continuation in, a position of public employment for arbitrary and capricious reasons, or for reasons that conflict with fundamental constitutional rights.[86] The first Supreme Court decision to take this approach was the 1952 case of *Wieman v. Updegraff*.[87] The Court, faced with an arbitrary refusal by state officials to pay the salaries of teachers and other public employees who refused to subscribe to a loyalty oath, stated that to assert the "facile generaliza-

---

broad to the extent that it makes mere membership in the Communist party prima facie evidence of disqualification for employment. Keyishian v. Board of Regents, 385 U.S. 589, 591, 609-610 (1967).

[82] 342 U.S. at 492 (citations omitted).

[83] 330 U.S. at 111-12.

[84] 342 U.S. at 508.

[85] *Id.*

[86] *See* Note, *The First Amendment and Public Employees — An Emerging Constitutional Right to be a Policeman?*, 37 GEO. WASH. L. REV. 409 (1968). *See also* Comment, *supra* note 55; Note, *supra* note 50.

[87] 344 U.S. 183 (1952).

tion that there is no constitutionally protected right to public employment is to obscure the issue."[88] There "need [be no] pause to consider whether an abstract right to public employment exists. It is sufficient to say that constitutional protection does extend to the public servant whose exclusion . . . is patently arbitrary or discriminatory."[89] Mr. Justice Black, concurring, further stated: "We must have freedom of speech for all or we will in the long run have it for none but the cringing and the craven. . . . [T]he right to speak on matters of public concern must be wholly free or eventually be wholly lost."[90]

By 1967, in *Keyishian v. Board of Regents*,[91] the dissenting opinion in *Adler* had become escalated to the majority opinion of the Court. The *Keyishian* Court — clearly rejecting the premise that "public employment, including academic employment, may be conditioned upon the surrender of constitutional rights which could not be abridged by direct government action"[92] — held unconstitutional a complex statutory and regulatory scheme which was to "prevent the appointment or retention of 'subversive' persons in state employment."[93] In reaching this decision the Court stated: "Our Nation is deeply committed to safeguarding academic freedom, which is of transcendent value to all of us and not merely to the teachers concerned. That freedom is therefore a special concern of the First Amendment, which does not tolerate laws that cast a pall of orthodoxy over the classroom."[94]

In 1968, the Court, in *Pickering v. Board of Education*,[95] again addressed itself to first amendment rights. After a letter critical of the school administration was sent to a local newspaper by a tenured teacher, the school board dismissed the teacher on a determination that "the publication of the letter was 'detrimental to the ef-

---

[88] *Id.* at 191.

[89] *Id.* at 192; *accord*, Slochower v. Board of Higher Educ., 350 U.S. 551 (1956), where the Court, striking down a statute that required a teacher's dismissal for exercising his fifth amendment privilege against self-incrimination, stated: "To state that a person does not have a constitutional right to government employment is only to say that he must comply with the reasonable, lawful, and nondiscriminatory terms laid down by the proper authorities." *Id.* at 555.

[90] 344 U.S. at 193.

[91] 385 U.S. 589 (1967).

[92] *Id.* at 605. For a statement of the doctrine of unconstitutional conditions, see note 55 *supra*. *See also* O'Neil, *Unconstitutional Conditions: Welfare Benefits with Strings Attached*, 54 CALIF. L. REV. 443 (1966).

[93] 385 U.S. at 592.

[94] *Id.* at 603.

[95] 391 U.S. 563 (1968).

ficient operation and administration of the schools of the district'
. . . ."[96] The Court, dealing directly with the first amendment issue,
stated:

> To the extent that the Illinois Supreme Court's opinion may be
> read to suggest that teachers may constitutionally be compelled to
> relinquish the First Amendment rights they would otherwise enjoy
> as citizens to comment on matters of public interest in connection
> with the operation of the public schools in which they work, it pro-
> ceeds on a premise that has been unequivocally rejected in numer-
> ous prior decisions of this Court.[97]

In *Wieman, Keyishian,* and *Pickering* the Court did not rely upon
the privilege-right dichotomy. The Court did not assert that the due
process clause provides a "right" to teach; rather, the inquiry went
to whether there is a general obligation on the part of the government to act fairly with its employees. Utilizing the concept of a
"constitutionally protected interest,"[98] the Court could avoid the
necessity of finding a right to life, liberty, or property that was deprived without due process of law.[99] Once infringement of a constitutionally protected interest was at issue, due process could be used
to test the validity of the limitations put on the teacher's substantive
rights by questioning the reasonableness of their denial under the
circumstances.

   2. *A teacher's specific (positive) constitutional rights may be
limited only upon a showing that his activity interferes with an over-
riding public interest.* Confronted with the allegation that a teacher's
constitutional freedoms have been infringed, the court must proceed
to weigh the interest of the individual teacher against the interests of
the school system and determine what safeguards are constitutionally
required. This balancing of interests required by due process
"is not a mechanical instrument. It is not a yardstick. It is a process."[100] "Its exact boundaries are undefinable, and its content varies
according to specific factual contexts."[101]

---

[96] *Id.* at 564.

[97] *Id.* at 568.

[98] *See, e.g.,* Cafeteria Workers v. McElroy, 367 U.S. 886, 894-95, 900 (1961). *See
also* Roth v. Board of Regent of State College, 310 F. Supp. 972 (W.D. Wis. 1970).

[99] *See* Pickering v. Board of Educ., 391 U.S. 563, 568 (1968). *See also* Roth v.
Board of Regents of State Colleges, 310 F. Supp. 972, 976 (W.D. Wis. 1970).

[100] Joint Anti-Fascist Refugee Comm. v. McGrath, 341 U.S. 123, 163 (1951)
(Frankfurter, J., concurring).

[101] Hannah v. Larche, 363 U.S. 420, 442 (1960).

In *Pickering v. Board of Education*,[102] the Court pointed out that "the State has interests as an employer in regulating the speech of its employees that differ significantly from those it possesses in connection with regulation of the speech of the citizenry in general." The test is to "balance . . . the interests of the teacher, as a citizen . . . and the interest of the State, as an employer . . . ."[103] The standard used in this particular case was: Where the "employment is only tangentially and insubstantially involved in the subject matter of the public communication made by a teacher . . . it is necessary to regard the teacher as the member of the general public he seeks to be."[104] Recognizing that at times the interests of the state in efficient public service and the interests of a teacher in free speech may be in conflict, the Court found that, in this case, the teacher's statements were entitled to the same protections as if made by a member of the general public; therefore, his dismissal by the board was not justifiable.[105]

---

[102] 391 U.S. 563 (1968).

[103] *Id.* at 568; *accord*, Cafeteria Workers v. McElroy, 367 U.S. 886, 896-98 (1961), where the Court utilized a similar balancing approach to deny relief to a "security risk" whose employment at a defense plant had been terminated.

[104] 391 U.S. at 574.

[105] The Court also conceded, however, that "[i]t is possible to conceive of some positions in public employment in which the need for confidentiality is so great that even completely correct public statements might furnish a permissible ground for dismissal." *Id.* at 570 n.3.

Subsequent to its decision in *Pickering*, the Supreme Court set aside two state court decisions with instructions to reconsider the cases in the light of the principles announced in *Pickering*. In Puentes v. Board of Educ., 24 App. Div. 2d 628 (2d Dep't 1965), *aff'd mem.*, 18 N.Y.2d 906, 223 N.E.2d 45, 276 N.Y.S.2d 638 (1966), *vacated and remanded per curiam*, 392 U.S. 653 (1968), *rev'd mem.*, 24 N.Y.2d 996, 250 N.E.2d 232, 302 N.Y.S.2d 824 (1969), the president of the teachers' federation had been suspended without pay because he wrote a letter (containing some inaccuracies, as did the statements in *Pickering*) critical of the board's failure to renew the contract of a probationary teacher. The Supreme Court vacated the judgment and remanded for further consideration. Puentes v. Board of Educ., 392 U.S. 653 (1968). Upon remand [24 N.Y.2d 996, 250 N.E.2d 232, 302 N.Y.S.2d 824 (1969)] the court of appeals reversed its prior decision, finding that the inaccuracies in the letter were related to reports to which the teacher had no access and hence were not the result of reckless or intentional falsehood. The court said: "Indiscreet bombast in an argumentative letter, to the limited extent present here, is insufficient to sanction disciplinary action. Otherwise, those who criticize in an area where criticism is permissible would either be discouraged from exercising their right or would be required to do so in such innocuous terms as would make the criticism seem ineffective or obsequious." *Id.* at 998-99, 250 N.E.2d at 233, 302 N.Y.S.2d at 826. Since the contents of the letter were arguably within the free speech protection laid down in *Pickering*, the court ordered reinstatement of the teacher.

In an Alaska case, Watts v. Seward School Bd., 395 P.2d 372 (Alas. 1964), *remanded per curiam*, 381 U.S. 126 (1965), *aff'd*, 421 P.2d 586, *reh. denied*, 423 P.2d 678 (Alas. 1967), *vacated and remanded per curiam*, 391 U.S. 592 (1968), *aff'd*, 454 P.2d 732 (Alas. 1969), *cert. denied*, 397 U.S. 921 (1970), teachers were dismissed for distributing an open letter containing false statements disparaging the superintendent. Here too the Supreme Court vacated judgment and remanded for further consideration.

The *Pickering* doctrine was followed in *Los Angeles Teachers Union v. Los Angeles City Board of Education.*[106] Members of the Los Angeles Teachers Union wished to circulate, during duty-free periods, petitions directed to state officials seeking an increase in state support of public education. The school board refused to allow the circulation on the grounds that a controversial petition would cause unrest among the staff, and that the circulation would disturb teachers who were trying to work. The union sought a court order to compel the board to permit the petition to circulate. Quoting from *Pickering*, the Supreme Court of California said that it "must strike 'a balance between the interests of the teacher, as a citizen, in commenting upon matters of public concern and the interest of the State, as an employer, in promoting the efficiency of the public services it performs through its employees.' "[107] In striking this balance the California court held that the government had no valid interest in restricting this speech-related activity simply in order to avert the sort of disturbance which is inevitably generated by the expression of ideas that are controversial. The court directed the school board to allow the teachers to circulate the petitions.

Balancing approaches similar to those in *Pickering* and *Los Angeles Teachers Union* have also been used by federal district courts. In *Friedman v. Union Free School District,*[108] an action was brought by the Bay Shore Classroom Teachers' Association challenging the right of the board of education to prohibit distribution in teachers' mailboxes of publications by the Association other than "routine internal distributions." The Association claimed that the distribution rule deprived teachers of their right to free speech in violation of the first and 14th amendments. The school board argued that as owner of the school premises it had the absolute right to direct how its facilities could be used, and that the distribution rule was necessary to keep the school premises free and clean of all litter. The court, citing prior holdings of the Supreme Court which had

---

Watts v. Seward School Bd., 391 U.S. 592 (1968). The Supreme Court of Alaska, upon remand [454 P.2d 732 (Alas. 1969), *cert. denied*, 397 U.S. 921 (1970)], reaffirmed its prior decision, holding that the situation did not fall under the *Pickering* doctrine in that the statements and actions of the teachers were detrimental to the school district and caused disharmony among the staff. None of the statements concerned matters on which the public voted; rather, they were in the nature of grievances which should have been pursued through established school procedures. For these reasons the teachers' dismissals were held to be justified.

106 71 Cal. 2d 551, 455 P.2d 827, 78 Cal. Rptr. 723 (1969).

107 *Id.* at 558, 455 P.2d at 831, 78 Cal. Rptr. at 727.

108 314 F. Supp. 223 (E.D.N.Y. 1970).

stated that such authority as claimed by the board must be exercised consistently with fundamental constitutional safeguards, found that the interests of the school board could hardly be deemed so substantial as to justify denial of first amendment rights. The court held the distribution rule to be "void on its face and in its application as an overbroad prohibition of the First Amendment rights . . . ."[109]

In *Roth v. Board of Regents of State Colleges*,[110] a district court ordered the school board to provide a nontenured teacher with a statement of the reasons for nonrenewal of his contract and a hearing at which those reasons could be challenged by the teacher. Relying on *Pickering*, the court noted: "A teacher's freedom of speech cannot be limited unless it can be shown that his utterances harm a substantial public interest."[111] Because the plaintiff was a nontenured university professor, the case also illustrates that courts have become highly sensitive to interferences with any teachers's specific constitutional rights, whether the teacher is tenured or not.[112]

3. *Tenured and nontenured teachers alike are protected against deprivation of their specific (positive) constitutional rights.* This view was taken as early as 1947 in *Bomar v. Keyes*.[113] There a probationary teacher was discharged under a New York statute because of her absence while exercising her privilege to serve on a federal jury. The law under which she was discharged allowed the discharge of a probationary teacher for any reason or for no reason at all.[114] An appeal to the commissioner of education was dismissed on the ground that the teacher "had not secured permanent tenure."[115] On appeal to the second circuit under section 1983 of the Civil Rights Act of 1871,[116] Judge Learned Hand stated that even if "her discharge by the Board was not a breach of contract . . . . it may have been the termination of an expectancy of continued employment, and that is an injury to an interest which the law will

---

109 *Id.* at 229.

110 310 F. Supp. 972 (W.D. Wis. 1970).

111 *Id.* at 980-81.

112 *See id.* at 976; Pred v. Board of Public Instruction, 415 F.2d 851 (5th Cir. 1969); McLaughlin v. Tilendis, 398 F.2d 287 (7th Cir. 1968); Johnson v. Branch, 364 F.2d 177 (4th Cir. 1966), *cert. denied*, 385 U.S. 1003 (1967); Bomar v. Keyes, 162 F.2d 136 (2d Cir.), *cert. denied*, 332 U.S. 825 (1947); Lucia v. Duggan, 303 F. Supp. 112 (D. Mass. 1969).

113 162 F.2d 136 (2d Cir.), *cert. denied*, 332 U.S. 825 (1947).

114 *Id.* at 139.

115 *Id.* at 138.

116 42 U.S.C. § 1983 (1964).

protect against invasion by acts themselves unlawful, such as the denial of a federal privilege."[117]

In *Shelton v. Tucker*,[118] the Supreme Court held invalid a state statute that required teachers in state-supported schools and colleges to file an affidavit listing all of their organizational affiliations over the preceding 5 years. A class action was brought by a teacher whose contract was not renewed because he refused to file the required affidavit. Holding that the statute deprived teachers of their right to associational freedom as protected by the 14th amendment, the Court alluded to the absence of tenure protections in Arkansas:

> These provisions [of the state statute] must be considered against the existing system of teacher employment required by Arkansas law. Teachers there are hired on a year-to-year basis. They are not covered by a civil service system, and they have no job security beyond the end of each school year.[119]

Although the implication by the Court that the consititutional protection afforded a teacher is in some fashion determined by looking to the existence of state tenure laws seems specious, the Court's language, nevertheless, seems to carry with it the notion that the constitutional rights of a nontenured teacher require even closer protection by the courts than those of the tenured teacher since the nontenured teacher is subject to more employment pressures.

Similarly, in *Johnson v. Branch*,[120] a teacher's yearly contract was not renewed because of her involvement in civil rights activities. The state statute under consideration did not provide for tenure and provided that all contracts were for only 1 year, renewable at the discretion of the school authorities. The Court of Appeals for the Fourth Circuit, in directing the school board to renew the teacher's contract, stated that it is "beyond cavil that the state may not force the plaintiff to choose between exercising her legitimate constitutional rights and her right of equality of opportunity to hold public employment."[121]

In *McLaughlin v. Tilendis*[122] — an action brought by probation-

---

117 162 F.2d at 139. Judge Hand pointed out that "[c]ertainly there are 'reasonable' limits to the exercise of her privilege; but the question whether she kept within such limits . . . must be tried . . . ." *Id.*

118 364 U.S. 479 (1960).

119 *Id.* at 482.

120 364 F.2d 177 (4th Cir. 1966), *cert. denied*, 385 U.S. 1003 (1967).

121 *Id.* at 180.

122 398 F.2d 287 (7th Cir. 1968). *See also* Pred. v. Board of Public Instruction, 415 F.2d 851 (5th Cir. 1969), reversing the trial court's dismissal of a suit by teachers

ary teachers under section 1983 of the Civil Rights Act of 1871[123] — the Court of Appeals for the Seventh Circuit held that a teacher's right to join a union is protected by the first amendment. Thus, the school board could not dismiss or refuse to renew the contract of a nontenured teacher because of his exercise of that constitutional right.

In the recent case of *Jones v. Hopper*,[124] however, the Court of Appeals for the Tenth Circuit seemed to revert to a tenure-nontenure distinction, allowing conditions to be placed on a nontenured teacher that presumably would be unconstitutional if placed on a tenured teacher. Jones, a nontenured associate professor, sued the president and the board of trustees of the state college for damages arising from their refusal to renew a contract of employment for the coming academic year. The complaint alleged that Jones was denied a renewal of his contract for the sole reason that he sought to exercise his constitutional rights of speech, publication, and religion.[125] The district court dismissed the case for failure to state a claim upon which relief could be granted, and the Court of Appeals for the Tenth Circuit affirmed. The latter court held that in the absence of tenure or an existing contract of employment, the refusal to renew his contract does not deprive a teacher of any constitutional rights for purposes of section 1983 of the Civil Rights Act of 1871.[126] The court appeared to recognize extremely broad discretionary power in the university administration when it stated: "Because of the special needs of the university, both public and private, great discretion must be given it in decisions about the renewal of contracts during the probationary period. In deciding whether to rehire or grant tenure, the considerations involved go well beyond a judgment about general teaching competency."[127] Although the decision may be explained by the traditional caution of courts not to delve into the maze of symbiotic relationships that may exist among the various component constituencies of a university, the effect of such judicial

---

alleging that their contracts were not renewed because of their participation in a teachers' association and their advocacy of campus freedom.

[123] 42 U.S.C. § 1983 (1964).

[124] 410 F.2d 1323 (10th Cir. 1969) (per curiam), *cert. denied*, 397 U.S. 991 (1970).

[125] The complaint specifically alleged that the nonrenewal decision was based on Jones' objection to the disqualification of an applicant for the English department because he was an Oriental, Jones' newspaper attack upon the English department's textbook, his founding of a student-faculty publication which criticized the Viet Nam war and commented on other controversial matters, and his support for a student who claimed conscientious objector status. *Id.* at 1326.

[126] 42 U.S.C. § 1983 (1964).

[127] 410 F.2d at 1329, *quoting Developments in the Law — Academic Freedom*, *supra* note 20, at 1101.

timidity is to jeopardize the position of any nontenured teacher. Such a judicial posture can only result in a first amendment chilling effect, thus inhibiting an otherwise free exchange of ideas.

The *Jones* decision, however, seems to represent the minority position; it is inconsistent with cases that preceded it, as reviewed above, and with subsequent state and federal decisions. In *Williams v. School District*,[128] a nontenured high school teacher alleged that she was not reemployed in a Missouri school system because of a speech that she had made before the Classical Association. The speech, which was subsequently published in the association's journal, included an evaluation of the comparative emphasis placed on athletics as opposed to scholarly pursuits in the public schools. The superintendent told the teacher that he found the speech offensive and that he would recommend that she not be reemployed. The trial court dismissed the entire complaint, and the teacher appealed. The Supreme Court of Missouri held that while the board does not have to reemploy a teacher, does not have to set out grounds for nonretention, and does not have to grant the teacher a hearing upon nonretention, "a school board's right not to rehire a teacher must not be on grounds that are violative of a teacher's constitutional right."[129] Accordingly, the court ordered the reinstatement of that part of the teacher's complaint that charged violation of a constitutional right and remanded the case for a trial on that issue.

The *Williams* court relied heavily upon the Supreme Court's decision in *Pickering v. Board of Education*,[130] which involved facts similar to those before the Missouri court. Although *Pickering* dealt with the dismissal of a tenured teacher, the broad language of the opinion suggests (as the *Williams* court apparently found) that the Court did not intend to limit the protection of first amendment rights to tenured teachers.

In *Roth v. Board of Regents of State Colleges*,[131] Judge Doyle stated that "substantive constitutional protection is unaffected by the presence or absence of tenure under state law."[132] Similarly, in *Gouge v. Joint School District*,[133] Judge Doyle said that the satisfaction of the requisites of state law is not determinative of "whether

---

128 447 S.W.2d 256 (Mo. 1969).

129 *Id.* at 265.

130 391 U.S. 563 (1968); *see* text accompanying notes 95-97, 102-05 *supra*.

131 310 F. Supp. 972 (W.D. Wis. 1970); *see* text accompanying notes 110-12 *supra*.

132 310 F. Supp. at 976; *see* cases cited in note 112 *supra*.

133 310 F. Supp. 984 (W.D. Wis. 1970).

the defendants met the minimum requirements of substantive . . . due process . . . in coming to the decision not to renew the plaintiffs' contracts."[134]

A federal district court in Indiana, in the case of *Roberts v. Lake Central School Corp.*,[135] found that the constitutional rights of a nontenured elementary school teacher had been abridged when a school system refused to rehire him because of a comment respecting the school board's bargaining tactics that he had made before a teachers' association. The principal of the school called the teacher in, charged that the statement was untrue, and demanded an apology; the teacher refused. When the teacher again refused to apologize before the superintendent, he was told that his nonretention would be recommended. The district court, finding that the comment did not threaten the efficient operation of the school, ordered the teacher reemployed. The court stated that if school boards were permitted not to renew teachers' contracts because of critical statements, "there would be a serious impairment in the freedom of teachers to speak out on issues concerning them."[136]

In light of the above discussion it becomes fairly clear that, whether a teacher is tenured or nontenured, most courts will not tolerate a termination or nonrenewal of a teacher's contract by a state agency when such action is spurred by the teacher's exercise of a specific constitutional right. However, what of the teacher who cannot allege infringement of a specific constitutional right, but only that the school administration's termination or nonrenewal of his contract was arbitrary and capricious? How may the Constitution protect him? If the teacher is tenured, the courts will generally find it unnecessary to reach basic constitutional issues; rather, they can ensure fairness by demanding strict adherence to the existing administrative safeguards, and, if necessary, interpreting the tenure requirements in such a way that rational treatment is most likely to be afforded an employee. Where the teacher in question is nontenured, however, courts have differed in their result. Some find a general due process right; some do not.

Mr. Justice Cardozo has characterized the protection of the individual from arbitrary action by the state as the very essence of due process.[137] The Supreme Court in *Wieman v. Updegraff*,[138] reaf-

---

[134] *Id.* at 989.
[135] 317 F. Supp. 63 (N.D. Ind. 1970).
[136] *Id.* at 65.
[137] Ohio Bell Tel. Co. v. Public Util. Comm'n, 301 U.S. 292, 302 (1937).
[138] 344 U.S. 183 (1952); *see* text accompanying notes 87-90 *supra*.

firmed that position with the statement: "[C]onstitutional protection does extend to the public servant whose exclusion pursuant to a statute is patently arbitrary or discriminatory."[139]   And recently, in *Norton v. Macy*,[140] where a civil service employee was dismissed as unfit because of his alleged homosexual activity, the Court of Appeals for the District of Columbia Circuit stated: "The Government's obligation to accord due process sets at least minimal substantive limits on its prerogative to dismiss its employees: it forbids all dismissals which are arbitrary and capricious."[141]

4. *A teacher, whether tenured or nontenured, should be protected by the due process clause of the 14th amendment against dismissal or nonretention which is arbitrary, capricious, or wholly without basis in fact.*   In *Birnbaum v. Trussell*,[142] the Court of Appeals for the Second Circuit reasoned that "whenever there is a substantial interest, other than employment by the state, involved in the discharge of a public employee, he [cannot] be removed . . . on arbitrary grounds . . . ."[143] Here, where a physician had been dismissed from a municipal hospital due to his alleged anti-Negro bias and without a hearing on the specific allegations, the court found two vital interests were threatened: reputation and the ability to pursue a profession effectively.   The court stated: "Both are ordinarily accorded meticulous protection . . . to prevent direct injury by arbitrary state action."[144]

Because of the teaching profession's limited employment opportunities — the state being the main and often the sole employer — a teacher's discharge for an arbitrary or capricious reason would be no less damaging to his future career than a discharge for untested allegations of racial prejudice would be to a doctor's career.   Thus, in *Lucia v. Duggan*,[145] where a nontenured teacher was summarily dis-

---

[139] 344 U.S. at 192.

[140] 417 F.2d 1161 (D.C. Cir. 1969).

[141] *Id.* at 1164.   In making its finding the court emphasized the fact that a "badge of infamy" may attach to alleged homosexuality.

It should be noted that the Court of Appeals for the District of Columbia Circuit has taken the most critical view of administrative terminations based upon conduct unrelated to employment, such as homosexuality.   The Court of Appeals for the Fifth Circuit, on the other hand, has accepted the contention that private homosexual acts can be the basis for discharge.   Anonymous v. Macy, 398 F.2d 317 (5th Cir. 1968), *cert. denied*, 393 U.S. 1041 (1969).

[142] 371 F.2d 672 (2d Cir. 1966).

[143] *Id.* at 678.

[144] *Id.* at 678-79 n.13.

[145] 303 F. Supp. 112 (D. Mass. 1969).

missed for wearing a beard, Judge Garrity, citing the *Birnbaum* decision, stated:

> Whatever the derivation and scope of [the nontenured teacher's] alleged freedom to wear a beard, it is at least an interest of his, especially in combination with his professional reputation as a school teacher, which may not be taken from him without due process of law. . . . Plaintiff's interest in wearing a beard and in his career as a teacher is not nullified by his having been employed less than the three years required to achieve tenure status.[146]

But in *Freeman v. Gould Special School District*,[147] the eighth circuit reached a different result. Six Negro teachers in Lincoln County, Arkansas asserted that the decision of the school board not to renew their contracts of employment was based on racial discrimination. Arkansas law did not provide for a tenure system; teachers were employed under annual contracts with automatic renewal unless written notice to the contrary was given within a prescribed time.[148] The court declared that in the absence of a tenure statute a local school board has the absolute right to decline to employ or reemploy any teacher as long as its decision is not violative of a specific constititutional right such as race, religion, freedom of association, or the right against self-incrimination.[149] The court found no evidence to support the teachers' allegation that the board's decision was racially discriminatory; rather, the decision appeared to be based on the recommendation of the local Negro principal, with whom the teachers had had several personal conflicts. Absent evidence of discrimination, the court held that no federal question was presented; the board's decision, even if it was arbitrary and capricious, violated none of the teachers' rights. Noting that "there are many public employees who are separated from their employment by a purely arbitrary decision," the court rejected the teachers' contention that "the Board must accord due process, both substantive and procedural, in all of its operative procedures."[150] The onus of an imminent flood of litigation must have lurked in the *Freeman* court's mind when it observed that under a contrary decision, "there could only be . . . a discharge for cause, with the school board carrying the burden of showing that the discharge was for a permissible rea-

---

[146] *Id.* at 117-18.

[147] 405 F.2d 1153 (8th Cir.), *cert. denied*, 396 U.S. 843 (1969).

[148] It should be noted that subsequent to the decision in *Freeman* a statewide teacher tenure law was adopted by the Arkansas legislature. *See* NATIONAL EDUCATION ASS'N OF THE UNITED STATES, *supra* note 9, at 33.

[149] 405 F.2d at 1159.

[150] *Id.* at 1160.

son."[151] The court felt that such a holding would render the tenure laws useless in the states which had adopted them.

The *Freeman* court had to distinguish the Supreme Court decision of *Slochower v. Board of Higher Education*.[152] The court did so by stating that the *Slochower* case "applied to a tenure situation and an unconstitutional city charter provision" which mandated the discharge of city employees who relied upon the fifth amendment.[153] The court also had to contend with *Schware v. Board of Bar Examiners*,[154] which held that a general due process right protecting a person against arbitrary, capricious, or unreasonable state action exists in the area of state licensing. The majority in *Freeman* distinguished that case on the ground that it "dealt with the general right to practice a profession, and did not deal with the narrower question of a right to specific employment."[155]

Judge Lay, dissenting in *Freeman*, met the tenure issue head-on:

> The majority opinion assumes that the protective cloak of the due process clause as enunciated in *Slochower* . . . does not apply to a public school teacher who is without tenure . . . . I disagree. Constitutional rights of public school teachers are not conditioned upon state tenure laws. The entire discussion of "tenure" is irrelevant to the facts here. *Slochower* does not turn upon recognition of tenure laws but upon the denial of the "protection of the individual against arbitrary action" which violates due process of law.[156]

Judge Lay felt that a school board cannot arbitrarily or capriciously refuse to renew a teacher's contract. He asserted that "the right to the specified job is not in issue; rather, the focal stake is the personal liberty to pursue one's employment without arbitrary vilification and reckless exclusion by the state."[157] The dissent further contended that the extension of this limited general due process right to the area of public employment would not result in either a flood of

---

[151] *Id.*

[152] 350 U.S. 551 (1956). In *Slochower*, the Court, in a 5-4 decision, held unconstitutional the summary dismissal of a tenured teacher under a New York City Charter provision that provided for the automatic dismissal of any city employee exercising his fifth amendment privilege against self incrimination to avoid answering a question relating to his official conduct. Because no inference of guilt could be made from the exercise of the privilege, the Court found the dismissal "wholly without support." *Id.* at 559.

[153] 405 F.2d at 1159.

[154] 353 U.S. 232 (1957) (a state cannot deny a person the opportunity to take a bar examination except for reasons which are related to a valid state purpose).

[155] 405 F.2d at 1159.

[156] *Id.* at 1163.

[157] *Id.* at 1165 (emphasis omitted).

litigation or an imposed tenure system as feared by the majority. In particular, Judge Lay pointed out that "[w]hen the board's discretion is challenged, the burden of proof always remains on the plaintiff to demonstrate impermissible grounds" for the board's action.[158]

Despite the stand taken by the *Freeman* majority, the principal announced by the *Birnbaum* court has found recent application. In *Roth v. Board of Regents of State Colleges*,[159] Judge Doyle stated: "The balancing test of *Cafeteria Workers v. McElroy* [367 U.S. 886 (1960)] compels the conclusion that under the due process clause of the Fourteenth Amendment the decision not to retain a professor employed by a state university may not rest on a basis wholly unsupported in fact . . . ."[160] He noted that this standard should be considerably less severe than the standard of "cause" as applied in the dismissal of tenured professors. Thus, it cannot be said that the prescribed protections constitute judicially-imposed tenure for all teachers. Judge Doyle then quoted the controlling language from *Birnbaum*: "[W]henever there is a substantial interest, other than employment by the state, involved in the discharge of a public employee, he [cannot] be removed . . . on arbitrary grounds . . . ."[161] Judge Doyle reasserted this position with regard to elementary school teachers in *Gouge v. Joint School District*.[162]

5. *A teacher should be protected by the due process clause of the 14th amendment against a dismissal or nonretention decision which is wholly without reason.* Although the Supreme Court has never had to decide the specific question of whether a dismissal or nonretention for no reason is subject to challenge, it has had occasion to speak on the issue. In *Vitarelli v. Seaton*,[163] for example, a government employee had been suspended from the Department of the Interior as a "security risk." Although the Court ordered the employee reinstated because the secretary did not comply with departmental regulations, it indicated in dictum that there is no constitutional proscription against summary dismissal of an unprotected

---

158 *Id.* at 1167.

159 310 F. Supp. 972 (W.D. Wis. 1970). *See also* Hetrick v. Martin, 322 F. Supp. 545 (E.D. Ky. 1971), denying defendants' motion to dismiss a suit by a teacher whose contract was not renewed because she was "unsociable" and her assignments were "inconclusive." Mrs. Hetrick alleged that her nonretention was in fact based on her classroom discussions of the Viet Nam war and the draft system.

160 310 F. Supp. at 979.

161 *Id.*

162 310 F. Supp. 984, 991 (W.D. Wis. 1970).

163 359 U.S. 535 (1959).

employee for no stated reason.[164]   One could argue, however, that since there is always a reason for action, regardless of how obscure, a dismissal that is totally unexplained and alleged to be for "no reason" is the essence of arbitrariness and capriciousness.

Chief Justice Weintraub, in his concurring opinion in *Zimmerman v. Board of Education*,[165] although refusing to pass on the question, does suggest the availability of such an argument:

> [I]f we may inquire into "unreasonableness" [of the dismissal], it would seem to follow that there must be a "reason," i.e., "cause" for refusal to continue the teacher into a tenure status. That course has its difficulties. It would not mean the court would not recognize a wide range of "reasons" or would lightly disagree with the employer's finding that the "reason" in fact existed. . . . [However, it may] involve some practical problems in the administration of a school system.
>
> I think the question might well be left for another day . . . .[166]

Support for this protection against dismissal or nonretention for no reason is found in recent cases which have held that a nontenured teacher must be informed of the charges against him prior to the termination of his employment. In both *Roth v. Board of Regents of State Colleges*[167] and *Gouge v. Joint School District*,[168] Judge Doyle expressed the view that a teacher is protected by the due process clause against nonrenewal which is "wholly without reason."[169]

The *Lucia v. Duggan*[170] case vividly exhibits the interest of the teacher in not being dismissed without reason. The court, after finding that the dismissed teacher had "attempted unsuccessfully to secure employment elsewhere as a public school teacher,"[171] stated: "It is fairly inferable that one reason, if not the only one, why plaintiff has been unable to secure employment as a public school teacher is because he was dismissed by the . . . school committee for no stated reasons."[172]

Moreover, under a dismissal or nonretention for no reason, it is more difficult for the teacher to prove that the motive of the school administration was constitutionally proscribed. And knowing that

---

[164] *Id.* at 539-40.

[165] 38 N.J. 65; 183 A.2d 25 (1962), *cert. denied*, 371 U.S. 956 (1963).

[166] *Id.* at 80, 183 A.2d at 33 (concurring opinion).

[167] 310 F. Supp. 972 (W.D. Wis. 1970).

[168] 310 F. Supp. 984 (W.D. Wis. 1970).

[169] 310 F. Supp. at 979, 991.

[170] 303 F. Supp. 112 (D. Mass. 1969).

[171] *Id.* at 116.

[172] *Id.*

it must give a reason for its actions, the administration will be wary of dismissing a teacher for exercising a specific constitutional right.

It might be argued that requiring that dismissal or nonretention be based upon some stated reason affords the nontenured teacher the full protection enjoyed by tenured teachers, who can be dismissed only for cause. This argument was recently met by the Rhode Island commissioner of education in *Domenicone v. School Committee*.[173] There, a probationary teacher, after requesting a statement of charges and a hearing concerning nonrenewal of his contract, was told by the school board that such notice and a hearing were afforded only to tenured teachers or to teachers dismissed during the school year, and not to probationary teachers whose contracts were not renewed. The commissioner of education did not accept this distinction: "The provision in the [state statute] . . . which states that a teacher who has acquired tenure shall not be dismissed without good and just cause should not be construed to imply that a teacher who has not acquired tenure may be dismissed without cause."[174] But the commissioner did believe that the cause for dismissal of a nontenured teacher could be less than that required to dismiss a tenured teacher. He concluded that "simple justice as provided not only by the laws of this state but by the Constitution of the United States demands that [the teacher] know the cause for dismissal or non-renewal of contract."[175]

6. *With regard to a teacher's substantive due process protections, it should be immaterial whether his employment is terminated during a given contract period, or not renewed for a subsequent period.* In *Jones v. Hopper*[176] the petitioner relied on *Bomar v. Keyes*[177] in support of the contention that he was denied an "expectancy" of continued employment when his contract was not renewed. Noting that Bomar, a nontenured teacher, was dismissed during her contract period, the *Jones* court distinguished that case on the ground that the "interest" protected was a contract of employment and the "expectancy" was that of continuing employment until the expiration of the contract. The *Jones* court found no "interest" to be pro-

---

173 Opinion of the Rhode Island Commissioner of Education (May 20, 1970), *reviewed in* 48 NEA RESEARCH BULL. 90 (Oct. 1970).

174 *Id.*, 48 NEA RESEARCH BULL. at 91-92.

175 *Id.*, 48 NEA RESEARCH BULL. at 92.

176 410 F.2d 1323 (10th Cir. 1969), *cert. denied*, 397 U.S. 991 (1970).

177 162 F.2d 136 (2d Cir.), *cert. denied*, 332 U.S. 825 (1947).

tected where nonrenewal of a nontenured teacher's contract is based on arbitrary or retaliatory reasons.[178]

Better reasoned opinions were given in the *Roth v. Board of Regents of State Colleges*[179] and *McLaughlin v. Tilendis*[180] cases, where the courts found that substantive constitutional protection makes no distinction as to "whether employment is terminated during a given contract period, or not renewed for a subsequent period."[181]   And in *Domenicone v. School Committee*,[182] the commissioner stated that the only difference between nonrenewal and discharge is the point in time of the action taken against the teacher; therefore, in practice they are the same.   Although the *Roth* and *McLaughlin* courts were referring to the protection of first amendment rights, the same protection should be afforded to any rights which have emerged as substantive due process requirements.   A nontenured teacher's protection against actions which are arbitrary, capricious, without basis in fact, or, as in *Domenicone*, for no stated reason, should apply in both dismissal and nonrenewal situations.

In summary, the evolving guidelines for substantive due process require that where the dismissal or nonretention of a faculty member, tenured or nontenured, impinges upon a specific constitutional right, the state shall not prevail unless it can show that the teacher's exercise of such a constitutionally protected right harms a substantial public interest.   Of course, this requires a rational connection between the proscribed activity and the particular interests of the educational system.   Where no specific constitutional right is at issue, but rather the administration's action is arbitrary, capricious, without basis in fact, or based upon no stated reason, the courts have looked to other factors such as damage to reputation and career opportunities in order to invoke the due process clause.   Although the courts differ in their results where the balancing does not involve specific (positive) constitutional rights, the more progressive courts have recognized that dismissal or nonretention for arbitrary or capricious reasons, or for no reason, can effectively mask a constitutionally impermissible discharge.   Where the hidden reason for such a discharge is the teacher's exercise of a first amendment right, the

---

[178] 410 F.2d at 1327-29.

[179] 310 F. Supp. 972 (W.D. Wis. 1970).

[180] 398 F.2d 287 (7th Cir. 1968).

[181] 310 F. Supp. at 976; *see* 398 F.2d at 289.

[182] Opinion of the Rhode Island Commissioner of Education (May 20, 1970), *reviewed in* 48 NEA RESEARCH BULL. 90, (Oct. 1970).

dismissal or nonretention could have a significant chilling effect on the exercise of those rights by nontenured teachers.[183]

C. *Procedural Due Process*

In order to properly safeguard a person's substantive rights, the due process clause provides that certain procedural requirements must be satisfied. As Mr. Justice Frankfurter once observed: "The history of liberty has largely been the history of observance of procedural safeguards."[184] Nevertheless, the Supreme Court has been somewhat vague in dealing with the procedural rights of government employees. Moreover, in the area of education, administrators have effectively argued that the question of a teacher's competence is one peculiarly within the discretion of the teacher's superiors since such competence is judgmental and is not readily susceptible to factual determination in an adversarial proceeding. However, as the courts more clearly articulate constitutional principles of procedural due process and recognize that even sincere administrators are often arbitrary, they are becoming more dubious of the academic administrator's assertion that the esoteric relationship between the administration and the teacher should not be subject to judicial review. This trend is evinced by the increasing number of cases in which the courts are recognizing the teacher's right to 14th amendment procedural due process protections.[185] The protections discussed below have emerged from such cases.

---

[183] Generally, first amendment freedoms, and the chilling thereof, have been scrupulously protected. *See* Dombrowski v. Pfister, 380 U.S. 479 (1965); Smith v. California, 361 U.S. 147 (1959); Thornhill v. Alabama, 310 U.S. 88 (1940).

[184] McNabb v. United States, 318 U.S. 332, 347 (1943). Historically, procedural due process may be traced directly as far back as 1215 when, in the Magna Carta, the Crown agreed, as to a limited class of persons, not to proceed summarily but only after notice and a hearing given in accordance with "the law of the land."

[185] *See, e.g.*, Lucia v. Duggan, 303 F. Supp. 112 (D. Mass. 1969). "The particular circumstances of a dismissal of a public school teacher provide compelling reasons for application of a doctrine of procedural due process." *Id.* at 118. *See also* Roth v. Board of Regents of State Colleges, 310 F. Supp. 972 (W.D. Wis. 1970); Gouge v. Joint School Dist., 310 F. Supp. 984 (W.D. Wis. 1970). *But cf.* Vitarelli v. Seaton, 359 U.S. 535 (1959), where the Court implied that so long as procedural rules for the dismissal of government employees (here an unprotected employee of the Department of the Interior) are present, the administrator must comply with those procedures; absent such rules, the Constitution places no restrictions on dismissals of unprotected employees.

Mr. Justice Brennan's dissenting opinion in Cafeteria Workers v. McElroy, 367 U.S. 886, 899 (1961), reveals the vulnerability of government employees' substantive rights in the absence of procedural safeguards. In that case the majority upheld the summary dismissal of a short-order cook employed at a defense plant because she failed to meet certain regulatory and contractual "security requirements." Mr. Justice Brennan observed:

1. *Notice of the specific reasons for the institution's intended nonretention of the teacher is required.* The inference is present in several cases that information as to cause and an opportunity to dispute the stated cause must be afforded where the dismissal will grievously affect the public employee's career opportunities. In *Birnbaum v. Trussell*,[186] the court stated that "whenever there is a substantial interest, other than employment by the state, involved in the discharge of a public employee, he [cannot] be removed . . . without a procedure calculated to determine whether legitimate grounds do exist."[187] In a footnote, the court further stated: "It is clear that [the] refusal to give appellant a copy of the charges was as much a denial of his rights as an absolute refusal to allow him a hearing."[188]

In *Lucia v. Duggan*,[189] the plaintiff was not told that his refusal to remove his beard would result in his dismissal. Plaintiff was forced to guess what the charges against him were and what action, if any, the school committee might take. The court, finding a violation of due process stated: "On the latter point, at least, plaintiff may have guessed wrong. No reason has been advanced by the defendants as to why plaintiff should have been forced to make these guesses."[190]

In *Roth v. Board of Regents of State Colleges*,[191] Judge Doyle stated: "Substantive constitutional protection for a university professor against nonretention in violation of his First Amendment rights or arbitrary non-retention is useless without procedural safeguards. . . . [M]inimal procedural due process includes a statement of the

---

[T]he mere assertion by government that exclusion is for a valid reason forecloses further inquiry. That is, unless the government official is foolish enough to admit what he is doing — and few will be so foolish after today's decision — he may employ "security requirements" as a blind behind which to dismiss at will for the most discriminatory of causes.

— Such a result in effect nullifies the substantive right — not to be arbitrarily injured by Government — which the Court purports to recognize. What sort of a right is it which enjoys absolutely no procedural protection? *Id.* at 900.

[186] 371 F.2d 672 (2d Cir. 1966).

[187] *Id.* at 678.

[188] *Id.* at 679 n.15. "Whatever knowledge Dr. Birnbaum may have gleaned about the charges against him from hospital rumors was not the 'notice' which the due process clause requires. A party against whom the Government is proceeding is entitled to be apprised by the Government, with some precision and specificity, of its reasons for so doing." *Id.*

[189] 303 F. Supp. 112 (1969).

[190] *Id.* at 118.

[191] 310 F. Supp. 972 (W.D. Wis. 1970).

reasons why the university intends not to retain the professor . . . ."[102]
The same principle was held to apply to elementary school teachers
in *Gouge v. Joint School District*.[193]

In a decision of the Court of Appeals for the Fifth Circuit, *Ferguson v. Thomas*,[194] the rights of a nontenured teacher to procedural
due process were again considered. Although in this instance the
dismissal of a university professor for cause was upheld, the appellate court listed the minimal requirements of procedural due process
for one who has an expectancy of continued employment. Where
the termination for cause is opposed, these requirements include notice of "the cause or causes for termination in sufficient detail to
fairly enable [the teacher] to show any error that may exist . . . ."[195]

2. *The teacher should be given a hearing and notice thereof.*
Generally speaking the courts do not delineate a right to notice of a
hearing separate from a right to the hearing itself. But it has been
specifically stated in both the *Roth* and *Gouge* cases that minimal
procedural due process requires that "notice of a hearing" be provided the teacher.[196] Of course, the right to notice of a hearing will
be dependent upon finding a right to the hearing itself.

In *Birnbaum* the court noted the significance of a hearing when
it stated that "it is readily apparent that whatever injury appellant
has suffered was a result of his being denied a hearing. . . . [A]
full hearing was the only way appellant's substantial interests could
have been protected . . . ."[197] The court held that denial of such a
hearing afforded Birnbaum a right of action for injuries suffered in
consequence thereof.[198] The courts in *Roth*, *Gouge*, and *Ferguson*
also found that minimal procedural due process includes a hearing.[199]

---

192 *Id.* at 979-80. The *Roth* court was quick to point out that "[i]t should clearly
be understood that any more stringent requirements imposed by statute, custom, or
otherwise, such as a showing of 'cause' in the case of a tenured professor, are unaffected
by this statement of minimal procedural requirements embodied in the due process
clause of the Fourteenth Amendment." *Id.* at 980 n.3.

193 310 F. Supp. 984, 992 (W.D. Wis. 1970).

194 430 F.2d 852 (5th Cir. 1970).

195 *Id* at 856, *followed in* Lucas v. Chapman, 430 F.2d 945 (5th Cir. 1970) (nontenured principal with 11 years of employment in the school system should have been
accorded *Ferguson* minimal due process standards when his 1-year contract was not
renewed after he criticized the school board at a PTA meeting).

196 Roth v. Board of Regents of State Colleges, 310 F. Supp. 972, 980 (W.D. Wis.
1970); Gouge v. Joint School Dist., 310 F. Supp. 984, 992 (W.D. Wis. 1970).

197 Birnbaum v. Trussell, 371 F.2d 672, 679 (2d Cir. 1966).

198 *Id.*

199 Ferguson v. Thomas, 430 F.2d 852, 856 (5th Cir. 1970); Roth v. Board of
Regents of State Colleges, 310 F. Supp. 972, 980 (W.D. Wis. 1970); Gouge v. Joint
School Dist., 310 F. Supp. 984, 992 (W.D. Wis. 1970).

In contrast, the Supreme Court, in *Cafeteria Workers v. McElroy*,[200] upheld the denial of a hearing to a short-order cook who had been dismissed because she did not meet the "security requirements" of the defense plant where she worked. The Court stated that it was satisfied that "under the circumstances of this case such a procedure was not constitutonally required."[201]   However, in a vigorous dissent, Mr. Justice Brennan, quoting from *Joint Anti-Fascist Refugee Committee v. McGrath*,[202] stated: "[T]he right to be heard before being condemned to suffer grievous loss of any kind, even though it may not involve the stigma and hardships of a criminal conviction, is a principle basic to our society."[203]

A more recent example of a court upholding the denial of a hearing may be found in *DeCanio v. School Committee*.[204]   The Supreme Court of Massachusetts, adhering to the majority opinion in *Cafeteria Workers* and disagreeing with the *Roth* and *Gouge* decisions, upheld a lower court decision denying six nontenured teachers the right to a hearing. The teachers had been suspended for 7 days due to their unauthorized absence when they joined parents and citizens in a "liberation school." At a hearing on the suspensions, their request for a continuance and a public hearing was denied, the school committee voting instead to terminate the teachers' contracts. The committee also voted to hold a closed hearing on the dismissals, but the teachers declined to attend. (Due to lack of notice of the specific charges against the plaintiffs, the trial judge did not view this refusal to attend the closed hearing as a waiver by the teachers.)   Instead, they brought a suit seeking reinstatement.[205]

The teachers contended that the lack of a hearing on the dismissal deprived them of due process. The Massachusetts court disagreed with the decision of the district court in the *Roth* and *Gouge* cases and said that it "chose to follow the greater weight of authority," noting that "[m]ost of the cases in which the question [of the dismissal of a nontenured teacher] has been considered have concluded that in the absence of a statute to the contrary a probationary

---

200 367 U.S. 886 (1961).

201 *Id.* at 894.

202 341 U.S. 123, 168 (1951) (Frankfurter, J., concurring).

203 367 U.S. at 901.

204 260 N.E.2d 676 (Mass. 1970), *cert. denied*, 39 U.S.L.W. 3374 (U.S. Mar. 2, 1971).   It should be noted that subsequent to the *DeCanio* decision the Massachusetts legislature enacted statutory changes granting additional rights to probationary teachers. *See* MASS. GEN. LAWS ANN. ch. 71, §§ 42, 42B (Supp. 1971).

205 260 N.E.2d at 678.

teacher may be dismissed without a hearing."[206]   The court concluded that the Massachusetts statute, which provided a hearing to tenured teachers but not to nontenured teachers, did not violate the Constitution of the United States.[207]

3. *The teacher should have the opportunity to be present at the hearing and respond to the stated reasons for nonretention.* A significant case dealing with the right to confrontation is *Greene v. McElroy.*[208] In *Greene* the Government's revocation of an aeronautical engineer's security clearance, without a full hearing, resulted in termination of his employment. The Supreme Court held that the security clearance revocation, which was based on information received from unidentified persons, deprived Greene of "the traditional procedural safeguards of confrontation and cross-examination."[209] In so deciding, the Court stated that among "relatively immutable" principles of our jurisprudence is one which holds that "where governmental action seriously injures an individual and the reasonableness of the action depends on fact findings, the evidence used to prove the Government's case must be disclosed to the individual so that he has an opportunity to show that it is untrue."[210]

The rule espoused in *Greene* has likewise been followed in cases involving teachers. In the *Roth* case, for example, the court held "that minimal procedural due process includes . . . a hearing at which [the teacher] may respond to the stated reasons [for nonretention] . . . if the professor appears at the appointed time and place. At such a hearing the professor must have a reasonable opportunity to submit evidence relevant to the stated reasons."[211] The same prin-

---

[206] *Id.* at 680-81.

[207] *Id.* at 681.

[208] 360 U.S. 474 (1959).

[209] *Id.* at 493.

[210] *Id.* at 496.

[211] Roth v. Board of Regents of State Colleges, 310 F. Supp. 972, 980 (W.D. Wis. 1970).

Although the courts do not appear to have dealt with the issue, it seems clear that the nontenured teacher's right to be present at the hearing should be complimented by the right to also have legal counsel present at the hearing. The right to counsel serves to insure that the teacher is afforded maximum fairness at the hearing and that his interests are most effectively served by his appearance. Committee A of the American Association of University Professors (AAUP) has alluded to the nontenured teacher's right to counsel in its 1968 *Recommended Institutional Regulations on Academic Freedom and Tenure*, 54 A.A.U.P. BULL. 448 (1968). Section 10 of the proposed regulations provides that where a nontenured faculty member "alleges that considerations violative of academic freedom significantly contributed to a decision not to reappoint him" and his allegations have not been resolved by informal methods, if the appropriate "committee so recommends, the matter will be heard in the manner set forth in Regulations 5 and 6 . . . ." *Id.* at 451. Section 5(c)(3), one of the regulations referred to

ciple was held to apply to elementary school teachers in *Gouge*. And in *Ferguson*, the fifth circuit stated that the nontenured teacher "must be accorded a meaningful opportunity to be heard in his own defense . . . ." In this respect he must be "advised of the names and nature of the testimony of witnesses against him . . . ."[212]

In summary, the emerging substantive rights of nontenured teachers can be realized only if they are protected by the procedural due process requirements of (1) notice of the specific reasons for dismissal or nonretention, (2) a hearing on those reasons and notice of such a hearing, and (3) the opportunity to be present at the hearing and to respond to the stated reasons for dismissal or nonretention. These procedural requirements are basic standards which the more sagacious courts have recognized as being necessary to protect the teacher's interests.

The requirements discussed above are by no means exhaustive of the procedural safeguards which could be invoked to protect the substantive rights of teachers. There has been judicial reference to more refined procedural requirements which would further protect the interests of faculty members. Those suggested safeguards would require (1) that the ultimate decision of the board rest upon the charges of which the teacher was notified,[213] (2) that the ultimate decision of the board be based on a finding of facts which were submitted at the hearing,[214] and (3) that the hearing be held by an impartial tribunal.[215] Although even the most prescient courts have not uniformly recognized these broader requirements, the adoption

---

above, provides: "During the proceeding the faculty member will be permitted to have an academic advisor and counsel of his own choice." *Id.* at 450.

212 Ferguson v. Thomas, 430 F.2d 852, 856 (5th Cir. 1970).

213 In Gouge v. Joint School District, 310 F. Supp. 984 (W.D. Wis. 1970), Judge Doyle stated that the "necessary corollary" to the requirement of a statement of the charges against a nontenured teacher is that "the Board's ultimate decision may not rest on a basis of which the teacher was never notified nor may it rest on a basis to which the teacher had no opportunity to respond." *Id.* at 992.

214 "[T]he district court . . . must judge the constitutionality of [the Board's] action on the basis of the facts which were before the Board and on its logic." Johnson v. Branch, 364 F.2d 177, 181 (4th Cir. 1966), *cert. denied*, 385 U.S. 1003 (1967).

The district court opinion of the *Johnson* case, 242 F. Supp. 721 (E.D.N.C. 1965), reveals the disadvantage of not having a full record of the initial hearing. As is often the case, the trial court had to conduct an extended finding of facts de novo to determine what facts were before the board when it decided not to renew the plaintiff's contract.

215 In Ferguson v. Thomas, 430 F.2d 852 (5th Cir. 1970), the Court of Appeals for the Fifth Circuit said that teachers with an expectancy of reemployment should be afforded a "hearing . . . before a tribunal that both possesses some academic expertise and has an apparent impartiality toward the charges." *Id.* at 856.

of such safeguards may be forthcoming if the courts seek to fully protect the interests of nontenured teachers.

School authorities might argue that the emerging protections for nontenured teachers demand that every teacher be afforded the elaborate and time-consuming procedures formerly required only in the discharge of tenured teachers. It might thus be urged that the burden of preparing for, and actually conducting, numerous adversarial hearings, as well as the publicity surrounding such proceedings, would seriously disrupt the school's educational activities. Although it is true that the evolving procedural requirements for nontenured teachers do place additional demands upon school authorities, there are several factors which should prevent these demands from seriously interfering with the educational process. Initially, it must be remembered that the burden of proof and the burden of going forward at the hearing remain on the nontenured teacher who challenges his nonretention.[216] Because these burdens remain with the teacher, school authorities will not be required to prepare a full and persuasive case comparable to that required where a tenured teacher is discharged. Moreover, the undesirable publicity surrounding the hearings could be mitigated by the frequent use of *in camera* proceedings. Finally, the procedural requirements discussed above are not intended to foreclose the opportunity for the nontenured teacher to knowingly and voluntarily waive his procedural rights when he is informed of the decision not to reemploy him.[217]

Regardless of the ultimate refinements of the procedural safeguards and the degree of judicial involvement therewith, educational

---

[216] In Roth v. Board of Regents of State Colleges, 310 F. Supp. 972 W.D. Wis. 1970), Judge Doyle stated:

The burden of going forward and the burden of proof rests with the professor. Only if he makes a reasonable showing that the stated reasons are wholly inappropriate as a basis for decision or that they are wholly without basis in fact would the university administration become obliged to show that the stated reasons are not inappropriate or that they have a basis in fact. *Id.* at 980.

[217] *See id.* at 980 n.2, where Judge Doyle noted:

I do not intend to foreclose more considerate procedures, which permit the professor to waive procedural rights, voluntarily and knowingly. For example, the initial notice that non-retention is being considered may say that if the professor makes a written request, within a stated interval, a written statement of reasons will be supplied him, and that he will be provided with hearing at which he may respond; otherwise, he will simply be furnished with a letter announcing the decision without a statement of reasons. Also, even at the point at which a written statement of reasons is furnished, the professor may be advised that, if he makes a request for a hearing within a stated interval, a hearing will be scheduled; otherwise, the procedure will end with the written notice of non-retention and the reasons therefor.

institutions at all levels should take it upon themselves to insure that procedural due process is afforded to all of their teachers. The confidence that the educational institution's constituents place in a fair hearing militates that such procedural protection be recognized not only for the benefit of the teacher, but also for the benefit of the school itself by insuring that the integrity of its educational system is being maintained.

V. Conclusion

Academic freedom — enveloping the freedoms of study, research, opinion, discussion, expression, publication, speech, teaching, writing, and communication — is a fundamental element of the infrastructure of a democratic society which can only be adequately protected where the proclivity to arbitrary administrative action is effectively precluded. Thus, the courts, recognizing that "[a]cademic freedom would avail us little if those teachers most likely to exercise it may be weeded out of the scholastic garden before they fall within the protective embrace of the tenure statutes,"[218] are securing both the tenured and nontenured teachers' substantive and procedural due process protections. In this process the more enlightened court decisions suggest that too often questions concerning the particular state's tenure or contract law vis-a-vis the teacher serve to obfuscate the *raison d'etre* of the due process clause: "[D]ue process of law is not for the sole benefit of an accused. It is the best insurance . . . against those blunders which leave lasting stains on a system of justice but which are bound to occur on *ex parte* considerations."[219]

The court opinions which recognize the pervasive nature of the due process clause as a protector of both man's dignity[220] and the integrity of a system of justice[221] have the force of an idea whose time has come. The concept of constitutional tenure brings the copious benefits of academic freedom closer to realization for all of society.

---

[218] Frakt, *Non-tenured Teachers and the Constitution*, 18 KAN. L. REV. 27 (1969).

[219] Shaughnessy v. United States *ex rel.* Mezei, 345 U.S. 206, 224-25 (1953) (Jackson, J., dissenting).

[220] Kadish, *Methodology and Criteria in Due Process Adjudication — A Survey and Criticism*, 66 YALE L.J. 319, 347 (1957).

[221] *Id.* at 346.

TOWARD A LAW
OF ACADEMIC STATUS

Matthew W. Finkin

TOWARD A LAW OF ACADEMIC STATUS

MATTHEW W. FINKIN*

INTRODUCTION

The history of judicial treatment of institutional disputes concerning professorial rights or privileges has not been earmarked by a consistent or particularly sensitive legal theory.[1] As William Murphy pointed out, a body of decisional law dating from the days "before tenure plans came into widespread use and acceptance, at a time when employer prerogatives in all areas were largely unlimited, and professors too were considered to be mere hired hands"[2] provided little protection for the professoriate. The Wisconsin Supreme Court had held, for example, that the statutory power of a governing board to remove a faculty member at its pleasure comprised a part of the professor's contract of employment; a contract of appointment of a year's duration was held therefore as beyond the board's power, although it did observe a thirty day notice of termination provision.[3] A similar notice provision was held to be beyond the governing board's authority by one court, reasoning that if the board could bind itself for three months, it could bind itself for a year or longer.[4]

Two cases of more recent vintage, arising in the Dakotas, reflect

---

* A.B., Ohio Wesleyan, 1963; LL.B., N.Y.U., 1967.
Graduate Fellow, Yale University Law School. On leave from position as Associate Counsel, AAUP. The opinions herein expressed are not necessarily those of the Association.

1. *See, e.g.,* C. BYSE & L. JOUGHIN, TENURE IN AMERICAN HIGHER EDUCATION 71 (1959); Fellman, *Academic Freedom and the Law,* 1961 WIS. L. REV. 3; Note, *Academic Freedom and the Law,* 46 YALE L.J. 670 (1937).

2. Murphy, *Educational Freedom in the Courts,* 49 AAUP BULL. 309, 312 (1963).

3. Gillan v. Board of Regents, 88 Wis. 7, 58 N.W. 1042 (1894). *See also* Head v. University, 86 U.S. (19 Wall.) 526 (1873); Hyslop v. Board of Regents, 23 Idaho 341, 129 P. 1073 (1913); University of Mississippi v. Deister, 115 Miss. 469, 76 So. 526 (1917); Hartigan v. Board of Regents, 49 W. Va. 14, 38 S.E. 698 (1901).

4. Devol v. Board of Regents, 6 Ariz. 259, 56 P. 737 (1899). *But see* Board of Regents v. Mudge, 21 Kan. 223 (1878); State Bd. of Agriculture v. Meyers, 20 Colo. App. 139, 77 P. 372 (1904) (which allowed recovery of damages for the notice period required by board regulation which was held to be within its statutory power).

the continuing confrontation of the 19th century perspective with the realities of 20th century academic life. In *Posin v. State Board of Higher Education*,[5] a state statute provided for the establishment of rules and regulations for the governance of the institution by the faculty, subject to the rules established by the board. Accordingly, the faculty of North Dakota Agricultural College adopted a tenure plan which was approved by the board. When four tenured professors sought review of their dismissals, the court held that the tenure regulations could not limit the "full authority" to dismiss faculty granted to the governing board. In *Worzella v. Board of Regents*,[6] the Supreme Court of South Dakota held the tenure system adopted by the governing board for the South Dakota state colleges to be an unlawful delegation of the board's power to employ and dismiss and thus denied relief to a professor who had acquired tenure under the regulations and who had been dismissed without adherence to the procedures provided in them.

In private institutions a similar perspective was reflected in *Bradley v. New York University*,[7] which involved the dismissal of a professor of more than twenty years' service who had been convicted of contempt of Congress for failure to produce records of an organization of which he had been an officer and which had been subpoenaed by a congressional committee. New York University had adopted a "Statement of Policy in Regard to Academic Freedom and Tenure" contained in the University's *Faculty Handbook*. It provided in pertinent part:

> The Council [Board of Trustees] of New York University has authorized the following statement of policy in regard to academic freedom and tenure at New York University. *It should be emphasized that this is a statement of policy and not a draft of a contract* between the Council of the University on the one hand and the University Senate for and on behalf of present and future members of the University staff on the other hand.[8]

---

5. 86 N.W.2d 31 (N.D. 1957).

6. 77 S.D. 447, 93 N.W.2d 411 (1958). For a critique of this decision see Byse, *Academic Freedom, Tenure and the Law: A Comment on Worzell v. Board of Regents,* 73 Harv. L. Rev. 304 (1959). For an argument that the absence of legal enforceability of tenure is not essential to its maintenance see *Academic Tenure at South Dakota's State Supported Colleges and University,* 5 S.D. L. Rev. 31 (1960).

7. 124 N.Y.S.2d 238 (Sup. Ct. 1953), *aff'd mem.,* 283 App. Div. 671, 127 N.Y.S.2d 845, *aff'd,* 307 N.Y. 620, 120 N.E.2d 828 (1954).

8. *Id.* at 242.

The court held that the Statement of Policy took effect subsequent to the dismissal and thus the aggrieved faculty member could not claim the benefit of it. As an alternative ground, however, the court concluded that the express language indicated that the Statement did not create a binding obligation.[9]

It was in this largely inhospitable context that the profession moved to establish its standards of academic freedom and tenure and secure institutional acceptance of them in practice if not at law. The last full codification of these norms is found in the 1940 *Statement of Principles on Academic Freedom and Tenure*[10] drafted jointly by the American Association of University Professors (AAUP) and the Association of American Colleges (AAC) and now officially endorsed by eighty-two educational organizations and disciplinary societies. It has been supplemented by additional statements and by a set of formal Interpretive Comments issued by the AAUP and AAC in 1970. Moreover, the AAUP offers advice and assistance pursuant to these standards and when requested will attempt to mediate disputes arising under them. In situations involving serious possible departures from the 1940 *Statement* which have proved resistent to settlement, the Association undertakes investigation through an ad hoc committee reporting to its national Committee A on Academic Freedom and Tenure.[11] The national committee reviews the conclusions of its ad hoc investigating committees and the published reports constitute a body of professional "common" or customary law of academic freedom and tenure.[12]

---

9. The decision is obscured even more by the court's conclusion that the procedural requirements of the *Statement* were adhered to in any event and that no departure from its terms had been shown.

10. The *Statement* may be found in POLICY DOCUMENTS AND REPORTS OF THE AMERICAN ASSOCIATION OF UNIVERSITY PROFESSORS 1-4 (1970) [hereinafter cited as POLICY DOCUMENTS], accompanied by the Interpretive Comments. For treatment of the 1940 *Statement* in the history of academic freedom and tenure see R. HOFSTADTER & W. METZGER, THE DEVELOPMENT OF ACADEMIC FREEDOM IN THE UNITED STATES 480-90 (1955).

11. For an outline of the Association's case procedures see ACADEMIC FREEDOM AND TENURE: A HANDBOOK OF THE AMERICAN ASSOCIATION OF UNIVERSITY PROFESSORS 11-29 (L. Joughin ed. 1969).

12. For a further discussion of the role of the 1940 *Statement* in higher education see Belasco, *The American Association of University Professors: A Private Dispute Settlement Agency*, 18 IND. & LAB. REL. REV. 535 (1965); *Developments in the Law— Academic Freedom*, 81 HARV. L. REV. 1045, 1105-12 (1968); Emerson & Haber, *Academic Freedom and the Faculty Member as a Citizen*, in ACADEMIC FREEDOM: THE SCHOLAR'S PLACE IN MODERN SOCIETY 95, 104 (Baade ed. 1964).

The development of this scheme of private ordering was accompanied by some hesitation on the part of the professional association to seek actively judicial redress. As Robert Carr pointed out, one reason was the organization's concern that "what the courts give, they may take away, and that having thus given and taken away, academic freedom may be left in a weaker position than it was before it became a concern of the law."[13] Another was the preference for internal regulation over review by bodies which had not demonstrated sensitivity to academic values.[14]

In light of recent moves by the United States Supreme Court to expand the constitutional rights of public employees, including professors employed in publicly operated institutions of higher learning, the theory of academic freedom has begun to be reassessed.[15] As a result there has emerged a view of academic freedom as itself an aspect of the Constitution, focusing first on institutional action taken due to the professor's activities as a citizen, and more recently viewing substantive "on-the-job" academic freedom as a subset of first amendment rights.[16]

This discussion will juxtapose the profession's customary standards with developing constitutional doctrine on these two issues. It will then turn to nonconstitutional means of protecting academic interests and will discuss an emerging body of cases dealing with the contractual rights of university faculty. In both the constitutional and nonconstitutional areas it will appear that established academic custom and practice may play a significant role.

---

13. Carr, *Academic Freedom, The American Association of University Professors, and The United States Supreme Court*, 45 AAUP BULL. 5, 20 (1959).

14. *See, e.g.,* Kay v. Board of Higher Educ., 173 Misc. 943, 18 N.Y.S.2d 821 (Sup. Ct. 1940), in holding illegal the appointment of Bertrand Russell to the City College of New York as a "direct violation of the public health, safety, and morals of the people . . . ." *Id.* at 953, 18 N.Y.S.2d at 831. *See also* Jones v. Board of Control, 131 S.2d 713 (Fla. 1961) (dicta concerning academic freedom).

15. Fract, *Non-Tenure Teachers and the Constitution*, 18 U. KAN. L. REV. 27 (1969); Murphy, *Academic Freedom—An Emerging Constitutional Right*, in ACADEMIC FREEDOM: THE SCHOLAR'S PLACE IN MODERN SOCIETY, *supra* note 12, at 17; Pettigrew, *"Constitutional Tenure:" Toward a Realization of Academic Freedom*, 22 CASE W. RES. L. REV. 475 (1971); Van Alstyne, *The Constitutional Rights of Teachers and Professors*, 1970 DUKE L.J. 841.

16. Van Alstyne, *A Comment on the Specific Theory of Academic Freedom and the General Issue of Civil Liberty*, to appear in 405 ANNALS —— (1972). The author is indebted to Professor Van Alstyne for making a copy of his manuscript available.

I. Constitutional Developments

A. *Freedom as a Citizen*

The 1940 *Statement* provides in pertinent part:

> The college or university teacher is a citizen, a member of a learned profession, and an officer of an educational institution. When he speaks or writes as a citizen, he should be free from institutional censorship or discipline, but his special position in the community imposes special obligations. As a man of learning and an educational officer, he should remember that the public may judge his profession and his institution by his utterances. Hence he should at all times be accurate, should exercise appropriate restraint, should show respect for the opinions of others, and should make every effort to indicate that he is not an institutional spokesman.[17]

In 1963 an ad hoc committee investigating the dismissal of a professor at the University of Illinois for writing a letter to the student press concerning student sexual conduct, concluded that the 1940 *Statement's* standard of "academic responsibility" was in essence admonitory and could not itself serve as a basis for discipline.[18] A majority of Committee A disagreed.[19] The position of the Committee has, however, been modified in subsequent statements of policy. The recently appended Interpretive Comments, for example, incorporate language from Committee A's *Statement on Extramural Utterances* issued in 1964:

> The controlling principle is that a faculty member's expression of opinion as a citizen cannot constitute grounds for dismissal unless it clearly demonstrates the faculty member's unfitness for his position. Extramural utterances rarely bear upon the faculty member's fitness for his position. Moreover, a final decision should take into account the faculty member's entire record as a teacher and scholar.[20]

Further clarification is provided in the model institutional regulations approved by Committee A requiring that

> Adequate cause for a dismissal will be related directly and substantially, to the fitness of the faculty member in his professional capacity

---

17. Policy Documents, *supra* note 10, at 2.
18. *Academic Freedom and Tenure: The University of Illinois*, 49 AAUP Bull. 25 (1963).
19. *Id.* at 40-43.
20. Policy Documents, *supra* note 10, at 3.

as a teacher and researcher. Dismissal will not be used to restrain faculty members in the exercise of academic freedom or other rights of American citizens.[21]

Professor William Van Alstyne has argued, however, that a professor's aprofessional utterances as a citizen should be viewed as being outside the doctrine of academic freedom. To apply a professional standard of care, as the 1940 *Statement* appears to do, is to hold the professor to a higher standard than the average citizen and is, in effect, to invite institutional scrutiny of his aprofessional activities.[22]

Some support for this argument is provided by the action of the Board of Regents of the University of California which relied explicitly on the "academic responsibility" provisions of the 1940 *Statement* in deciding not to renew the appointment of Acting Assistant Professor Angela Davis in the University of California at Los Angeles.[23] The Board concluded that some of Miss Davis' extramural utterances were "so extreme, so antithetical to the protection of academic freedom and so obviously and deliberately false in several respects as to be inconsistent with qualification for appointment"[24] to the faculty.

The AAUP's investigating committee found that each of the Board's specific allegations failed to withstand a literal analysis. More important, the committee report pointed out that an infraction of

---

21. *Id.* at 16.

22. Van Alstyne, *supra* note 16. Professor Van Alstyne observes that the distinction between professional and aprofessional activity can be elusive. Some cases do deal with activity which falls within an aprofessional categorization. *See, e.g., Academic Freedom and Tenure: A Successfully Resolved Case at Northern Michigan University,* 55 AAUP BULL. 374 (1969) (active opposition to the university's plans for community redevelopment); *Academic Freedom and Tenure: Lincoln College,* 50 AAUP BULL. 244 (1964) (picketing a U.S. post office in protest of the blockade of Cuba). Some cases deal with speech or activity that is both aprofessional and apolitical. *See, e.g., Academic Freedom and Tenure: Broward Junior College (Fla.),* 55 AAUP BULL. 71 (1969) (art instructor's opinions on homosexuality), and *Academic Freedom and Tenure: St. Mary's College (Minn.),* 54 AAUP BULL. 37 (1968) (lay faculty member marries in civil ceremony). For a fuller discussion of the problems in this area, see O'Neil, *The Private Lives of Public Employees,* 51 ORE. L. REV. 70 (1971). Other cases are more difficult to categorize. *See, e.g., Academic Freedom and Tenure: Oklahoma State University,* 56 AAUP BULL. 62 (1970) (relationship of professor of journalism to the outside press on stories concerning university affairs), and *Academic Freedom and Tenure: The University of Hawaii,* 55 AAUP BULL. 29 (1969) (role of faculty advisor to radical student organization). To the extent that a precise categorization may be required before the applicable standard may be determined, the elusive case may prove troublesome.

23. *Academic Freedom and Tenure: The University of California at Los Angeles,* 57 AAUP BULL. 382 (1971).

24. *Id.* at 415.

AAUP standards as a basis for discipline must show not only irresponsibility in terms of that standard but also a necessary relationship between the extramural utterance and the faculty member's fitness for an academic position based on his entire record.

> Thus, institutional sanctions imposed for extramural utterances can be a violation of academic freedom even when the utterances themselves fall short of the standards of the profession; for it is central to that freedom that the faculty member, when speaking as a citizen, "should be free from institutional censorship or discipline" except insofar as his behavior is shown, on the whole record, to be incompatible with fitness for his position.[25]

In sum, while the "academic responsibility" aspect of the 1940 *Statement* does imply a degree of institutional accountability for aprofessional utterance, it is clear that such utterance does no more than invite attention in rare cases to the faculty member's fitness on which latter question alone would institutional action be warranted. The difficulty with this position, according to Van Alstyne, is that it seems to imply a higher degree of institutional accountability than is desirable and suggests that the operative constitutional standard is narrower than that implied by AAUP standards.

The constitutional standard is best adumbrated in *Pickering v. Board of Education*,[26] which held that a teacher's speech on issues of public importance could not furnish the basis for dismissal from public employment absent proof of false statements knowingly or recklessly made. The decision is, however, carefully limited. The Court is at pains to note: (1) it is not appropriate to lay down a general standard to judge public utterances made by public employees which may be critical of their superiors; and, (2) a balancing of interests between the teacher as citizen and the state as employer must be made.[27] The Court then delineates the considerations weighed in its decision: (1) a close working relationship with the person or persons against whom the statements are directed posing a problem of discipline or harmony was not involved; (2) the utterance did not actually foment controversy or conflict (the Court noted that the letter involved was greeted with "massive apathy and total disbelief" and had earlier noted that no evidence of the effect of the publication on the community or

---

25. *Id.* at 398.
26. 391 U.S. 563 (1968).
27. *Id.* at 568-69.

on the administration of the school system had been introduced) ;
(3) the subject of the public utterance was a matter of legitimate public concern on which open debate is vital, particularly as the matter
was the subject of a popular vote; and, (4) the inaccuracies in the
utterance concerned matters of public record about which the teacher's employment did not lend greater authority than any other citizen.[28]

Thus the *Pickering* standard would require a showing that the
teacher's extramural utterance or activity either impeded the performance of the teacher's duties or interfered with the regular operation
of the school. Dismissal for criticizing a school's emphasis on athletics
in a learned journal would state a constitutional claim[29] as would the
denial of a salary increase for publishing a letter in *Redbook* magazine in which the author identifies himself as a professor at a public
institution, praises an article on premarital sex, and expresses intent
to use the author's comments in class.[30] Neither of these cases seem
to depart from what would be otherwise protected by customary
standards. Alternatively, the nonrenewal of a high school teacher who
created animosities with other teachers, used profanity, was abusive
and inebriated on teacher social occasions, and who used his classroom as a forum to promote the activities of a teacher union "to
sanction polygamy, to attack marriage, to criticize other teachers and
to sway and influence the minds of young people without a full and
proper explanation of both sides of the issue,"[31] was held to run
afoul of *Pickering* standards. On the other hand, the use of college
letterhead to charge the institution with unethical practices in a communication to the state psychological association could, it seems,
be properly relied on in part by college authorities in a decision not
to renew a faculty member for "lack of judgment."[32]

It is particularly noteworthy that the *Pickering* Court observed
in a footnote that the utterances involved were not

so without foundation as to call into question [the faculty member's]

---

28. Professor Van Alstyne has been highly critical of portions of the *Pickering* test;
see Van Alstyne, *supra* note 15.
29. Williams v. School Dist. of Springfield, 447 S.W.2d 256 (Mo. 1969).
30. Jarvey v. Martin, 336 F. Supp. 1350 (W.D. Va. 1972).
31. Knarr v. Board of School Trustees, 317 F. Supp. 832, 836 (N.D. Ind. 1970).
32. Local 1600, AFT v. Byrd, 456 F.2d 882, 888-89 n.7 (7th Cir.), *cert. denied,*
93 S. Ct. 56 (1972). *Cf.* the treatment of use of college letterhead in a letter to the
headquarters of the Boys' Clubs of America to protest racial segregation in the local
Boys' Club in Magnolia, Arkansas, in *Academic Freedom and Tenure: Southern State
College (Arkansas),* 57 AAUP BULL. 40 (1971).

fitness to perform his duties in the classroom. In such a case, of course, the statements would merely be evidence of the teacher's general competence, or lack thereof, and not an independent basis for dismissal.[33]

Thus, while an extramural utterance would not constitute an independent basis for dismissal, it could raise a question of the teacher's fitness and thereby lead to ultimate dismissal. This seems to be indistinguishable from the 1940 *Statement* as it has been refined and applied.

Further, while the 1940 *Statement* limits any review occasioned by aprofessional speech to the faculty member's fitness or competence based on his entire record and not on a single incident alone, *Pickering* actually appears to pose a more restrictive standard by permitting such inquiry to focus on disruption of harmonious relations within the institution or of its efficient operation.[34] Thus where

---

33. 391 U.S. at 573 n.5.

34. *See* Rozman v. Elliott, 335 F. Supp. 1086 (D. Neb. 1971) (nonrenewal of nontenured professor who "intruded" himself into negotiations between students and administration during occupancy by students of ROTC building); Knarr v. Board of School Trustees, 317 F. Supp. 832 (N.D. Ind. 1970). *Compare* Jergeson v. Board of Trustees, 476 P.2d 481 (Wyo. 1970) (dismissal of high school teacher after hearing on charges including the content of an issue of the student newspaper for which he was faculty advisor and which, the court concludes, the trustees could find interfered with the discipline of the school), *with Academic Freedom and Tenure: The University of Hawaii, supra* note 22 (concerning the revocation of a letter of intent to grant tenure to a professor who served as advisor to a student organization which issued a statement calling for subversion of the military and a campaign to sabotage the war effort in Vietnam).

Thus the cases following *Pickering* have perforce to concern themselves with matters of working relationships, discipline and harmony. *See* Watts v. Seward School Bd., 395 P.2d 372 (Alas. 1964), *remanded,* 381 U.S. 126 (1965), *aff'd,* 421 P.2d 586 (Alas. 1966), *vacated and remanded in light of Pickering,* 391 U.S. 592 (1968), *aff'd,* 454 P.2d 732 (Alas. 1969) (court found efforts of two teachers to oust the superintendent of schools were directed toward a person with whom they would be in working contact and that a question of maintaining discipline was involved). *See also* Meehan v. Macy, 392 F.2d 822 (D.C. Cir. 1968), *remanded in light of Pickering,* 425 F.2d 472 (D.C. Cir. 1969) (circulation of material critical of the governor of the Canal Zone by a police officer relating to and during an international dispute); Tepedino v. Dumpson, 24 N.Y.2d 705, 249 N.E.2d 751, 301 N.Y.S.2d 967 (1969) (suspension of social worker for letter critical of department caseload and procedures directed to the federal department of Health, Education and Welfare; Chief Judge Fuld points out that there was no showing of interference with the welfare program, of neglect of duty, or "that the letter created discipline problems or disharmony" among fellow employees, *id.* at 710, 249 N.E.2d at 753, 301 N.Y.S.2d at 970; Puentes v. Board of Educ., 18 N.Y.2d 906, 223 N.E.2d 45, 276 N.Y.S.2d 638 (1966), *remanded in light of Pickering,* 392 U.S. 653 (1968), *rev'd,* 24 N.Y.2d 996, 250 N.E.2d 232, 302 N.Y.S.2d 824 (1969) (letter of criticism circulated within school system); Brukiewa v. Police Comm'r, 257 Md. 36, 263 A.2d 210 (1970) (police officer critical of the

Pickering may become troublesome is in the area of internal utterances: *i.e.*, where the faculty members speaks not as a private citizen to an issue of general public interest but, in a sense, as an institutional citizen criticizing the administration of the institution's affairs.[35] It is in this area that the application of the test of disharmony or interference requires an appreciation of the nature of a university, which has not been lacking in some cases.[36] Thus the profession's customary standards deriving from the particular circumstances of higher learning may serve as a basis for modifying the potentially disturbing aspects of *Pickering*. On the other hand, if *Pickering* is in effect a less restrictive standard, it should serve to inform and thus modify the profession's customary standard, which, in turn, could serve as an implied term in contracts of academic employment to which constitutional standards would be otherwise inapplicable.[37]

---

commissioner during television interview; the dissent would distinguish a policeman from a teacher whose employment implies the "right to exercise the *maximum* of the right of free speech," *id.* at 75, 263 A.2d at 299; *In re* Chalk, 441 Pa. 376, 272 A.2d 457 (1971) (suspension of social worker for speech critical of the agency and urging recipients to agitate).

35. It is an area to which the AAUP's attention has been extensively directed. *See, e.g., Academic Freedom and Tenure: St. John's University (N.Y.)*, 52 AAUP BULL. 12 (1966) (use of public address system in University cafeteria to speak on administration-faculty relations and other activities petitioning or criticizing the administration); *Academic Freedom and Tenure: Amarillo College*, 53 AAUP BULL. 292 (1967) (allegation of improper letter directed to members of the administration, inability to get along with department chairman, and the making of derogatory remarks about the college's former president during a farewell party); *Academic Freedom and Tenure: Dean Junior College*, 53 AAUP BULL. 64 (1967) (continuance of faculty member was alleged to make the work of incoming department head more difficult); *Academic Freedom and Tenure: Lorain County Community College (Elyria, Ohio)*, 54 AAUP BULL. 49 (1968) (nonrenewal due to opposition to the president's policy on securing regional accreditation); *Academic Freedom and Tenure: Southeastern Louisiana College*, 55 AAUP BULL. 369 (1969) (termination of faculty member who had substantial friction with his department head and who had a reputation for irritating the administration).

36. *See, e.g.,* State *ex rel.* Richardson v. Board of Regents, 70 Nev. 347, 269 P.2d 265 (1954); State *ex rel.* Ball v. McPhee, 6 Wis. 2d 190, 94 N.W.2d 711 (1959).

37. Constitutional standards have not been applied to private institutions under the "state action" test. *See* O'Neil, *Private Universities and Public Law*, 19 BUFFALO L. REV. 155 (1970); Schubert, *State Action and the Private University*, 24 RUTGERS L. REV. 323 (1970). The distinction appears to retain its vitality in higher education despite anomalous results as in Powe y. Miles, 407 F.2d 73 (2d Cir. 1968). *See* Blackburn v. Fisk University, 443 F.2d 121 (6th Cir. 1971); Brownley v. Gettysburg College, 338 F. Supp. 725 (M.D. Pa. 1972); Rowe v. Chandler, 332 F. Supp. 336 (D. Kan. 1971) (College of Emporia). *But see* Coleman v. Wagner College, 429 F.2d 1120 (2d Cir. 1970) (where state law requiring the adoption of disciplinary rules by private colleges was sufficient state action to compel constitutional compliance) *and* Ryan v. Hofstra University, 67 Misc. 2d 651, 324 N.Y.S.2d 964 (Sup. Ct. 1971), *order clarified,* 68 Misc. 2d 890, 328 N.Y.S.2d 339 (Sup. Ct. 1972) which, as an alternative ground, clearly holds the fourteenth amendment applicable to a private institution on the basis

B. *Freedom "On-the-Job"*

A series of recent cases concerning secondary education now lends support to the identification of substantive academic freedom as a distinct subset of first amendment rights.

In *Parducci v. Rutland*[38] a teacher had been dismissed for assigning Kurt Vonnegut's *Welcome to the Monkey House* to his eleventh grade class to acquaint them with the genre of the short story. The court clearly identified academic freedom as a first amendment right and relied on *Tinker v. Des Moines Independent Community School District*[39] as setting the guidelines for balancing the institutional and individual interests in determining the result. Accordingly, the court undertook to determine whether the assignment materially and substantially interfered with the requirements of appropriate discipline and concluded that it did not.[40] In so doing the court made its own determination of the literary merit of the work and its own findings of the degree of disruption occasioned by its use. In *Keefe v. Geanakos*[41] the First Circuit enjoined the suspension of a high school teacher who had assigned an article in *Atlantic Monthly* to a senior class. The text, by an apparently established psychiatrist, used a "vulgar term for an incestuous son" which was nevertheless found in five books in the school library. The court found the article "scholarly, thoughtful and thought-provoking"[42] and used for educational pur-

---

of the university's general relationship to the state and the public interest in private higher education. The excellent opinion is slightly marred, however, by the confusion of the concept of institutional autonomy with academic freedom.

38. 316 F. Supp. 352 (M.D. Ala. 1970). *Contra,* Parker v. Board of Educ., 237 F. Supp. 222 (D. Md.), *aff'd on other grounds,* 348 F.2d 464 (4th Cir. 1965), *cert. denied,* 382 U.S. 1030 (1966). But: "The need for teachers to have freedom in what they teach rises from the very heart of the first amendment." Hostrop v. Board of Junior College Dist. No. 515, 337 F. Supp. 977, 980 (N.D. Ill. 1972).

39. 393 U.S. 503 (1969).

40. It is curious that the court applies as a standard of on-the-job professional utterance one developed for a nonprofessional political utterance. A similar result on seemingly nonconstitutional grounds was reached in Oakland Unified School Dist. v. Olicker, 25 Cal. App. 3d 1098, 102 Cal. Rptr. 421 (1st Dist. 1972) concerning whether a teacher's distribution to an eighth grade class of their own writings, some of which concerned blatantly sexual subjects, constituted "evident unfitness." The court rejected the constitutional argument but applied as a test whether the teaching technique "disrupted or impaired the discipline of defendant's [teacher's] students or the teaching process." *Id.* at 1110, 102 Cal. Rptr. at 429-30. The court concluded that there was no evidence of such disruption or of a violation of any school regulation. The vigorous dissent argued that despite the majority's contention, "[c]omfort is given to defendant's contention that she was protected by her 'academic freedom.'" *Id.* at 1116, 102 Cal. Rptr. at 433.

41. 418 F.2d 359 (1st Cir. 1969).

42. *Id.* at 361.

poses, not to provoke. In *Mailloux v. Kiley*[43] the same court concluded that a high school teacher could not be discharged for using teaching methods which were not universally approved but against which no explicit prohibition had been issued.

A conclusion drawn from these cases by one commentator seems inescapable: the effect of these decisions is to

> carve an area of autonomy in the classroom in which teachers teach free of interference from school authorities and parents alike, so long as the teachers can convince a federal court that their classroom expression is relevant to their curricular assignment, is balanced and has educational value.[44]

This implies, however, that "the court has the last word on educational value concerning the curriculum."[45] As Judge Wyzanski saw it, *Keefe* and *Parducci* establish two kinds of academic freedom:

> the substantive right of a teacher to choose a teaching method which *in the court's view* served a demonstrated educational purpose; and the procedural right of a teacher not to be discharged for the use of a teaching method which was not proscribed by a regulation, and as to which it was not proven that he should have had notice that its use was prohibited.[46]

The customary professional standard in higher education has also recognized a high degree of autonomy in the classroom. According to the 1940 *Statement*: "The teacher is entitled to freedom in the classroom in discussing his subject, but he should be careful not to introduce into his teaching controversial matter which has no relation to his subject."[47] The Interpretive Comment clarifies that

> The intent of this statement is not to discourage what is "controversial." Controversy is at the heart of the free academic inquiry which the entire statement is designed to foster. The passage serves to underscore the need for the teacher to avoid persistently intruding material which has no relation to his subject.[48]

---

43. 448 F.2d 1242 (1st Cir. 1971).

44. Nahmod, *First Amendment Protection for Learning and Teaching: The Scope of Judicial Review*, 18 WAYNE L. REV. 1479, 1499 (1972).

45. *Id.*

46. Mailloux v. Kiley, 323 F. Supp. 1387, 1390 (D. Mass. 1971) (emphasis added). The First Circuit chose to treat the case, concerning the use of a taboo word in an eleventh grade English class, wholly on grounds of prior notice. 448 F.2d 1242 (1st Cir. 1971). *See* text at *supra* note 43.

47. *Supra* note 10.

48. *Id.*

Under this standard a teacher is somewhat freer than the foregoing cases might indicate in his subject matter and teaching method. Indeed, a proscription, even if based on some body of professional opinion, might itself constitute a violation of the professional standard.[49] Thus a university case must bear the burden of distinguishing the precedents established in secondary education and it seems that a productive avenue for such distinction lies in the unique customs and functions of higher education. Judge Wyzanski explicitly distinguished a university setting from the secondary school by its tradition of independence, the usually higher intellectual qualification of faculty and broader discretion in teaching method.[50] This he related to the differences in function between the two kinds of institutions—the former geared largely to the acquisition of new knowledge and a mutual testing and exploration of ideas by faculty and students, the latter geared primarily for the transmission of established knowledge through traditional techniques and, to some extent, the indoctrination of existing values. Here, then, academic custom may assist in informing constitutionally cognizable rights in higher education. Moreover, reliance on such a body of custom much reduces the problem of scope of judicial review which perforce has serious implications for the conduct of the institution.[51]

---

49. *See* Wolfe v. O'Neill, 336 F. Supp. 1255 (D. Alas. 1972) (an allegation by an assistant professor of English that the expression of ideas in disagreement with those held by the University of Alaska's English Department occasioned his nonrenewal was held to state a claim under the first amendment).

50. Mailloux v. Kiley, 323 F. Supp. 1387, 1392 (D. Mass. 1971). *Accord* Palo Verde Unified School Dist. v. Hensey, 9 Cal. App. 3d 967, 88 Cal. Rptr. 570 (4th Dist. 1970) (dicta) concerning the dismissal of a junior college teacher primarily for several incidents involving his use of language in the classroom. The court consistently points out it is dealing with the junior college level but also finds that some of the teacher's conduct transgressed the "limits of bad taste and vulgarity." *Id.* at 974, 88 Cal. Rptr. at 575; McEnteggart v. Cataldo, 451 F.2d 1109 (1st Cir. 1971) where an academic department voted 5-0 to recommend the nonrenewal of the plaintiff's appointment due to his inability to get along with his colleagues, with which assessment the administration of a state college concurred. The court held that the standards approved in Drown v. Portsmouth School Dist., 451 F.2d 1106 (1st Cir. 1971), applied "with due recognition that a college presents a different context and has a different educational mission." It affirmed the dismissal of the action noting that, "[t]he department may well . . . be purchasing harmony at the expense of scholarly potential. Even so, the college can surely prefer harmony in deciding which of its nontenured faculty members will be granted new contracts. The reason is not trivial or unrelated to working relationships within the college." *Id.* at 1111.

51. *See* Nahmod, *supra* note 44. The Second Circuit takes a somewhat different view of *Keefe* and *Parducci:* "To the extent that these cases hold that first amendment rights have been violated whenever a district court disagrees with the judgment of school officials as to the propriety of material assigned by a teacher to students, we are

II. NONCONSTITUTIONAL PROTECTION

Other means of achieving judicial protection for academic freedom and tenure have been considered. Professor Cowan's provocative tort theory[52] has apparently not been pursued with vigor and thus appears to remain in gestation. The possibility of vindicating academic interests through contract confronted a predominantly unresponsive judicial reaction based, not surprisingly, on a body of unhelpful traditional contract doctrine.[53]

Some recent cases indicate, however, an emerging judicial sensitivity to the realities of academic life. The entering wedge seems to center on the legal effect of standards for notice of nonrenewal of nontenured faculty appointments adopted by the institution's governing board or followed in practice. In *Zimmerman v. Minot State College*,[54] the Supreme Court of North Dakota held that the rules for notice of nonreappointment adopted by the State Board of Higher Education were binding on it and affirmed an award of damages for the failure to provide timely notice to a nontenured instructor whose appointment was terminated due to declining enrollment in her department. The State Board had adopted a Policy Statement on Tenure in 1964, incorporating AAUP standards including a provision that no less than twelve months' notice for faculty beyond the second year of probationary service be afforded. A statute then applicable to higher education provided that notice of nonrenewal was to be afforded no earlier

---

not in accord." Presidents Council, Dist. 25 v. Community School Bd. No. 25, 457 F.2d 289, 293-94 (2d Cir. 1972). As Judge Mulligan, a former law school dean, put it, "Academic freedom is scarcely fostered by the intrusion of three or even nine federal jurists making curricular . . . choices for the community of scholars." *Id.* at 292.

52. Cowan, *Interference with Academic Freedom: The Pre-Natal History of a Tort*, 4 WAYNE L. REV. 205 (1958).

53. *See* Breen v. Larson College, 137 Conn. 152, 75 A.2d 39 (1950) (dismissal of a dean for writing letters to parents critical of the president in which the court speaks of the employee's duty of loyalty to the employer); Rhine v. International Young Men's Christian Ass'n College, 339 Mass. 610, 162 N.E.2d 56 (1959) (acceptance of an additional year's terminal appointment beyond the maximum probationary period does not confer tenure); Thomas v. Catawba College, 248 N.C. 609, 104 S.E.2d 175 (1958) (dismissal for cause by institution which purported to follow AAUP standards in which the court finds the dismissed professor had elected his remedy by accepting a year's salary, as required in a dismissal by AAUP standards, in lieu of a suit for damages which, the court concludes, would have been limited to a year's salary as fixed damages in any event). For a discussion of the obstacles presented by resort to a contract theory see T. EMERSON, D. HABER & N. DORSEN, POLITICAL AND CIVIL RIGHTS IN THE UNITED STATES 972 (1967); C. BYSE & L. JOUGHIN, *supra* note 1.

54. 198 N.W.2d 108 (N.D. 1972).

than February 15 of the school year. The two provisions were, the court observed, "patently inconsistent." Relying on *Posin v. State Board of Higher Education*,[55] the court noted that the authority of the Board, derived from the state constitution and statutes, included the "full authority" over institutions under its control including the specific power to appoint faculty, fix their terms of office and *adopt rules for the governance of the institution*. The court concluded, following established rules of statutory construction, that policies adopted pursuant to such specific statutory authority took precedence over a conflicting general provision.

The case is noteworthy in two respects. First, it held that the faculty member's employment relationship had to be examined in the context of the Board's Statement of Policy, included in the *Faculty Handbook* which the faculty member received when she was appointed and which, the court concluded, comprised a part of her contract. Second, though relying on *Posin*, the result seriously erodes if not eviscerates the logic of *Posin*:

> It is argued [said the *Posin* court] that the provisions of the College constitution have the force and effect of law. It is, however, at most only a rule or regulation approved by the Board. We think it clear that the College constitution, considered as a rule or regulation, does not have, and cannot have, the effect of diminishing, limiting, restricting or qualifying the power and authority vested in the Board . . . .[56]

In *Pima College v. Sinclair*,[57] the faculty handbook and calendar provided a March 1 date for notification of nonreappointment. The college, though required by the state-wide governing board to adopt policies governing renewal, nonrenewal and tenure, had neglected to do so. An officer of the administration testified, however, that the college generally adhered to the state's teacher tenure law,[58] which did not itself apply to higher education[59] and which provided a March 15 notification date. The plaintiff faculty member had received notice on March 11. The court said that reference to the teacher tenure act was warranted inasmuch as some policy was required and the college gen-

55. 86 N.W.2d 31 (N.D. 1957).
56. *Id.* at 35.
57. 17 Ariz. App. 213, 496 P.2d 639 (1972).
58. Ariz. Rev. Stat. Ann. § 15-251 et seq. (1956).
59. Kaufman v. Pima Junior College, 14 Ariz. App. 475, 484 P.2d 244 (1971).

erally followed it, save for the disparity in notification dates. Accordingly it held the college to its established practice and ordered the faculty member reinstated.

What is thus far the most inciteful discussion of the contract of academic appointment is provided by the District of Columbia Circuit Court in *Greene v. Howard University*.[60] Five nontenured faculty members were notified in June that their appointments would not be renewed at the close of the then current academic year. The University's *Faculty Handbook* provided that written notice would be afforded before April 15 but "without contractual obligation to do so." The administration argued that its disclaimer of contractual obligation for the provision of timely written notice relieved it of any liability therefor. The court disagreed, observing:

> Contracts are written, and are to be read, by reference to the norms of conduct and expectations founded upon them. This is especially true of contracts in and among a community of scholars, which is what a university is. The readings of the market place are not invariably apt in this non-commercial context.[61]

The court noted that the practices and customs of the institution could be raised to the level of contractual obligation and noted also that the faculty members had relied on them. The court was also particularly aware of the assertion in the *Faculty Handbook* of the University's acceptance of AAUP standards for notice as a guiding principle. It concluded:

> The employment contracts of appellants here comprehend as essential parts of themselves the hiring policies and practices of the University as embodied in its employment regulations and customs. . . . Those provisions [of the *Faculty Handbook*] seem to us to contemplate a hearing before separating from the academic community for alleged misconduct one who, although a non-tenure employee, has acquired a different dimension of relationship because

---

60. 412 F.2d 1128 (D.C. Cir. 1969).
61. *Id.* at 1135. *See also* Bruno v. Detroit Inst. of Technology, 36 Mich. App. 61, 193 N.W.2d 322 (1971) where a faculty member in his seventh year of service was offered a two-year appointment at a stipulated salary for the first year, the second year's salary to be reviewed. At the conclusion of the first year he was offered the same salary for the second year and when he objected his appointment was terminated due to the lack of a contract. The court looked to the conduct of the parties, noting that employment contracts should be strictly contrued against those preparing them. Given the institution's *practice* of annual raises it held that the faculty member had a contract for at least the stipulaed annual amount in both years.

of the expectations inherent in the University's failure to give notice contemplated by its own regulations.[62]

Explicitly following *Greene,* the Court of Appeals of New Mexico held that the provisions of the *Faculty Handbook* of Eastern New Mexico University comprise a part of the faculty member's contract of employment.[63] Thus the administration was obliged to follow its established procedures for the nonreappointment of a nontenured faculty member, even though it had argued that its provisions were for "administrative" purposes only. The court disagreed with the Regents' argument that the *Greene* rule with respect to the *Handbook* itself or to the "course of conduct" of the parties could not apply to a governmental body.[64]

Against this background, the action of the Supreme Court of Illinois in *Fooden v. Board of Governors of State Colleges and Universities*[65] must be viewed as quixotic. Two faculty members in their second year of service in Chicago State College were given timely notice of nonrenewal. They charged *inter alia* that the procedures employed in reaching these decisions were not in accord with college policy which, they alleged, included AAUP standards, and that the reasons for the action were constitutionally impermissible. The responding

---

62. *Id.* From a different perspective, failure to adhere to institutional notice provisions was found to have constitutional implications in Roumani v. Leestamper, 330 F. Supp. 1248 (D. Mass. 1971), requiring the provision of a particularized statement of charges and a hearing.

63. Hillis v. Meister, 82 N.M. 474, 483 P.2d 1314 (1971); *accord* Smith v. Losee, Civil No. C283-69 (D. Utah, Jan. 27, 1972). *See also* Downs v. Conway School Dist., 328 F. Supp. 338 (E.D. Ark. 1971) (holding *inter alia* that the school's published policies comprise a part of the teacher's contract of employment); Griffin v. Board of Trustees of St. Mary's College, 258 Md. 276, 265 A.2d 757 (1970) (appeal denied on procedural ground but *dicta* agrees that rights could be claimed under a statement of policy adopted by the Board incorporating AAUP standards but disagrees that a departure from the policy was shown).

64. *Cf.* Gadzella v. Neumaier, 67 Misc. 2d 585, 324 N.Y.S.2d 600 (Sup. Ct. 1971), in which the court declined to view a course of conduct as giving rise to a legal right. Plaintiff had been appointed to an administrative position in which one serves at the pleasure of the appointing authority. She claimed academic status and tenure as a result of reliance on the manner in which her salary was computed and the manner of her listing on the salary roster. The court notes that only the Trustees or the Chancellor of the University can award academic tenure and that even the local campus president lacked that authority. As she had never received an appointment to the academic staff the administration was not, as she alleged, estopped to deny that she had achieved tenure. The decision seems far broader than the facts would warrant. The case appears best explained on the narrower ground that a mere listing on a salary roster is insufficient to maintain a "course of conduct" treating an administrator as a faculty member.

65. 48 Ill. 2d 580, 272 N.E.2d 497 (1971), *cert. denied,* 408 U.S. 943 (1972).

affidavit of the Board of Governors denied *inter alia* that the faculty constitution was binding on the Board or that the Board had adopted or approved AAUP standards as policy. The court affirmed the grant of summary judgment for the Board on the ground that no factual issues were presented:

> We find that the Board's affidavit clearly refutes this contention [on the applicability of AAUP policy] and that, as a matter of law, the [plaintiffs'] contract was specifically made subject only to the "By-Laws, Governing Policies and Practices of the Board," and that the Board's sole duty thereunder was to provide the notice of nonretention within the required time. Plaintiffs' allegations in their complaint on this matter constitute nothing more than statements of conclusions and do not present a genuine issue of fact in the face of the uncontroverted facts set forth in the Board's affidavit.[66]

Curiously, the court seemed to accept on the one hand that the institution was bound to follow its established policies and practices but on the other concluded that the Board's affidavit was alone dispositive of whether a particular policy or practice existed.[67]

The decision of the United States Supreme Court in *Perry v. Sindermann*[68] lends additional weight to the judicial recognition of a professional or at least an institutional customary law. Professor Sinder-

---

66. *Id.* at 588-89, 272 N.E.2d at 501 (two judges dissenting).

67. A similarly restrictive interpretation of institutional policy was provided by the Supreme Court of Tennesee in Sprunt v. Members of the Bd. of Trustees, 223 Tenn. App. 210, 443 S.W.2d 464 (1969). The plaintiff had been Professor and Chairman of Pathology since 1944. Under the Board's policy, amended during plaintiff's tenure, a faculty member retires at age 65 unless continued on a year-to-year basis by the Board with mandatory retirement at age 70. The plaintiff, who had apparently been so continued, reached age 68 in August, 1968, and was retired at the end of that month. He argued that his retirement was for "cause" in that it was occasioned by a recommendation from his dean urging his retirement due to a dispute between them. The court held that the Board's motives were irrelevant inasmuch as it had complete discretion to retire a faculty member after age 65 "whatever the motives of the Trustees in so doing." *Id.* at 213, 443 S.W.2d at 466. It does not appear from the opinion that institutional policy on academic freedom, including the academic of superannuated faculty, was presented to or considered by the court. The court seems to treat a superannuated faculty member who *loses* his tenure by continuing on an annual basis after retirement as if he were a nontenured faculty member first coming into the institution. This is a murky area in terms of national practice. *See Statement of Principals on Retirement and Insurance Plans,* POLICY DOCUMENTS, *supra* note 10, at 70. It is clear, however, that a decision not to continue a superannuated faculty member for reasons violative of academic freedom is no less violative of academic freedom merely because the faculty member is superannuated. The case is mitigated by the fact that the Trustees did allow the plaintiff to appear before them accompanied by counsel to present his arguments before it took action.

68. 408 U.S. 593 (1972).

mann had been a teacher in the Texas state college system for ten years, the last four of which had been at Odessa Junior College, serving on one year renewable appointments. In May of his last year he was given notice of nonrenewal and the Board of Regents issued a press release alleging that the decision was due to his insubordination. Professor Sindermann sought redress on both substantive and procedural grounds: *i.e.*, that the reason for the action was violative of constitutional rights and that the failure of the Board to provide a hearing was violative of fourteenth amendment guarantees of due process. On the former the Court agreed that a claim had been stated. On the latter it was faced with its decision in *Board of Regents v. Roth*[69] that a nontenured faculty member in his first year of service on a one-year appointment had not such a "property" interest as to require, as a constitutional matter, notice and a hearing before the nonrenewal could be effected. Professor Sindermann relied, however, on the college's *Faculty Guide* which, while reciting that the college had "no tenure system," went on to assure of the administration's wishes that the faculty member "feel that he has permanent tenure" as long as he performs satisfactorily, is cooperative and is "happy in his work." He relied further on guidelines issued by the Coordinating Board of the Texas College and University System which incorporated much of the language of AAUP standards. The Court acknowledged that while an explicit tenure provision is evidence of such entitlement or "property" as to require cause for a dismissal to be shown, its absence may not necessarily forclose the possibility of showing such an interest.

> A teacher, like the respondent, who has held his position for a number of years, might be able to show from the circumstances of this service—and from other relevant facts—that he has a legitimate claim of entitlement to job tenure. Just as this Court has found there to be a "common law of a particular industry of a particular plant" that may supplement a collective-bargaining agreement, *Steelworkers v. Warrior & Gulf Co.*, 363 U.S. 574, 579, so there may be an unwritten "common-law" in a particular university that certain employees shall have the equivalent of tenure.[70]

The analogy to *Steelworkers* is both striking and useful.[71] Collec-

---

69. 408 U.S. 564 (1972).
70. 408 U.S. 593, 602 (1972).
71. It is understandable that *Greene* should make no reference to *Steelworkers* given *Greene's* clear reliance on *professional* custom. It is puzzling, however, that *Sindermann* should have made no note of *Greene*.

tive agreements are characteristically incomplete, frequently embody ambiguous language, and cannot explicitly provide for every possible situation which may arise. "The end result," observes one leading authority, "is a document with broad rules, a miscellany of gaps, unclear language, and unsettled issues. To the parties it represents agreement, even though they know that it is only the gateway to the resolution of remaining disagreements."[72] Others have remarked on the governmental character of the collective agreement.[73] Similarly, the "terms and conditions" of an academic appointment are found, as *Greene* and related cases suggest, in institutional policies, practices and customs as colored by the practices, standards and customs of the profession as a whole. The language of institutional policies, handbooks and other regulatory provisions is frequently the product of a species of negotiation with internal faculty governing bodies and, equally, may leave much to be desired by way of clarity but doubtless represents the terms on which the faculty, administration and governing board understand they will deal with one another. Such internal faculty bodies may play a role in decisions affecting faculty status and discipline as a matter either of regulation or custom. Thus upon appointment, an institutional *status* is conferred on the faculty member which may yield rights to participate in as well as criticize institutional decisions. These rights, in a fashion analagous to those enjoyed under a collective agreement, comprise a portion of the bundle of rights conferred upon consummation of a contract of academic appointment.

This approach was treated unsympathetically, if obliquely, in a case involving the decision of the Regents of the University of California to deny academic credit for a course, half the lectures of which were to be given by Eldridge Cleaver.[74] The course had been approved through the established faculty machinery of the Berkeley Division of the Academic Senate in early September, 1968. On September 20, the Regents adopted two resolutions. The first prohibited anyone from lecturing for more than one occasion in an academic quarter in a course

---

72. Summers, *Collective Agreements and the Law of Contracts*, 78 YALE L.J. 525, 529 (1969).

73. *See, e.g.,* Chamberlain, *Collective Bargaining and the Concept of Contract*, 48 COLUM. L. REV. 829 (1948); Cox, *The Legal Nature of Collective Bargaining Agreements*, 57 MICH. L. REV. 1 (1958). *See also* P. SELZNICK, LAW, SOCIËTY, AND INDUSTRIAL JUSTICE ch. 4 (1969).

74. Searle v. Regents of the Univ. of Calif., 23 Cal. App. 3d 448, 100 Cal. Rptr. 194 (1st Dist. 1972). The course was entitled, "Dehumanization and Regeneration in the American Social Order."

for credit unless he holds an academic appointment. The second provided that if the course in question did not meet that requirement academic credit would not be given. The course was offered as approved and after credit was denied sixteen students (who had taken the course) and six faculty (otherwise unidentified save that four had been given responsibility to supervise the course) sought to compel the grant of credit.

The court was guided by its intepretation of the constitutional mandate that the Regents have " 'full powers of organization and government' of the university."[75] It noted that the Regents had established procedures for the repeal or amendment of its standing orders (pursuant to which the faculty exercise responsibility for the curriculum) and that it had failed to follow these procedures in adopting its September 20 resolutions. The court held, however, that these procedural requirements were merely for the Board's own guidance and benefit and cannot limit the Board's authority. Further, taking note of *Greene* the court pointed out that "it is not pleaded or suggested that any faculty appellant regarded or relied upon the standing order as to the amendment procedure as a term and condition of his employment."[76] Even had it been so regarded, the court suggests that the Regents' reservation of authority would also have comprised a part of the contract thereby negating the result urged. Finally, the court chose to characterize the controversy as "essentially whether the regents or the faculty shall control university policy in determining whether credit is to be given for courses conducted by non-members of the faculty. In light of the constitutional grant of power to the regents, we have no hesitation in holding that this power is vested in them."[77]

In effect, the court's approach here is indistinguishable from that of the Supreme Court of North Dakota in *Posin*[78] which that court has itself now abandoned.[79] Indeed, the court's statement of the issue here returns to the perspective of the 19th century cases noted at the outset

---

75. *Id.* at 195.
76. *Id.* at 196.
77. *Id.*
78. 86 N.W.2d 31 (N.D. 1957).
79. 198 N.W.2d 108 (N.D. 1972). *See also* the court's treatment of the argument that procedural requirements adopted by a governing board are simply for its own "administrative" convenience in Hillis v. Meister, 82 N.M. 474, 483 P.2d 1314 (1971).

in viewing the dispute in essence as one of managerial prerogative. That characterization blurs the really serious aspects of the case. Clearly, the regents' general reliance on the faculty's experience in curricular matters found in the relevant standing order and its adoption of rules governing any reconsideration of that reliance by way of amending the standing order are relevant to the sound exercise of the discretion given the regents by state law. To give effect to those procedural requirements does not involve the courts in the merits of the decision nor does it require that the faculty position be adhered to but does insure that the ultimate decision is adequately considered consistent with the Board's own rules. Moreover, contrary to the court's passing reference, *Greene* (and the cases following it) would logically seem to comprehend the inclusion of institutional policies and practices concerning curricular development as a term of faculty appointment. Though such matters are not bargained-for, anymore than "hiring practices" or tenure policies, they clearly go to the faculty's professional intramural responsibilities. From that point of view it is doubtful that the general reservation of unfettered authority should save the Board from compliance with its established policies and practices.

In reviewing this section, it is interesting to note that prior to many of the decisions discussed herein the *Harvard Law Review* concluded that "the courts could attempt to fashion a special body of law explicitly defining the professional rights and obligations of members of the academic community—either within such traditional legal categories as contract or tort or by the formulation of a branch of the law of private associations."[80] While a tort approach remains undeveloped it now appears that a contract theory incorporating the customs and practices of the profession is being pressed with some consistency toward that end.[81] Such a theory holds the promise of effecting a jointure of

---

80. *See Developments in the Law—Academic Freedom, supra* note 12 at 1051. Given the governmental character of the faculty's collective role in the life of the institution, which may be assimilated into the individual faculty member's contract of employment, the contract theory here presented does partake of a law of association. In Galton v. College of Pharmaceutical Sciences, 70 Misc. 2d 12, 332 N.Y.S.2d 909 (Sup. Ct. 1972), for example, it was held that plaintiff students, faculty, alumni, and student and faculty organizations had standing to secure judicial review of the decision to close down the college, an affiliate of Columbia University. *Cf.* Searle v. Regents of the Univ. of Calif., 23 Cal. App. 3d 448, 100 Cal. Rptr. 194 (1st Dist. 1972).

81. *See* Whitson v. Hartford Seminary Foundation, No. 175492 (Conn. Super. Ct., Hartford County, filed Mar. 30, 1972) (action to enjoin alterations in educational program and resultant curtailment in faculty without faculty participation as provided for

the common law with the profession's customary law; but that jointure can be fully effected only after the questions of the scope of the custom and the fashioning of an effective remedy have been satisfactorily resolved.

A. Scope of Custom

Justice Stewart's opinion in *Sindermann,* while relying on language speaking to the "common law" of an industry as well as of a particular plant, goes on to conclude that there may be a common law "in a particular university,"[82] pursuant to which Sindermann might have de facto tenure. Similarly, the Illinois Supreme Court's posture in *Fooden*[83] seems restricted to a consideration of purely local practice. Neither opinion really confronts the issue, however, nor does any sound reason manifest itself why a body of national custom should not be so recognized particularly when one contemplates that the American professoriate is fundamentally a national profession.[84] No

---

by charter and AAUP standards) (later settled out-of-court); Cook County Teachers Union v. Board of Governors, Case No. 2350-67 (Ill. Cir. Ct., Sangamon County, 1967) (action for mandamus to compel the issuance of a contract of academic employment to Professor Staughton Lynd based in part on the meaning given an exchange of letters between officers of the administration and Professor Lynd by the "customs, practices, and traditions of the academic community" including particularly AAUP standards) (later settled out-of-court); Erar v. Assumption College, No. 4314 (Super. Ct., Worcester, Mass.) (action to enjoin termination of tenured faculty member for alleged financial exigency as violation of the terms of the *Faculty Handbook* comprising part of the faculty member's contract of employment and governing the dismissal of tenured faculty) (later successfully resolved, November, 1971); Sharples v. Wayne State Univ., Civil No. 199-485R (Mich. Cir. Ct., Wayne County, Feb. 4, 1972) (action to enjoin the nonrenewal of 281 nontenured faculty based on institutional custom and the standards of the profession nationally requiring faculty participation in the nonrenewal decisions) (later settled out-of-court); Muscarella v. Metropolitan Museum of Art, No. 20960/72, (Sup. Ct., New York County, filed Sept. 29, 1972) (action to enjoin dismissal of curator who had been granted "academic tenure" pursuant to museum policy); *In re* Schulman, No. 10131/70 (Sup. Ct., New York County, June 26, 1970) (action to compel renewal of appointment based on first amendment violation and incorporating, *inter alia,* failure to provide an internal hearing pursuant to AAUP standards as requested by the Faculty Senate of the City College of New York and failure to abide by other procedures found in institutional regulations and customs) (later settled out-of-court).

82. 408 U.S. 593, 602 (1972).

83. 48 Ill. 2d 580, 272 N.E.2d 497 (1971).

84. *See* D. Brown, The Mobile Professors (1967); T. Caplow & R. McGee, The Academic Marketplace (1965); H. D. Marshall, The Mobility of College Faculty (1964). *See generally* C. Jencks & D. Reisman, The Academic Revolution chs. I, IV (1968). *See also* cases cited in note 81 *supra,* in several of which AAUP standards were expressly relied on. Moreover, in many of the cases discussed AAUP standards have been adopted in institutional policies by reference or verbatim. Perry v.

real obstacle seems presented where resort to such a body of custom is used to give meaning to the broad language of institutional policy or to fill the interstices of such provisions, *i.e.*, what one commentator referred to in the commercial context as *translational* and *additive* functions.[85] In so proceeding, consideration of evidence concerning the meaning of national custom most prominently found in AAUP standards and interpretations would be in order.[86]

Sindermann, 408 U.S. 593 (1972) (language of the Texas Governing Board statement); Greene v. Howard Univ., 412 F.2d 1128 (D.C. Cir. 1969); Mendez v. Trustees of Boston Univ., —— Mass. ——, 285 N.E.2d 446 (1972); Griffin v. St. Mary's College, 258 Md. 276, 265 A.2d 757 (1970); Thomas v. Catawba College, 248 N.C. 609, 104 S.E.2d 175 (1958). *See also* Holliman v. Martin, 330 F. Supp. 1 (W.D. Va. 1971):

> In the present case, there was no express provision as to termination of employment in the contract received by Mrs. Holliman . . . her "contract" consisted of a salutary greeting, an offer of employment, a recital of the proposed salary, and a statement that the faculty was to be governed by the American Association of University Professors' 1940 Statement of Principles on Academic Freedom and Tenure.

Id. at 8. *See also* Board of Trustees v. Davis, 396 F.2d 730 (8th Cir. 1968) later settled by a Joint Stipulation for Dismissal, No. PB-66-C-76 (E.D. Ark.) reciting that the Board of Trustees of Arkansas A & M College "have heretofore bound themselves and again hereby commit the Board of Trustees . . . to be guided and controlled" by AAUP policy. The ruling of the Illinois Supreme Court in Fooden v. Board of Governors of State Colleges and Universities, 48 Ill. 2d 580, 272 N.E.2d 497 (1971), *cert. denied*, 408 U.S. 943 (1972), foreclosed the attempt to show that the board had in fact adopted or followed AAUP standards.

On the impact of AAUP standards, compare the conclusions drawn by Byse and Joughin concerning the tenure plans in effect at 80 predominantly private "traditional" colleges and universities in 1959, *supra* note 1, at 68-70, with the results of a sample of 413 more varied institutions in 1972. Furniss, *Faculty Tenure and Contract Systems: Current Practice*, A.C.E. SPECIAL REPORT (July 27, 1972):

> It may be that, in the past, the policies and practices of large numbers of institutions were inadequate or repressive. This survey indicates, however, that AAUP policies with respect to length of probationary period, credit for prior service, written reasons for nonrenewal, and the availability of appeal procedures are widely observed. . . .

Id. at 2.

The AAUP's judicial work has also been increasingly recognized. Belasco, *supra* note 12, reports that in the six-year period of roughly 1950-1956 the Association processed 363 complaints. In the 1971-1972 year the Association processed 1139 complaints; approximately 50% of those pursued to active mediation with the respective administrations were successfully resolved. *Report of Committee A, 1971-1972*, 58 AAUP BULL. 145, 145-46 (1972). Regrettably, the Association does not publish its successfully resolved cases in a fashion from which it is possible to abstract a body of operational principle.

85. Note, *Custom and Trade Usage: Its Application to Commercial Dealings and the Common Law*, 55 COLUM. L. REV. 1192, 1195-96 (1955). Some institutions are so new as to lack well-defined purely local practices. *See* Schultz v. Palmberg, 317 F. Supp. 659 (D. Wyo. 1970) (college in its second year).

86. *See* the cases discussed in *supra* note 81. This may require a more active program of litigation than the AAUP has thus far embarked upon. Regrettably, the legal com-

In *Mendez v. Trustees of Boston University*,[87] for example, a non-tenured instructor of nursing who had served in the institution for three years was informed in May that attendance for faculty discussions the following September 1 was required. A month later she was notified of the renewal of her appointment for the ensuing academic year. She failed to report, however, until September 10, during which time the administration's efforts to reach her proved unavailing. Her absence, apparently unexplained, was not due to circumstances beyond her control. Accordingly, her contract was terminated for her failure to appear and she sought redress based on the administration's failure to pursue the termination procedures embodied in the *Faculty Manual* explicitly incorporating AAUP standards. The Supreme Judicial Court of Massachusetts agreed that the one page "Faculty Appointment Form" does not spell out the details of the relationship between the faculty member and the institution and agreed further that the *Faculty Manual* comprises a part of the contract of employment. It observed, however, that the review machinery does not apply to one who "resigns his position"[88] and concurred with the trial court that the plaintiff, having in effect abandoned the agreement, could not claim the benefit of it—particularly where no services had been rendered. Thus the court treated the termination of a faculty member renewed for a fourth year of service as if she had failed to appear for an initial one-year appointment. Although this seems to be the kind of case where evidence of national custom would be in order, particularly in view of the fact that AAUP standards formed a part of the contract of employment, it does not appear that such evidence was presented or referred to.

The more serious issue is posed where local rules or practices are in explicit contravention of national norms. As Professor Van Alstyne points out, the Supreme Court in *Roth* treats an initial one-year non-tenured appointment as if it were a special one-year terminal appointment.[89] This treatment appears consistent nevertheless with the spe-

---

munity will be denied the resolution of this issue in *Sindermann* which might have served as a useful guidepost particularly on the question of the effect of the Texas Coordinating Board's statement incorporating national practice. Professor Sindermann has settled his case. *In Town to Get Check—Sindermann Politely Declines Job At O.C.*, The Odessa American, Nov. 12, 1972 at 1.

87. —— Mass. ——, 285 N.E.2d 446 (1972).

88. *Id.* at ——, 285 N.E.2d at 448.

89. Van Alstyne, *The Supreme Court Speaks to the Untenured: A Comment on Board of Regents v. Roth and Perry v. Sindermann*, 58 AAUP Bull. 267, 268 (1972).

cific regulations in effect for Wisconsin State University at Oshkosh, although local practice tends to indicate a somewhat different treatment.[90] It seems likely that for most matters, particularly those of a procedural character, specific local provisions will be controlling. It remains to be seen, as the Constitution is extended to protect academic freedom in publicly operated institutions, whether the public policy so clearly favoring the exercise of academic freedom will elevate the doctrine to the status of a "common law custom" forming an essential part of employment contracts in situations where the Constitution has not been held applicable.[91]

B. *Effective Remedy*

A contract theory confronts the common law rule against specific performance of contracts for personal services.[92] As one commentator has pointed out, the basis for the rule seems inapplicable in this area.[93] First, damages are rarely adequate. Wholly apart from the disruption of the faculty member's life and injury to his reputation the institutional action may have a chilling effect on the exercise of academic rights by other faculty members. Second, the rationale of difficulty of supervising a decree of specific performance ill fits the circumstances of a highly autonomous faculty member. Moreover, what is frequently sought is reinstatement pending the presentation of charges and a hearing—matters with which the courts have some experience. Third, it is anomalous that reinstatement may be awarded by an arbitrator for breach of a collective agreement incorporating the "common law" of the profession but not by a court, with its greater responsibility

---

90. That is, only 4 of 442 nontenured faculty were actually not renewed at Oshkosh that year. *Id.*

91. One commentator has argued that academic freedom may be viewed simply as an implied term in the contract of academic employment. "It is essential that the man hired to traffic in ideas not be fired for doing so." York, *The Legal Nature of Academic Freedom*, 48 BRIEF 246 (1953).

92. RESTATEMENT OF CONTRACTS § 379 (1932); CORBIN, CORBIN ON CONTRACTS § 1204 (1964). *See also* Barden v. Junior College Dist. No. 520, —— Ill. App. 2d ——, 271 N.E.2d 680 (1970); Felch v. Findlay College, 119 Ohio App. 357, 200 N.E.2d 353 (1964) (explicitly follows Restatement in denying injunction by tenured faculty dismissed without compliance with hearing procedures which court accepts as part of the employment contract); Sprunt v. Members of the Bd. of Trustees of the University of Tennessee, 223 Tenn. 210, 443 S.W.2d 464 (1969).

93. Comment, *Academic Tenure: The Search for Standards*, 39 S. CAL. L. REV. 593, 603 (1966).

for bringing public policy to bear,[94] presented with the same departure under an individual contract incorporating the same customs. Finally, it should be noted that the common law rule is being eroded by the complexities of modern business transactions.[95] It is, again, anomalous that an automobile dealer of many years standing can enjoin the termination of his relationship with the manufacturer until adequate cause is shown but not a university professor of as many years standing. By so acting in the former case the courts seem to recognize what is tantamount to a tenure system, but by declining to do so in the latter fail to give effect to an explicit award of tenure.[96]

Some tentative movement in this direction may be discerned. In remanding for findings of damages, *Greene*[97] seems to rely more on the impracticality of ordering a hearing at that late date than on the recitation of the common law rule. Moreover, the court in *Pima College*[98] was of the view that since, as a matter of custom, an appointment would be automatically renewed once the nonrenewal date had passed and as the institution's customary nonrenewal date had been exceeded the appointment was renewed as a matter of law. Thus the court concluded that it could order reinstatement by way of mandamus inasmuch as no discretionary act was called for.[99] Interestingly, it appears that the Board of Regents in *Hillis*[100] had argued that the failure to abide by its procedures could properly result in a reversal of the decision to terminate but not in an award of damages.

---

94. On the respective roles of arbitrator and judge see Blumrosen, *Public Policy Considerations in Labor Arbitration Cases*, 14 RUTGERS L. REV. 217 (1960); Seitz, *The Arbitrator's Responsibility for Public Policy*, 19 ARB. J. 23 (1964); Shulman, *Reason, Contract, and Law in Labor Relations*, 68 HARV. L. REV. 999 (1955).

95. *See, e.g.*, Semmes Motors, Inc. v. Ford Motor Co., 429 F.2d 1197 (2d Cir. 1970); Dahlberg Bros., Inc. v. Ford Motor Co., 272 Minn. 264, 137 N.W.2d 314 (1965) (auto dealer franchises); Fleischer v. James Drug Stores, Inc., 1 N.J. 138, 62 A.2d 383 (1948) (participation in retailing cooperative); Harmon v. Tanner Motor Tours, 79 Nev. 4, 377 P.2d 622 (1963) (ten-year exclusive franchise awarded by board of county commissioners).

96. One may speculate whether it would be easier to distinguish the rule if faculty were deemed "independent contractors" rather than employees. One administration has explicitly argued that faculty are independent contractors and not employees in attempting to pursuade the National Labor Relations Board not to extend jurisdiction to the faculty. Brief of the employer at 3-5, *In re* New York University, Civ. Nos. 2-RC-15719, 2-RC-15757 (NLRB, Aug. 14, 1972).

97. 412 F.2d at 1135.

98. 17 Ariz. App. at 216, 496 P.2d at 641.

99. A similar result was achieved on a contract theory in State *ex rel.* Keeney v. Ayers, 108 Mont. 547, 92 P.2d 306 (1939). The dissent relies on the common law rule against specific performance of contracts for personal service.

100. Hillis v. Meister, 82 N.M. 474, 483 P.2d 1314 (1971).

Conclusions

The extension of constitutional protection from aprofessional to professional activity, in tandem with a developing contract theory incorporating the practice and custom of the profession, have the potential of shaping a body of law particularly sensitive to the needs of the academic milieu. They hold the promise of effecting a jointure of the common law with a body of practice developed by a profession heretofore chary of judicial redress. Interestingly, these developments come at a time when the profession is greatly troubled[101] and, as the foregoing indicates, when resort to the courts is becoming increasingly commonplace.

More than a decade ago, Byse and Joughin urged judicial recognition of certain concomitants of *status* in the institution.[102] The emerging contract theory in particular is capable of maturing into a law of academic status. Whether it will do so will depend in good measure on the degree of acceptance of the profession's customary law and the willingness of courts to fashion an adequate remedy.

---

101. For a far too simplistic outline of some of the reasons for the profession's unease, see Finkin, *The Dilemma of the Professoriate*, 17 Vill. L. Rev. 1010 (1972).

102. *See* C. Byse & L. Joughin, *supra* note 1, at 137-38.

THE SUPREME COURT SPEAKS
TO THE UNTENURED

A Comment on
Board of Regents v. *Roth*
and
Perry v. *Sindermann*

William Van Alstyne

The Supreme Court Speaks to the Untenured:
A Comment on Board of Regents v. Roth and Perry v. Sindermann

William Van Alstyne

On June 29th, 1972, the Supreme Court handed down its first decisions directed to the procedural rights of untenured faculty. The results were mixed and not uncomplicated. (The full Opinions are printed at 406 U.S. ——, 92 S. Ct. 2694, 40 U.S.L.W. 5079.) In *Board of Regents* v. *Roth*, by a vote of five to three (Brennan, Douglas, and Marshall dissenting, the three Nixon appointees joining White and Stewart in the majority, Powell taking no part), the Court appeared to hold essentially that untenured faculty members have no constitutional right to any procedural observances in the nonrenewal of their appointments. In *Perry* v. *Sindermann*, however, the Court agreed unanimously that the technical absence of formal tenure was not conclusive of the faculty member's procedural rights and that proof of *de facto* tenure would entitle him to some degree of explanation and opportunity for reconsideration. In between, the Court appears to have left room for a concept of quasi-tenure applicable to significant numbers of regular faculty members, a *terra incognita* that may well raise serious practical questions for general institutional policy in cases of nonrenewal or nonreappointment. The larger implications of both cases may appropriately be pursued in the detailed analyses of the professional law journals. This Comment will confine itself to a brief review of the decisions plus a closing observation about their relevance to the AAUP's *Statement on Procedural Standards in the Renewal or Nonrenewal of Faculty Appointments*.

The Reductionism of Roth: The Untenured Faculty Member as a Limited Appointee Entitled to No Further Consideration

The constitutional issue of pretermination procedural rights was raised most starkly in *Roth*, a case involving an assistant professor of political science at Wisconsin State University-Oshkosh, who received unexplained notice in January of his first year of teaching advising him that he would not be reappointed for the next academic

WILLIAM VAN ALSTYNE, Professor of Law at Duke University, is Chairman of the Association's Committee A on Academic Freedom and Tenure.

year. The notice came shortly after Professor Roth had made a number of public statements critical of the University administrators and board of regents, and Professor Roth was one of only 4 (of 442) untenured faculty members at the University whose appointments were not renewed that year. In his complaint in the federal district court, Professor Roth alleged that the University's summary action of unexplained notice without opportunity for hearing or reconsideration violated the Fourteenth Amendment provision that no state shall deprive any person of life, liberty, or property, without due process of law.

The district court sustained Professor Roth's position to the extent of holding that *due* process required the University administration to respond to a request for an explanation of its decision to discontinue him and to grant him some opportunity to be heard on reconsideration of the matter, albeit with the burden being his to show that the stated reasons were either "wholly inappropriate as a basis for decision or that they [were] wholly without basis in fact." Only then, the district court added, "would the university administration become obliged to show that the stated reasons are not inappropriate or that they have a basis in fact." (310 F. Supp. 972, 980 [W.D. Wis. 1970]). The University appealed from this decision, but the court of appeals affirmed and the case thereafter went to the Supreme Court where it was consolidated with *Perry* v. *Sindermann* for argument.

The Supreme Court majority found it unnecessary to determine whether the district court had erred in its specification of the particular procedural rights it had determined to be required by *due* process. Rather, the majority held that the clause did not apply at all:

> [R]espondent has not shown that he was deprived of liberty or property protected by the Fourteenth Amendment. The judgment of the Court of Appeals, accordingly, is reversed.

Analytically, the majority treated Professor Roth's situation exactly on the same footing as that which would be appropriate in respect to a special or limited appointment for a single year, the kind of situation where even notice of nonreappointment would itself be anomalous because it could only be regarded by the special appointee himself as a gratuitous discourtesy. By placing Professor Roth in this different frame, as though he were not a regular appointee and as though there were no significant distinctions between his situation and that of a special one-year terminal appointment, the majority of the Supreme Court reduced his constitutionally cognizable substantive interests in reappointment to zero. It followed smoothly that the due process clause had not been triggered and thus, in a constitutional sense, no process of law was due Professor Roth at all.

The position of the majority was unaffected by the fact that nonrenewal of untenured faculty members at Oshkosh was apparently highly exceptional at the time, a point the district court had emphasized both in terms of its evidentiary force regarding the real implications of regular appointment at the institution and its relevance in measuring the real burden to the University to provide some opportunity for reconsideration in the occasional case of nonrenewal. That this matter was felt by the Supreme Court majority to be of too little significance, rather than that it might somehow have been overlooked, seems clear from the fact that a footnote in the majority Opinion obliquely refers to it. That the decision is indeed a significant one which will not be easy to distinguish or to limit is further attested by the fact that the majority was also aware of the coincidence that notice of nonrenewal followed shortly after Professor Roth's critical public utterances. (The district court had stressed the coincidence as lending additional weight to some right to explanation and pretermination review as an important means of protecting the faculty member's substantive First Amendment freedom of speech.) Finally, the majority was not inclined to view the case as distinguishable from one of a limited one-year special appointment in spite of the possible far greater difficulty Professor Roth might expect to encounter in finding a position somewhere else after unexplained termination from Oshkosh, following his very first year as a regular faculty member, a point also stressed by the district and circuit courts in holding in his favor. The different view of the Supreme Court majority appears in the trailing portion of still another footnote:

> Mere proof . . . that his record of nonretention in one job, taken alone, might make him somewhat less attractive to some other employers would hardly establish the kind of foreclosure of opportunities amounting to a deprivation of "liberty" [sufficient to entitle him to some measure of pretermination procedural due process].

Given the analytic basis of the decision, *Roth* necessarily deals a heavy blow to further claims by untenured faculty members to procedural rights in the consideration of reappointment, at least as a matter of constitutional right. Indeed, the Supreme Court's decision in this case not only reversed the judgment of the seventh circuit, but simultaneously rejected decisions from the fifth and first circuits (with federal appellate jurisdiction in the South and New England respectively) which had previously held that some measure of pretermination procedural due process was constitutionally required in circumstances like those in *Roth.*

Nevertheless, the different result in *Perry* v. *Sindermann* (decided the same day) complicates the picture a good deal and provides room for a number of important second thoughts.

The Realism of Sindermann: De Facto Tenure and the Importance of Collateral Effects

Neither his letter of appointment nor any state statute provided Professor Robert Sindermann with tenure as a regular faculty member at Odessa Junior College when, in May, 1969, the Texas Board of Regents voted not to renew the latest in the series of one-year appointments he had held at the College. A lead sentence in the College's official Faculty Guide itself declared, moreover, that "Odessa College has no tenure system." Professor Sindermann's situation at Odessa might therefore appear to have been indistinguishable from that of Professor Roth at Oshkosh. Accordingly, the same outcome might have been expected in the Supreme Court after the Texas Regents had secured review of the decision of the fifth circuit that had held in favor of Professor Sindermann's claim for some measure of pretermination procedural due process. (The two cases were also similar in the coincidence that Professor Sindermann's unexplained notice of nonrenewal followed shortly on the heels of news reports of his public and political activities.)

Unlike David Roth, however, Professor Sindermann was in his tenth year of full-time faculty service, the last four of which he had served at Odessa (including service for a time as cochairman of the department of government and social science). Notwithstanding the formal disclaimer of any tenure system, moreover, official publications of the College and of the Coordinating Board of the Texas College and University System clearly implied the existence of a *de facto* tenure policy at Odessa, a policy arguably covering Professor Sindermann since it adhered to AAUP standards in providing for credit for three years service at other institutions. Noting that Professor Sindermann alleged that he met the terms of that policy and had relied upon it, the Supreme Court first distinguished *Roth* in holding that here more than "a mere subjective 'expectancy' " of reappointment was involved. Accordingly, it held that proof by Sindermann that tenure protection was implied in fact in his case would be sufficient demonstration of an existing "property interest" in reappointment to trigger the Fourteenth Amendment and thus to require some degree of intramural procedural due process before he could be deprived of that interest.

Up to this point, the Sindermann Opinion is encouraging: dry legalism is not utterly dispositive of professional security and the technical absence of formally conferred *de jure* tenure is not always controlling of one's right to intramural procedural due process in case of nonreappointment. Even where the state may not have adopted a formal tenure system and a faculty member's letter of appointment may itself refer only to a specific term, the existence of an official policy or authoritative practice akin to tenure may imply some degree of intramural procedural due process as a matter of constitutional right.

Nevertheless, in what may be hoped to have been casual *dicta* added at the close of Mr. Justice Stewart's Opinion for the majority, the description of the *kind* of procedural due process constitutionally assured a faculty member under these circumstances is breathtakingly slight:

> Proof of such a property interest would not, of course, entitle him to reinstatement. But such proof would obligate college officials to grant a hearing at his request, where he could be informed of the grounds for his nonretention and challenge their sufficiency.

Thus, the Court appears to declare that even one with *de facto* tenure may not be entitled as a matter of constitutional right to any pretermination procedural due process. Rather, much like the Queen of Hearts in *Alice in Wonderland,* the administration may declare "sentence first, trial and verdict later." Moreover, the burden would apparently be placed upon the faculty member seeking reinstatement to overcome a presumption of regularity accompanying the statement of grounds for termination presented by the administration in that hearing. While it is very doubtful that the Court meant in any way also to imply that such a *post hoc* procedure with its reversal of the burden of proof is constitutionally sufficient where tenure has been conferred *de jure,* it nonetheless managed by this statement to take away much of the little good it had just done in identifying conditions of *de facto* tenure, by thus immediately eroding its strength in terms of its constitutionally required procedural entitlements.

A similar qualification characterized still another portion of the Opinions that otherwise acknowledged a limited constitutional right to procedural due process under special circumstances of nonrenewal. In *Roth,* the Court was careful to distinguish what it deemed to be the ordinary and foreseeable hardship of an unexplained nonrenewal at the end of an initial one-year academic appointment from other kinds of collateral consequences which would be sufficient to require procedural due process insofar as the university might itself be *directly* responsible for those collateral consequences. Specifically, Mr. Justice Stewart laid considerable stress on the fact that in declining to rehire Professor Roth "[t]he State . . . did not make any charge against him that might seriously damage his standing and association in his community":

> Had it done so, this would be a different case. For "[w]here a person's good name, reputation, honor or integrity is at stake because of what the government is doing to him, notice and an opportunity to be heard are essential."

Mr. Justice Stewart also stressed that the decision of non-renewal in Roth did not itself *authoritatively* foreclose Professor Roth from any other employment opportunities, *i.e.,* it did not operate as a matter of law to bar him from consideration elsewhere even assuming that other institutions might regard the fact of his nonreappointment at Oshkosh as a matter of some practical significance. He was quick to add, moreover, that the collateral effect of a larger legal consequence accompanying nonrenewal would describe a different case and might well require

the observance of procedural due process.

Even so, the character of intramural procedural due process which the presence of either of these collateral effects beyond *per se* nonrenewal may make available to the distressed faculty member is evidently limited to the possibility of securing relief only from the effects themselves. Success in refuting the institution's discrediting public statements in the course of a university hearing would still not entitle the faculty member to reinstatement. Again, the point is discoverable in a footnote:

> In such a case, due process would accord an opportunity to refute the charge before University officials.[12]

[12] The purpose of such notice and hearing is to provide the person an opportunity to clear his name. Once a person has cleared his name at a hearing, his employer, of course, may remain free to deny him future employment for other reasons.

The logic of this position is perfectly straightforward, namely, that water cannot rise higher than its source: since a *post hoc* hearing is constitutionally required only because of collateral injury to reputation resulting from damaging public statements by the institution and not at all because of nonrenewal *per se,* the relief it provides is solely for the benefit of reputation and not in contemplation of reinstatement. Although the Court did not expressly say so (and quoted *dicta* from other cases implying the contrary), moreover, the logic of its position may likewise imply that the only required purpose of providing a hearing where the decision of nonrenewal would authoritatively foreclose other employment would be to provide an opportunity to rescind that particular collateral effect without, however, securing reinstatement within the institution itself.

Even so, the result suggested above is very much open to doubt and subject to reasonable dispute. If a public institution failed to renew a faculty member's appointment solely because it originally believed certain things to be true which a fair hearing subsequently established to be false (even assuming that the opportunity to have proved them false would not have been provided except that it was constitutionally required because the institution made a public statement about the matter), continued refusal to renew the appointment might then be successfully challenged on the basis that it can only be explained as an arbitrary reaction, *i.e.,* as an arbitrary refusal to treat the faculty member on equal terms with others whose appointments were renewed, discriminating against him solely on the basis of an earlier belief of unfitness since refuted in a fair hearing. As the hearing itself was a matter of constitutional right, moreover, the institution could not hope to defend itself on the basis that the faculty member's decision to press for a hearing was itself sufficient evidence of lack of trust or temperamental incompatibility to decline to reinstate him.

The Terra Incognita of Quasi-Tenure and the Better Position of AAUP Policy

With all of this uncertainty stemming from the Opinions in *Roth* and *Sindermann,* there is yet another complexity that warrants examination. Between the ten-year instance of termination under an alleged policy of de facto tenure (as in *Sindermann*) and the first-year instance of nonreappointment under circumstances where the Court found that neither an explanation nor an opportunity for reconsideration is constitutionally required (as in *Roth*), there is a great deal of *terra incognita* where the majority of untenured faculty members and official institutional policies are actually to be found.

In *Roth*, Mr. Justice Stewart (writing for the majority) may well have been troubled by the lack of sufficient substance to David Roth's claim of any *officially* encouraged expectation of reappointment to fit it by analogy to a qualified or contingent "property" right, suitably to distinguish it from the claim of a disappointed first-time applicant or special appointee. The record in the *Roth* case, judged by Mr. Justice Stewart's characterization of it, left some things to be desired to the extent that it may not have indicated that there were official statements of criteria for reappointment and progress toward tenure consideration—statements which might have helped David Roth to provide a line of *constitutional* distinction in either of the two respects the majority of the Court evidently believed to be important. Designation of his appointment as a regular member of the faculty coupled with official assurances objectively encouraging him to anticipate reappointment upon satisfactory service as defined in reasonably attainable standards might have generated more substance to the view that he possessed a contingent property interest of which he could not be deprived without some measure of intramural due process. Similarly, official provision of standards contemplating reappointment in the absence of professional shortcoming or immoral conduct might have rendered an otherwise unexplained nonrenewal decision so great a slur upon the appointee's professional or personal standing as to be viewed as a deprivation of "liberty" (of reputation or contract) triggering the Fourteenth Amendment's guarantee of due process. It may not parse phrases too closely to aggregate all of Mr. Justice Stewart's qualifying observations about the record in the *Roth* case, for instance, in suggesting that the decision may yet permit meaningful distinctions to be made in the future:

> [O]n the record before us, all that clearly appears is that the respondent was not rehired for one year at one University. . . . [The terms of his appointment] did not provide for contract renewal absent "sufficient cause." Indeed, they made no provision for renewal whatsoever. . . . Nor, significantly, was there any state statute or University rule or policy that secured his interest in re-employment or that created any legitimate claim to it. . . . In the present case . . . there is no suggestion whatever that the respondent's interest in his "good name, reputation, honor or integrity" is at stake. . . . The District Court made an *assumption* "that non-retention by one university or college creates concrete and practical difficulties for a professor in his subsequent academic career. . . . But even assuming *arguendo* that such a "substantial adverse effect" under these circumstances would constitute a state imposed restriction on liberty, the record contains no support for these assumptions.

Given the overall conservative cast of the balance of the Opinion, it may read too much into these qualifying observations to suggest that they mark out obvious possibilities sharply to limit and to distinguish the basic holding. Nevertheless, they may imply that on a better record, under more compelling circumstances where the faculty member is well along the tenure track under policies explicitly encouraging reliance and practices consistent with that reliance, peremptory notice of nonreappointment may not be enough to quench the constitutional claim to more specific consideration than now at all.

Accordingly, the set of Opinions in *Roth* and *Sindermann* together with their full implications may now confront institutions of higher learning with a sharper choice: to avoid the "hazard" of even minimum constitutional procedures by strategically withdrawing any official encouragement of professional security for the faculty and retreating behind the ironplate of seried, short-term terminal contracts, thus to reserve a prerogative of procedural arbitrariness; or to systematize instead a policy of positive incentives with a willingness to provide some explanation and opportunity for reconsideration when so requested. It may be significant in this regard that in closing his Opinion, Mr. Justice Stewart went out of his way to note that the Court's decision was confined to a construction of the Constitution itself and that not all that the Constitution tolerates is necessarily "appropriate or wise in public colleges and universities." And again there is a footnote, by no means disapproving, comparing as an example the AAUP's *Statement on Procedural Standards in the Renewal or Nonrenewal of Faculty Appointments.*

A Postscript on the Substantive Constitutional Freedoms of the Faculty

Nothing in either *Roth* or *Sindermann* at all impairs the statutory right of a faculty member to secure full redress in an appropriate federal court upon proof of his allegation that his nonreappointment was significantly influenced by considerations foreclosed by the Bill of Rights or the Fourteenth Amendment. In both *Roth* and *Sindermann,* the Supreme Court remanded the cases to the federal district courts to consider the merits of each faculty member's first amendment claim that the decision of nonreappointment was in retaliation for critical public utterances which the faculty member alleged to be protected by the First Amendment. With no dissent to this proposition, Mr. Justice Stewart observed:

> The first question presented is whether the respondent's lack of a contractual or tenure right to re-employment, taken alone, defeats his claim that the nonrenewal of his contract violated the First and Fourteenth Amendments. We hold that it does not.

In this respect, the decision fully confirmed prior holdings of Supreme Court cases that lack of tenure has no effect upon the substantive equal protection of First Amendment rights, and it wholly lays to rest inconsistent *dicta* which had appeared in certain lower court decisions (*e.g., Jones* v. *Hopper*, 110 F.2d 1323 [10th Cir. 1970]). The problem does remain as a result of *Roth*, however, that the practical risk of retaliatory nonreappointment is doubtless enhanced insofar as no explanation or intramural hearing of any kind need be provided.

EMPLOYMENT
OF
NONTENURED FACULTY

Some Implications
of *Roth* and *Sindermann*

Carol Herrnstadt Shulman

Employment of Nontenured Faculty: Some Implications of *Roth* and *Sindermann*

By Carol Herrnstadt Shulman*

Introduction

In concurrent 1972 decisions authored by Justice Potter Stewart, the Supreme Court examined the right of nontenured teachers[1] in public institutions to a statement of reasons and collegiate due process hearings prior to nonrenewal of their contracts. These cases, *Board of Regents v. Roth*[2] and *Perry v. Sindermann*,[3] came before the Court at a time when there was considerable conflict among the various circuits concerning the rights to be accorded to such teachers.[4] They raised two major issues: whether the fourteenth amendment entitled teachers to institutional due process hearings prior to contract nonrenewal, and whether nonrenewal might be an infringement of free speech interests protected by the first amendment.

The Court held in *Roth* and *Sindermann* that nontenured teachers are entitled to due process protection[5] only under limited conditions: (1) when a teacher has been deprived of proven interests in "property" or "liberty" as these concepts have been interpreted under the fourteenth amendment; or (2) when an institu-

---

*Research Associate, ERIC Clearinghouse on Higher Education; B.A., 1966, City College of New York; M.A., 1967, University of North Carolina, Chapel Hill.

[1]A tenure system provides that:

> After the expiration of a probationary period, teachers, or investigators should have permanent or continuous tenure, and their service should be terminated only for adequate cause, except in the case of retirement for age, or under extraordinary circumstances because of financial exigencies.

American Ass'n of Univ. Professors, *Academic Freedom and Tenure, 1940 Statement of Principles and 1970 Interpretive Comments,* in A.A.U.P. Policy Documents and Reports 2 (1973).

[2]408 U.S. 564 (1972).

[3]408 U.S. 593 (1972).

[4]*See, e.g.,* Drown v. Portsmouth School Dist., 435 F.2d 1182 (1st Cir. 1970); Jones v. Hopper, 410 F.2d 1323 (10th Cir. 1969), *cert. denied,* 397 U.S. 991 (1970); Freeman v. Gould Special School Dist., 405 F.2d 1153 (8th Cir.), *cert. denied,* 396 U.S. 843 (1969).

[5]"Due process of law is a summarized constitutional guarantee of respect for those personal immunities which . . . are 'so rooted in the traditions and conscience of our people as to be ranked as fundamental.'" Rochin v. California, 342 U.S. 165, 169 (1952), *citing* Snyder v. Massachusetts, 291 U.S. 97, 105 (1934). The central meaning of procedural due process is that "parties whose rights are to be affected are entitled to be heard; and in order that they enjoy that right they must first be notified." Fuentes v. Shevin, 407 U.S. 67, 80 (1972), *citing* Baldwin v. Hale, 68 U.S. (1 Wall.) 223 (1864).

tion has directly violated a teacher's first amendment free speech interests.

This article will analyze the decisions in *Roth* and *Sindermann*, consider their impact on first and fourteenth amendment rights of nontenured teachers, and explore some of the policy implications raised by the decisions.

I.   ANALYSIS OF THE DECISIONS IN *Roth* AND *Sindermann*

A.   Board of Regents v. Roth

David Roth was employed under a 1-year contract for the 1968-69 academic year as an assistant professor at Wisconsin State University-Oshkosh. He did not have tenure, which is granted under Wisconsin statutes only after 4 years of continuous service.[6] Without a statement of reasons, Roth was notified in January 1969, that his contract would not be renewed for the next academic year. This notification followed a period of conflict on campus during which Roth had openly criticized the university administration. His suit in federal district court[7] claimed that his free speech and due process rights under the fourteenth amendment had been violated because his publicly expressed views were the reasons his contract was not renewed, and, in any case, he was entitled to an institutional hearing before a final decision on his contract could be made.[8] The district court agreed with the latter contention[9] and granted summary judgment ordering the university to provide Roth with a statement of reasons and to set a mutually agreeable date for a hearing.[10] The court of appeals affirmed.[11] In its review of *Roth,* the Supreme Court addressed itself only to Roth's due process rights under the fourteenth amendment and did not consider the free speech aspects of the case, which had caused the district court to deem summary judgment[12] inappropriate, since the facts surrounding the alleged interference with Roth's freedom of speech would have to be developed at trial.

The Supreme Court approached the case differently than did

---

[6]WIS. STAT. § 37.31 (1966).

[7]Roth v. Board of Regents, 310 F. Supp. 972 (W.D. Wis. 1970).

[8]*Id.* at 974.

[9]*Id.* at 983.

[10]*Id.* at 984.

[11]Roth v. Board of Regents, 446 F.2d 606 (7th Cir. 1970).

[12]Summary judgment is granted where there are no material facts in the controversy that need to be litigated and where the party asking for summary judgment is entitled to judgment as a matter of law. FED. R. CIV. P. 56.

the district court and the court of appeals. The lower courts had been concerned with weighing the plaintiff's interest in securing his job against the institution's need for unfettered discretion in its employment practices. The Court asserted that this weighing process must come only after a determination that there is either a "liberty" or "property" interest under the fourteenth amendment. Therefore, the Court examined the circumstances surrounding Roth's initial employment and his contract nonrenewal for the existence of such interests.

On the question of liberty, the Court recognized that term as meaning "generally to enjoy those privileges long recognized . . . as essential to the orderly pursuit of happiness by free men."[13] The Court held that if a teacher's liberty under this interpretation were impaired, he would be entitled to a due process hearing. Examples given by the Supreme Court of circumstances that would impair a teacher's liberty when his contract is not renewed are an accusation that "might seriously damage his standing and associations in his community,"[14] or a nonrenewal that "impose[s] on [the teacher] a stigma or other disability that foreclose[s] his freedom to take advantage of other employment opportunities."[15] The Court noted that while the district court and the court of appeals deemed nonretention itself to have a "substantial adverse effect" on a teacher, it found nothing in the record to support this belief. Therefore, the Court held that there was nothing in Roth's case to show that his liberty had been impaired.[16]

After reviewing decisions on property interests, the Court announced a standard to be used in determining the existence of such an interest:

> To have a property interest in a benefit, a person clearly must have more than an abstract need or desire for it. He must have more than a unilateral expectation of it. He must, instead, have a legitimate claim of entitlement to it.[17]

The Court found that such a claim emerges from the "rules or understandings" issued by an independent source, such as a state government.[18] In Roth's case, a property interest would have

---

[13]408 U.S. at 572, *quoting from* Meyer v. Nebraska, 262 U.S. 390, 399 (1923).
[14]408 U.S. at 573.
[15]*Id.*
[16]*Id.* at 574 & n.13.
[17]*Id.* at 577.
[18]*Id.*

to have been shown from the terms of his employment or the state statutes relating to granting tenure at public institutions. Roth's appointment, however, did not provide for employment beyond June 30, 1969, nor was there any renewal provision in his teaching contract. Despite Roth's observation that Wisconsin State University-Oshkosh generally rehires teachers who have 1-year contracts, the Court noted that the district court had found no "common law" of reemployment.[19] Therefore, the University's practices did not create the sort of expectation of renewal that would require a statement of reasons and a hearing on nonrenewal. State statutes also did not establish any right to reemployment for Roth. Given these considerations, the Court found that Roth did not have a "sufficient" property interest to entitle him to a statement of reasons and a hearing.[20] Accordingly, the Court reversed and remanded the case for further proceedings consistent with its decision.

In its conclusion, the Court made clear that its

> analysis of the respondent's constitutional rights in this case in no way indicates a view that an opportunity for a hearing or a statement of reasons for nonretention would, or would not, be appropriate or wise in public colleges and universities.[21]

B. Perry v. Sindermann

Sindermann presented the Court with a claim of free speech violations under the first and fourteenth amendments, as well as a charge that he was entitled to fourteenth amendment procedural due process. Because it dealt with different issues and with a substantially different set of circumstances in *Sindermann*, the Court's judgment was more favorable to the teacher than in *Roth*.

Robert Sindermann had been employed at Odessa Junior College in Odessa, Texas from 1965 through 1969 under a series of 1-year contracts. Odessa had no tenure system at that time.[22] He had previously worked for 6 years in the Texas state college system. During the 1968-69 academic year Sindermann testified before committees of the Texas legislature in his capacity as president of the Texas Junior College Teachers Association. He favored changing Odessa to a 1-year institution, a position opposed by the college's Board of Regents. In May 1969, Sindermann was

---

[19]*Id.* at 578 n.16.
[20]*Id.* at 578.
[21]*Id.* at 578-79.
[22]This situation has been changed. *See* note 68 and accompanying text *infra*.

notified that his contract would not be renewed, and the Board of Regents issued a press release setting forth allegations of insubordination by Sindermann. Despite its public stance, the board refused to provide Sindermann with an official statement of the reasons for nonrenewal of his contract or with an opportunity for a hearing.

In federal district court, Sindermann claimed that his nonrenewal was based on his public criticism of the Board of Regents and it therefore infringed upon his right of free speech. He also asserted that his fourteenth amendment right to procedural due process was violated by the college administration's refusal to provide a hearing. The district court's summary judgment for the college[23] was reversed because the court of appeals felt that a full hearing on the contested facts was necessary.[24] It further held that despite Sindermann's nontenured status, his contract nonrenewal would be impermissible if it violated his constitutionally protected free speech rights.

The Supreme Court agreed with the court of appeals that the district court had to investigate the facts of Sindermann's claim that his free speech rights had been violated. The Court declared it to be a well-established principle of constitutional law that a government "may not deny a benefit to a person on a basis that infringes his constitutionally protected interests—especially, his interest in freedom of speech."[25]

On the issue of Sindermann's right to a due process hearing, the Court held that he should have been given the opportunity to demonstrate that he had a property interest in continued employment, despite the absence of a formal tenure policy at Odessa. The Court defined such a property interest as follows:

> A person's interest in a benefit is a "property" interest for due process purposes if there are such rules or mutually explicit understandings that support his claim of entitlement to the benefit and that he may invoke at a hearing.[26]

It found that Sindermann's allegations based on factors such as his years of service in the Texas state college system and the policies and practices of Odessa Junior College might be suffi-

---

[23]Sindermann v. Perry, Civil No. MO-69-CA34 (W.D. Tex., Aug. 4, 1969).

[24]Sindermann v. Perry, 430 F.2d 939 (5th Cir. 1970).

[25]Perry v. Sindermann, 408 U.S. 593, 597 (1972).

[26]*Id.* at 601.

cient for him to prove a property interest.[27] In this regard, Sindermann had claimed that he had a form of job tenure because the guidelines of the Coordinating Board of the Texas College and University System provided for tenure after 7 years of service in institutions of higher education. (Sindermann had 10 years of service.) Odessa's faculty handbook declared:

> Odessa College has no tenure system. The Administration of the College wishes the faculty member to feel that he has permanent tenure . . . as long as he displays a cooperative attitude toward his co-workers and his supervisors, and as long as he is happy in his work.[28]

The Court therefore found that Sindermann had raised tenable claims to a property interest in continued employment.

The Court concluded that "[Sindermann] must be given an opportunity to prove the legitimacy of his claim of [property] entitlement in light of 'the policies and practices of the institution.' "[29] Such proof would require the college to grant him a hearing at which he would be given the reasons for his nonretention and would be able to "challenge their sufficiency."[30]

II. Implications of the Court's Interpretations of Liberty and Property

A. *Liberty*

As noted earlier, *Roth* held that for the nonrenewal of a teacher's contract to violate his liberty as guaranteed by the fourteenth amendment, it must cause serious damage to his reputation in the community or so stigmatize him as to impair his ability to obtain other employment.[31] Precisely what constitutes a stigma severe enough to be considered deprivation of liberty is not yet clear.

Both the district court[32] and the court of appeals[33] in *Roth* viewed nonretention as a serious impediment to a college teacher's career, but the Supreme Court stated:

> [O]n the record before us, all that clearly appears is that the respondent was not rehired for one year at one university. It stretches

---

[27]*Id.* at 599-601.
[28]*Id.* at 600.
[29]*Id.* at 603.
[30]*Id.*
[31]*See* note 15 and accompanying text *supra.*
[32]310 F. Supp. at 970.
[33]446 F.2d at 809.

the concept too far to suggest that a person is deprived of "liberty" when he simply is not rehired in one job but remains as free as before to seek another.[34]

Disagreeing with the majority opinion, Justice Douglas argued in his *Roth* dissent:

Nonrenewal of a teacher's contract is tantamount in effect to a dismissal and the consequences may be enormous. Nonrenewal can be a blemish that turns into a permanent scar and effectively limits any chance the teacher has of being rehired as a teacher, at least in his State.[35]

Others have also recognized the obstacles to future employment which may result from nonrenewal of a teacher's contract.[36] For example, Professor William Van Alstyne of Duke University Law School,[37] a distinguished commentator on matters relating to higher education, observed that the majority opinion in *Roth* fails to recognize the stigma of nonrenewal by treating Roth as if he had only a special, 1-year, limited appointment:

By placing Professor Roth in this different frame, as though he were not a regular appointee and as though there were no significant distinction between his situation and that of a special one-year terminal appointment, the majority of the Supreme Court reduced his constitutionally cognizable substantive interests in reappointment to zero.[38]

Laurence H. Kallen notes the Court's statement:

Mere proof, for example, that his [Roth's] record of nonretention in one job, taken alone, might make him somewhat less attractive to some other employers would hardly establish the kind of foreclosure of opportunities amounting to a deprivation of liberty.[39]

and asks: "[W]hat does this say about the teacher who is given notice of nonrenewal in January and by May has one hundred rejections to applications for employment?"[40]

---

[34] 408 U.S. at 575.

[35] *Id.* at 585 (Douglas, J., dissenting).

[36] *See, e.g.,* Kallen, *The Roth Decision: Does the Nontenured Teacher Have a Constitutional Right to a Hearing Before Nonrenewal?,* 61 ILL. B.J. 464 (1973); Levinson, *The Fourteenth Amendment, Fundamental Fairness, the Probationary Instructor, and the University of California — An Incompatible Foursome?,* 5 DAVIS L. REV. 608 (1972); Van Alstyne, *The Supreme Court Speaks to the Untenured: A Comment on Board of Regents v. Roth and Perry v. Sindermann,* 58 A.A.U.P. BULL. 268 (1972); Comment, *Constitutional Law — The Rights of the Untenured Teacher to Procedural Due Process Prior to Dismissal — Roth v. Board of Regents,* 7 RICHMOND L. REV. 357 (1972).

[37] Professor Van Alstyne was formerly Chairman of the American Association of University Professor's Committee on Academic Freedom and Tenure.

[38] Van Alstyne, *supra* note 36, at 268.

[39] Kallen, *supra* note 36, at 467.

[40] *Id.*

That the stigma caused by nonrenewal of a teacher's contract can indeed create difficulties in securing other employment is illustrated by the two case histories which follow.

In *Orr v. Trinter*[41] a Columbus, Ohio high school teacher whose contract was not renewed and who was not given a statement of reasons was unable to find a teaching position for the following year. He claimed that he

> will continue throughout the remainder of his professional career to suffer the [stigma] of having his professional qualifications [impugned] by the present action of the [school board] in refusing to renew his contract for unknown reasons, and will have his prospects of acquiring future teaching positions at other schools substantially impaired by the aforementioned actions . . . .[42]

The district court agreed and held that Orr was entitled to a statement of reasons and to a hearing,[43] but the court of appeals reversed,[44] holding that the school board's interest in freedom to hire was not outweighed by the teacher's interest in learning the reasons for nonrenewal.[45]

Mrs. Susan Russo, a high school art teacher in Henrietta, New York, also found that she was not able to find employment in her profession after her contract was not renewed. The reason given for nonrenewal was "insubordination." However, the court of appeals found that this reason was invalid because "Mrs. Russo's dismissal resulted directly from her refusal to engage in the school's daily flag ceremonies."[46] The court of appeals therefore reversed the lower court and remanded the case for proceedings not inconsistent with its opinion.[47] Despite this judicial finding, a highly satisfactory teacher observation report during her probationary year, and further scholastic achievement, Mrs.

---

[41]318 F. Supp. 1041 (S.D. Ohio 1970), *rev'd*, 444 F.2d 128 (6th Cir. 1971), *cert. denied*, 408 U.S. 943, 409 U.S. 898 (1972).

Two petitions for certiorari were filed. The first petition, submitted before the *Roth* and *Sindermann* decisions were handed down, raised the issue of whether Orr was entitled to a statement of reasons and procedural due process before nonrenewal. The second petition, submitted after the Court's decisions in *Roth* and *Sindermann* and after Orr's first petition was denied, raised the issue of first amendment violations, which was present in the original complaints but not examined by the district court.

[42]Petition for Writ of Certiorari at 5, Orr v. Trinter, 408 U.S. 943 (1972).

[43]318 F. Supp. at 1046-47.

[44]444 F.2d 128 (6th Cir. 1971).

[45]*Id.* at 135.

[46]Russo v. Central School Dist. No. 1, 469 F.2d 623, 630 (2d Cir. 1972), *cert. denied*, 411 U.S. 932 (1973).

[47]*Id.* at 634.

Russo has been unable to find work as an art teacher in and around Henrietta. She believes that work is available, but she has found that the controversy surrounding her nonrenewal has proved an insurmountable obstacle to employment as an art teacher. She has been told as much in job interviews.[48]

Although it is clear that nonrenewal can be a professional detriment, cases decided since *Roth* have not clearly settled the extent to which difficulty in reemployment—and, hence, how great the stigma of nonrenewal—constitutes deprivation of liberty.[49]

For example, in *Lipp v. Board of Education*[50] the Seventh Circuit held that an elementary school substitute teacher was not deprived of liberty when he was characterized as "anti-establishment" in a generally satisfactory efficiency rating, since the court did not consider the comment sufficient to damage his reputation so as to constitute a deprivation of liberty. Further, the court of appeals found that the comment did not prevent him from obtaining other employment in the school system.[51] Moreover, the court of appeals noted, "not every negative effect upon one's attractiveness to future employers violates due process if it results without a hearing."[52]

But in another 1972 decision, *Wilderman v. Nelson,*[53] the Eighth Circuit reviewed a case in which it found evidence "tending to show state action imposing a stigma upon Wilderman which may affect his future employment opportunities."[54] Wilderman, a welfare worker, was discharged, and his letter of dismissal, which cited his unfavorable attitude, was filed in several state offices. Also, a reference letter to a prospective employer "commented adversely upon [his] ability willingly to carry out his employer's policies."[55] The court held that the district court

---

[48]THE NEW YORKER, July 30, 1973, at 35.

[49]*See, e.g.,* Lipp v. Board of Educ., 470 F.2d 802 (7th Cir. 1972); Johnson v. Fraley, 470 F.2d 179 (4th Cir. 1972); Wilderman v. Nelson, 467 F.2d 1173 (8th Cir. 1972); McDowell v. Texas, 465 F.2d 1342 (5th Cir. 1971); Wellner v. Minnesota State Junior College Bd., No. 4-71 Civil 555 (D. Minn., Dec. 18, 1972); Franz v. Board of Educ., No. 772 Civil 151 (N.D. Ill., Aug. 10, 1972); Hostrop v. Board of Junior College Dist., 337 F. Supp. 977 (N.D. Ill. 1972).

[50]470 F.2d 802 (7th Cir. 1972).

[51]*Id.* at 805.

[52]*Id.*

[53]467 F.2d 1173 (8th Cir. 1972).

[54]*Id.* at 1176.

[55]*Id.*

"was not justified in summarily dismissing Wilderman's complaint insofar as it alleged a right to a pretermination hearing."[56]

An examination of *Roth*, *Sindermann*, and the other cases discussed in this section suggests that college administrations and school boards can minimize legal entanglements if they avoid impairing a teacher's reputation in his community or attaching such discredit to his nonrenewal that other job opportunities are foreclosed. Thus, college administrators and school boards may find that the best course legally is to say or publish nothing about a teacher whose appointment is not being renewed.[57]

B. *Property*

The Supreme Court's treatment of the deprivation of property question in *Roth* and *Sindermann* suggests that it is in the best interest of a school board or college administration to be very explicit in its employment policy concerning yearly contracts and probationary teachers. This conclusion is suggested by the different results reached in *Roth*, where clearly the teacher had not been granted tenure, and *Sindermann*, where the teacher was able to allege that he had tenure based on a de facto tenure system.

Although in *Roth* there had been an explicit tenure system, neither state statutes nor university regulations gave rise to a legitimate expectation by Roth of continued employment as a probationary teacher. Professor Van Alstyne notes, however, that the Court made this finding in the absence of any evidence to the contrary in the record. He suggests that there may be situations in which,

> on a better record, under more compelling circumstances, where the

---

[56]*Id.* The district court had granted summary judgment for the defendants. Wilderman v. Nelson, 335 F. Supp. 1381 (E.D. Mo. 1971).

[57]James F. Clark, of Ela, Christianson, Esch, Hart & Clark, counsel for the Wisconsin Association of School Boards, noted that the Supreme Court decisions "appear to have resulted in some reluctance on the part of school officials to give reasons for nonrenewal." Letter from James F. Clark to Carol Herrnstadt Shulman, July 10, 1973. His view is corroborated by Bruce F. Ehlke of Lawton & Cates, counsel for the Wisconsin Education Association. Letter from Bruce F. Ehlke to Carol Herrnstadt Shulman, Aug. 8, 1973. *See also* Shannon, *Due Process for Nontenured Teachers from the Board's Viewpoint,* in FRONTIERS OF SCHOOL LAW 15 (1973). However, Mr. Clark has also informed the author that reasons for nonrenewal were given to some plaintiffs following the court of appeals' decision in *Roth* and, in turn, these plaintiffs have amended their complaints following *Roth* and *Sindermann* to charge a deprivation of an interest in liberty without due process, because the reasons given for their nonrenewal damage their professional reputations.

faculty member is well along the tenure track under policies explicitly encouraging reliance, peremptory notice of nonreappointment may not be enough to quench the constitutional claim to more specific consideration than none at all.[58]

In order for schools with an explicit tenure system to avoid creating expectations of continued employment for probationary teachers, another writer has suggested following Harvard's example.[59] It hires more probationary teachers than can be used to fill the available and expected tenured positions, and stresses to them that tenure is only a "faint possibility." Since administrators at other institutions and teachers are aware of this competitive situation, Mr. Levinson believes that little stigma is attached to nonrenewal of these teachers' contracts, and that the same would be true for other institutions that adopt similar hiring policies.[60]

Institutions without explicit tenure systems may discover that they have created an expectancy of reemployment in some circumstances. A series of 1-year contracts may indicate a property interest in continued employment.[61] In *Johnson v. Fraley*[62] the court appeared to recognize what one authority has called the "quasi tenure" situation which had been acknowledged in the Supreme Court,[63] *i.e.*, official actions by the institution that lead a teacher to expect continued employment despite the legal barrier of mere periodic contracts.[64]

On the other hand, one court has found that a long period of employment under a series of 1-year contracts did not constitute de facto tenure.[65] In this case, the Fifth Circuit held that the complaint of a public school teacher who had been employed 22 years under 1-year contracts, but whose contract was not renewed for the 23d year, failed to state a claim upon which relief could be granted. The court further found that the teacher did not allege "the existence of rules or understandings promulgated or fostered by state officials which would justify any legitimate claim of entitlement of continued employment."[66]

---

[58]Van Alstyne, *supra* note 36, at 270.

[59]Levinson, *supra* note 36, at 619.

[60]*Id.*

[61]*See, e.g.,* Johnson v. Fraley, 470 F.2d 179 (4th Cir. 1972); Scheelhaase v. Woodbury Cent. Community School Dist. 349 F. Supp. 988 (N.D. Iowa 1972).

[62]470 F.2d 179 (4th Cir. 1972).

[63]Perry v. Sindermann, 408 U.S. 593, 601-02 (1972).

[64]Letter from William Van Alstyne to Carol Herrnstadt Shulman, July 12, 1973.

[65]Skidmore v. Shamrock Independent School Dist., 464 F.2d 605 (5th Cir. 1972). *See also* Lukac v. Acocks, 466 F.2d 577 (6th Cir. 1972).

[66]464 F.2d at 606.

These unpredictable results in contract nonrenewal cases may lead institutions without an explicit tenure system either to develop such a system or to adopt form contracts and an institutional policy that are very clear on the terms and conditions of employment. Such institutions may profit from Odessa College's unhappy example. Following the Supreme Court's decision in *Sindermann,* Odessa settled with Sindermann for $48,000 in back pay and court fees.[67] It has also, however, replaced its old statement of policy and contract system[68] with a formal tenure policy.[69]

III. IMPLICATIONS OF THE COURT'S TREATMENT OF THE FREE SPEECH QUESTION

In *Sindermann,* the Court did not rule on the allegation that nonrenewal was in reprisal for the exercise of free speech rights, since the district court had granted summary judgment for Odessa College. Thus, *Sindermann* does not directly speak to the question of pretermination proceedings on charges of free speech violations. But when *Sindermann* is read with *Roth,* it is evident that direct violations of free speech rights would require such pretermination hearings. In *Sindermann,* the Court noted:

> The Court of Appeals suggested that the respondent might have a due process right to some kind of hearing simply if he *asserts* to college officials that their decision was based on his constitutionally protected conduct. . . . We have rejected this approach in *Board of Regents v. Roth, ante . . . .*[70]

This reference is to an extensive footnote in *Roth,* which states in part: "Whatever may be a teacher's right of free speech, the interest in holding a teaching job at a state university, *simpliciter,* is not itself a free speech interest."[71] In *Sindermann,* however, the Court found that the "allegations represent a bona fide constitutional claim. . . . For this reason we hold that the grant of summary judgment against the respondent, without full exploration of this issue, was improper."[72]

Summary judgment was also held to be improper in a later case in which it was claimed that first amendment rights were

---

[67]Telephone conversation with Richard J. Clarkson (attorney for Robert Sindermann) in Odessa, Texas, Aug. 22, 1973.

[68]*See* text accompanying note 28 *supra.*

[69]Policy Statement on Academic Freedom, Tenure, and Responsibility of Odessa College, adopted by Board of Regents of Odessa College, March 27, 1972.

[70]408 U.S. at 599 n.5 (citation omitted).

[71]408 U.S. at 575 n.14.

violated. In *Chitwood v. Feaster*[73] nontenured teachers at a state college claimed that their contracts were not renewed because of their free speech activities and that they were entitled to a statement of reasons for nonrenewal. The court of appeals reversed the lower court decision that granted summary judgment for the college, holding that while the teachers were not entitled to a statement of reasons under *Roth,* their free speech claims, "although unsupported by hard evidence," must be heard.[74] The court of appeals noted:

> The concurrence of protected speech, which may be unpopular with college officials, and the termination of the employment contract seem to be enough, in the view of the Supreme Court, to occasion inquiry to determine whether or not the failure to renew was in fact caused by the protected speech.[75]

Not all speech by teachers is protected, however. For example, in *Duke v. North Texas State University*[76] a teaching assistant was not rehired because she had used profane language when criticizing the university and its administration. The university claimed that such language impaired her effectiveness as a teacher. The court of appeals held that:

> As a past and prospective instructor, Mrs. Duke owed the University a minimal duty of loyalty and civility to refrain from extremely . . . offensive remarks aimed at the administrators of the University. By her breach of this duty, the interests of the University outweighed her claim for protection.[77]

A similar decision was reached in another case involving similar issues, although the employee was not a teacher. In *Tygrett v. Washington*[78] the court also found for the employer, here the District of Columbia police force. Tygrett, a probationary officer, was dismissed after he announced that he would falsely call in sick, organize, and lead a "sick-out" unless certain personnel benefits were implemented. In finding for the employer, the district court noted: "[T]he First Amendment Right of Free Speech, whether in the context of employment or any other legitimate activity, is not absolute. Frequently the right to speak freely

---

[72]408 U.S. at 598.
[73]468 F.2d 357 (4th Cir. 1972).
[74]*Id.* at 361.
[75]*Id.*
[76]469 F.2d 829 (5th Cir.), *cert. denied,* 412 U.S. 932 (1973).
[77]*Id.* at 840.
[78]346 F. Supp. 1247 (D.D.C. 1972).

must be balanced against legitimate conflicting interests.''[79]

These cases demonstrate that teachers cannot be assured of success in court when seeking relief on the ground that their first amendment rights have been violated.

One significant effect of *Roth* and *Sindermann* may be to inhibit the bringing of such first amendment cases to court when contracts are not renewed. Roth's attorneys argued that if institutional proceedings were foreclosed to probationary teachers,

> few professors, faced with non-retention decisions, will seek judicial relief. Litigation and the attendant public exposure may be costly both in terms of money and personal embarrassment. Moreover, without a statement of reasons, the professor has only two alternatives: quietly acquiesce in the non-retention or begin a major law suit based on his suspicion that the reasons behind the non-retention were constitutionally impermissible.[80]

The National Education Association and Robert P. Sindermann, in their amici curiae brief in *Roth,* presented a similar argument about the "chilling effect" which results when litigation is the only available alternative in a nonretention dispute.[81] Their comments are directed to an opposing amicus argument of the Commonwealth of Massachusetts that a teacher has an adequate remedy in nonrenewal cases under section 1983.[82] Massachusetts appears to advocate this position in the belief that institutional proceedings in every nonrenewal case would be more burdensome

---

[79]*Id.* at 1250, *citing* Pickering v. Board of Educ., 391 U.S. 563 (1968). In *Pickering,* a teacher was dismissed by his school board because of his criticism of the board's activities. The Court, while finding for the teacher, also noted that

> it cannot be gainsaid that the State has interests as an employer in regulating the speech of its employees that differ significantly from those it possesses in connection with regulation of the citizenry in general. The problem in any case is to arrive at a balance between the interests of the teacher, as a citizen, in commenting upon matters of public concern and the interests of the State, as an employer, in promoting the efficiency of the public services it performs through its employees.

Id. at 568.

[80]Brief for Respondents at 8, Board of Regents v. Roth, 408 U.S. 564 (1972).

[81]Brief for National Education Association and Robert P. Sindermann as Amici Curiae at 3, Board of Regents v. Roth, 408 U.S. 564 (1972).

[82] Every person who, under color of any statute, ordinance, regulation, custom, or usage, or any State or Territory, subjects, or causes to be subjected, any citizen of the United States or other person within the jurisdiction thereof to the deprivation of any rights, privileges, or immunities secured by the Constitution and laws, shall be liable to the party injured in an action by law, suit in equity, or other proceeding for redress.

42 U.S.C. § 1983 (1970).

than occasional court proceedings.[83]

IV. POLICY IMPLICATIONS OF *Roth* AND *Sindermann*

The Supreme Court decisions in *Roth* and *Sindermann* establish the "constitutional boundary lines around the territory covered by procedural due process."[84] If institutions work within these "boundary lines," they will find that they have wide discretion in renewing the contracts of probationary teachers. On the other hand, probationary teachers confronted with the limits imposed by the Court's decisions will find that seeking relief through the courts is costly and yields unpredictable results.

Because there is a surplus of qualified college teachers,[85] *Roth* and *Sindermann* come at a time when institutions desire great flexibility in hiring, retaining, and dismissing faculty members. New concepts and needs in higher education in areas such as curricula, organization, and time spent in obtaining a degree also require colleges and universities to maintain flexibility in their programs. Under these circumstances, colleges and universities want to maintain a balance between tenured and nontenured faculty which will provide flexibility as well as stability.[86] If the Court had held that the mere fact of contract nonrenewal required a statement of reasons and an institutional hearing, institutions might have been overburdened with the work required for processing a substantial number of nonrenewal cases. They might then have been tempted to retain teachers simply to avoid the nonrenewal procedures, and as a consequence would have heavily tenured faculties with little flexibility. Such a situation might easily have arisen in an institution with a standard tenure policy of a 7-year probationary period after which the teacher must be granted tenure or not rehired, since the institution might have found it difficult to offer satisfactory reasons for nonrenewal after 7 years of continuous employment. In light of *Roth* and *Sindermann*, however, colleges and universities are legally free to develop employment policies that will provide the faculty mix most favorable to their own institutional goals.

---

[83]Brief for Massachusetts as Amicus Curiae at 7, Board of Regents v. Roth, 408 U.S. 564 (1972).

[84]Rosenblum, *Legal Dimensions of Tenure*, in COMMISSION ON ACADEMIC TENURE IN HIGHER EDUCATION, FACULTY TENURE: A REPORT AND RECOMMENDATIONS 160 (1973).

[85]T. FURNISS, STEADY-STATE STAFFING IN TENURE-GRANTING INSTITUTIONS AND RELATED PAPERS 2 (1973).

[86]*Id.*

As an alternative to tenure policies, colleges might consider the pure contract system of employment. This system was recently implemented by the Virginia community colleges which simultaneously abolished tenure for all faculty members who had not yet attained it.[87] The system's multiple contract plan does not contain any stated or implied promise of continuous employment beyond the term of a particular contract. The plan does, however, detail a procedure for appeal of a decision not to renew a contract. In view of *Sindermann,* institutions adopting this plan should not be found to have created an implied tenure-by-contract system.

In either a formal tenure or a contract system, the refusal of administrators to give reasons for nonrenewal,[88] coupled with the surplus of qualified college teachers, places probationary teachers at an obvious disadvanatage. However, in practice such teachers may not be at as great a disadvantage as these considerations suggest. There are pressures on universities not to adhere rigidly to the legal rights they have under the Court's decisions. First, the Court itself in *Roth* noted that its decision does not set university policy as to the "appropriate" action for a public institution to take in its treatment of employees.[89] It merely made clear that a hearing or statement of reasons would not inevitably be required when a nontenured teacher's contract was not renewed.

Second, it is important to note in this connection that many universities already provide a statement of reasons in nonrenewal cases. A survey conducted in April of 1972 by the American Council on Education's Higher Education Panel found that tenure systems are "nearly universal" in public and private universities and 4-year colleges, and that almost half of these institutions give written reasons for nonrenewal.[90] The survey also found that about 90 percent of these institutions had procedures for appeal following denial of tenure or contract nonrenewal, but that in only about 14 percent of these institutions had more than three appeals been taken during the preceding 30 months.[91]

Third, it is likely that teachers—and perhaps their un-

---

[87]Memorandum from Chancellor Dana B. Hamel to the presidents of the Virginia community college system, Sept. 20, 1972.

[88]*See, e.g.,* authorities cited note 57 *supra.*

[89]408 U.S. at 578. *See* note 21 and accompanying text *supra.*

[90]T. FURNISS, *supra* note 85, at 21. *See also* C. SHULMAN, COLLECTIVE BARGAINING ON CAMPUS (ERIC Clearinghouse on Higher Education No. 2, 1973).

[91]T. FURNISS, *supra* note 90.

ions—will exert pressure to continue and extend the probationary teacher's opportunities for redress. In this regard, William Van Alstyne has commented:

> The experience of the AAUP [American Association of University Professors] vividly demonstrates that . . . the lack of *any* intramural opportunity for hearing at all must ultimately undermine the untenured faculty member's constitutional freedom of speech and his academic freedom. Thus, we [AAUP] shall doubtless continue to stand by our own policy statement on this matter, whatever the prevailing fashion on the Court.[92]

The AAUP's position on this issue is, in fact, in opposition to the Court's rulings. But its position is apparently not out of favor with the Court, since the Court referred to the AAUP in its comment that institutional policy need not be limited by the *Roth* decision.[93]

Current AAUP policy classifies the question of nonrenewal under two separate headings: (1) cases in which the probationary teacher claims that his nonrenewal is based upon inadequate consideration of his qualifications; and (2) cases in which the probationary teacher charges that his nonrenewal resulted from considerations in violation of academic freedom or "governing policies on making appointments without prejudice with respect to race, sex, religion, or national origin."[94] In the first situation, the AAUP advises that the teacher be allowed to present his claim charging inadequate consideration of his qualifications to a designated faculty committee that will determine whether the original decision is in accordance with institutional standards. The faculty body may recommend a reconsideration of the decision, but will not "substitute its judgment on the merits for that of the [responsible] faculty body."[95] In the second situation, informal settlement of the teacher's charge should be attempted. If this is unsuccessful, a hearing may be held at which the faculty member has the burden of proof. If he makes a prima facie case, his supervisors must demonstrate the validity of their decision.[96] In either situation, the AAUP urges that a teacher, upon request, should receive a written statement of reasons for nonrenewal.

A more ambitious plan for the protection of nontenured fac-

---

[92]Letter from William Van Alstyne, *supra* note 64.

[93]408 U.S. at 579 n.15.

[94]A.A.U.P. POLICY DOCUMENTS AND REPORTS, *supra* note 1, at 19.

[95]*Id*. at 16.

[96]*Id*. at 19.

ulty members is found in a draft statement by the National Education Association (NEA).[97] This statement differs from the AAUP position in three ways: it places the burden of proof for justifying nonrenewal on the institution rather than the teacher; it gives the teacher the right to appeal the institution's decision to a neutral third party, *e.g.*, the American Arbitration Association; and, most significantly, it maintains that "the conferring of the initial annual contract upon a probationary employee does . . . carry with it an expectation of renewal so long as his work meets the predetermined standards of scholarship and teaching."[98] Both the NEA and the AAUP serve as collective bargaining agents for colleges and universities. It is predictable that in their contract negotiations they will press for guarantees to carry out their respective policies.

Conclusion

The Supreme Court's decisions in *Roth* and *Sindermann* place conservative interpretations on the fourteenth amendment concepts of liberty and property that limit probationary teachers' opportunities to obtain a statement of reasons and institutional due process hearings when their contracts are not renewed. Such teachers can, of course, resort to the courts, but success in court is unlikely if their institutions have acted knowledgeably in light of the Court's discussion of what will or will not constitute a violation of liberty or property interests.

In addition, when nontenured teachers allege that their nonretention was in retaliation for their exercise of first amendment rights, institutions are not, in general, legally required to offer due process hearings under the *Roth* and *Sindermann* decisions. *Sindermann* does provide, however, that allegations of contract nonrenewal for exercise of free speech rights must be heard in court without summary judgment against the teacher.[99] On the question of a property interest in continued employment, *Sindermann* holds that proof of an objective expectancy of de facto tenure entitles the teacher to an intramural hearing and a statement of reasons for contract nonrenewal.[100]

[97]National Education Association, *Due Process and Tenure in Institutions of Higher Education*, Today's Education, Feb. 1973, at 60.
[98]*Id.* at 61.
[99]408 U.S. at 598.
[100]*Id.* at 603.

The courts, therefore, are a nontenured teacher's first and last source of redress in most cases of violations of liberty and property interests and violations of first amendment rights. However, commentators have questioned whether it is desirable for higher education to rely so heavily on the courts for adjudication of its disputes. The Commission on Academic Tenure in Higher Education (the "Keast Commission") criticizes such dependence on the courts, because it demonstrates that an institution has not implemented satisfactory standards and procedures.[101] In addition, it claims that "frequent resort to court determination of personnel questions will surely erode institutional and faculty autonomy, thus jeopardizing the ability of faculties and institutions to govern themselves in the interest of their students and society generally."[102] Therefore, the commission recommends that colleges and universities develop policies and procedures for handling faculty personnel problems which will "minimize reliance on the courts."[103]

Much of the adverse effect of *Roth* and *Sindermann* on nontenured teachers may disappear as faculty collective bargaining units clarify in their contracts the rights of represented nontenured teachers to institutional hearings and statements of reasons in the event of contract nonrenewal. It remains to be seen, however, how the national pressures of the faculty labor market and the several professional faculty organizations will in fact affect institutional policies and practices in the nonrenewal of faculty contracts.

---

[101]The "Keast Commission" was established in 1971 under the sponsorship of the Association of American Colleges and the American Association of University Professors with a grant from the Ford Foundation. The commission examined the full range of issues concerning tenure: current status, criticisms, alternatives, and improvements. William R. Keast, chairman of the commission, is professor of English and Director of the Center for Higher Education of the University of Texas at Austin. The commission's report is COMMISSION ON ACADEMIC TENURE, FACULTY TENURE: A REPORT AND RECOMMENDATIONS (1973).

[102]*Id.* at 33.

[103]*Id.*

BOARD OF REGENTS
OF THE
KANSAS STATE AGRICULTURAL COLLEGE v.
B. F. MUDGE

*223   *BOARD OF REGENTS OF THE KANSAS STATE AGRICULTURAL COL-
LEGE *v.* B. F. MUDGE.

July Term, 1878.

1. **Agricultural College: Regents: Teachers: Salary.** The regents of
the Kansas State Agricultural College have the power to make a valid
contract for the employment of a professor or teacher for the period of
three months; and, although such contract or employment would not prevent the regents from discharging such professor or teacher prior to the
expiration of such three months, yet, if they should do so without any
sufficient cause, they would not relieve their board from paying such professor or teacher the full amount of the compensation agreed upon for
the three months.

2. ———— : **Liability: Contract.** The regents may also make a valid contract "that each professor shall give and receive three months' notice of
resignation or discharge, except in case of gross misconduct;" and where
the regents make such a contract with a professor, and then discharge
him without sufficient cause, and without giving him any previous notice, the board will be liable for his compensation for the next three
months after his discharge.[1]

3. ———— : **Implied Contract.** Where the board of regents passed a resolution tendering to M. a professorship, and afterwards passed another
resolution requiring "that each professor shall give and receive three
months' notice of resignation or discharge, except in case of gross misconduct," and M., having knowledge of these resolutions, entered upon
the discharge of the duties of his said professorship, *held* that, in the absence of any express contract, these facts are sufficient to authorize a
finding by the court and jury of an implied contract between the regents
and M. that M. should receive three months' notice before he should be
discharged, except in case of gross misconduct.

Error from Riley district court.

[1] As to the right of school-teachers to recover for wrongful discharge before
the expiration of their term, see Park v. Independent School-dist. No. 1, (Iowa,,
2 N. W. Rep. 567; Scott v. Joint School-dist. No. 16, (Wis.) 8 N. W. Rep. 898.

The case is stated in the opinion.

Green & Hessin, for plaintiff in error.

The plaintiff below was subject to any resolution the board of
*224   regents might pass terminating the relation between *the parties,
whenever, in the opinion of the board, the interest of the college
required the passage of such a resolution. The legislature has vested the
government of this college in the plaintiff in error, and made it, and no
other tribunal, the judge of what is for the interest of the institution;
and the relation existing between the plaintiff and defendant does not
result from any contract made and entered into by them, but from the
laws existing at the time for the government of the agricultural college,
creating professorships, fixing, increasing, and diminishing the regular
number of professors and teachers, and providing for the removal of the
president, and any professor or teacher, whenever the interest of the
college required it. Head v. University, 19 Wall. 526.

The judgment in this case must, we claim, be reversed for the admission of the resolution "that each professor shall give and receive three
months' notice of resignation or discharge, except in cases of gross misconduct." This resolution was passed September 4, 1873, and Prof.
Mudge was employed July 16, 1873. The objection was that the evidence was incompetent, and that the board of regents had no authority
to pass such a resolution under St. 1868, p. 75, § 4, entitled "An act
for the government of the Kansas State Agricultural College." This evidence was incompetent, for the reason that there is not one *scintilla* of
evidence offered on the part of the plaintiff below to show that Prof.
Mudge ever accepted the terms of this resolution, and agreed to comply
with the conditions therein expressed.

The board of regents, as the representative of the state, had no authority to pass said resolution. Section 4 of chapter 3, for the government
of the Kansas State Agricultural College, is as follows: "The regents
shall have power to enact ordinances, by-laws, and regulations for the
government of said college; to elect a president; to fix, increase, and diminish the regular number of professors and teachers; and to appoint
the same, and determine the amount of their salaries. They
*225   shall have *power to remove the president and any professor or
teacher, whenever the interest of the college shall require." The
resolution quoted above is in direct conflict with the latter part of this
section, and is an attempt to abridge the power therein expressly given
by the legislature to the regents of the college. The board of regents is
the creature of the act for the government of the college, dependent upon
said act for all its powers, and controlled by all the restrictions which the
act imposes. This act gives the board the power to remove any professor or teacher whenever the interest of the college requires, not by giving three months' notice of such intention, but whenever the authorities
governing the college deem it for the interest of the institution so to do.
The general principles defining the extent and mode of exercise of corporate powers are well settled. Corporations have only such powers as
are specially given by their charters. City of St. Louis v. Russell, 9

Mo. 507; Blair v. Perpetual Ins. Co., 10 Mo. 559; Ruggles v. Collier, 43 Mo. 353. It is well settled that the by-laws of a corporation must be in harmony with the general law of the state and with the provisions of its charter; and, whenever they come in conflict with either, the by-law must give way. Wood v. City of Brooklyn, 14 Barb. 428; City of New York v. Nichols, 4 Hill, 209; Town of Petersburg v. Metzker, 21 Ill. 205; Southport v. Ogden, 23 Conn. 128; Carr v. City of St. Louis, 9 Mo. 191; Com. v. Erie & N. E. R. Co., 27 Pa. St. 339; City of Burlington v. Kellar, 18 Iowa, 59.

McClure & Humphrey, for defendant in error.

Did the establishment of the regulation referred to transcend the power confided to this board? Section 4 of an act for the government of the agricultural college (page 75, Gen. St.) defines the powers of this body. It will be observed that this section vests in the board of regents extensive powers to establish all necessary regulations, rules, and provisions for the government of the institution; to appoint the president, professors, and teachers; to fix the number to be employed; to determine the amount of their salaries; and to remove them whenever the interest of the college shall require. The mode and character of government for the col*lege is left to the discretion of the board. The manner of appointing and removal of the president, professors, and teachers is also to be determined by the same body, and for this purpose they have the power to enact ordinances, by-laws, and regulations. Certain powers are granted to the board of regents, such as are necessary to the institution and maintenance of orderly government for the college, and the conduct and regulation of its various affairs and interests, but the particular mode and manner in which those powers shall be exercised is not prescribed by the law, but left to the determination of the board. The power of removal of the president and any professor or teacher is conferred; but whether such removal be summary, or at the lapse of any specified time after notice, except for specified causes, is wisely left to the judgment of the board of regents. The ground upon which the counsel for plaintiff place the theory of the non-liability of defendant, under the resolution recited, seems to be stated thus: "The state owns, controls, and governs the institution, and is not under any obligations of contract with any one." This proposition is true, only provided the state and board of regents are one and the same body; for we have already seen that the institution is controlled, not by the state, but by the regents, by virtue of powers conferred by the state. It involves the further supposition that the state, and also the board of regents, are incapable of entering into contract relations, or being bound thereby.

Was this proposition, concerning the notice to be given and received, assented to by Prof. Mudge? Prof. Mudge testifies: "I was notified of the resolution of notice about the time of its passage. The president mentioned the notice in the faculty meeting, just as we were breaking up." The president officially communicated to the members of the faculty, Prof. Mudge included, the resolution of the board of re-

gents, which directly affected each member.   It was not necessary, under
       the circumstances, that any member of the faculty should signify
*227   a formal acceptance of the terms of the *resolution.   He could
       not remain silent, and afterwards deny his assent, and no court
would permit him to do it.   From the presence of a party cognizant of
the matter, and not objecting, consent may be inferred.   Slocum v.
Lurty, Hemp. 431; Lattourett v. Cook, 1 Iowa, 3.   There was no question raised but that both parties understood that the terms of the resolution were accepted by all parties until it was raised in court upon a
supposed insufficiency of proof of the fact.   Both parties acted in accordance with such an understanding, which is itself sufficient proof of
assent.

       VALENTINE, J.   This was an action brought by B. F. Mudge against
the board of regents of the Kansas State Agricultural College.   The facts
of the case are substantially as follows: On July 16, 1873, the board of
regents adopted the following resolutions, to-wit:
       "Resolved, that Prof. Mudge be tendered the chair of geology and re-
lated sciences, at a salary of $1,600 per annum.
       "Resolved, that Prof. Mudge be allowed house, rent free, in consider-
ation of the extra services which he renders the college."
       On September 4, 1873, said board adopted the following resolution,
to-wit:
       "Resolved, that each professor shall give and receive three months'
notice of resignation or discharge, except in case of gross misconduct."
       At the beginning of the next school year, commencing in September,
1873, and in fact on the eleventh day of said September, though the exact day is not very definitely shown, Prof. Mudge commenced to perform services as professor of geology and associated sciences for said agricultural college.   At this time, and prior thereto, for more than seven
years, Prof. Mudge was and had been in the employment of the said
agricultural college, but in what capacity he was so employed is not
       shown.   From this time until February 6, 1874, he performed
*228   the duties of said professorship of geology *and kindred sciences.
       February 6, 1874, he was discharged by the board of regents from
his said professorship avowedly for gross misconduct, although in fact,
as was substantially found by the court below, he was not guilty of any
such misconduct.   For three months after the discharge Prof. Mudge
was out of employment, although he endeavored to obtain employment.
No written contract was ever executed between said regents and Prof.
Mudge, and no formal oral contract was ever entered into between them.
After the regents tendered to Prof. Mudge "the chair of geology and related sciences," he orally accepted the same, but when he accepted the
same is not shown.   It was not earlier, however, than August, 1873,
and may have been later.   The regents paid Prof. Mudge for his services
up to the time when they discharged him, but did not pay him for any
time afterwards.   Prof. Mudge then sued them for compensation for the
three months next succeeding his dismissal.   He recovered in the court

below, and obtained a judgment for $493.33. The board of regents now, as plaintiff in error, seek to have this judgment reversed by petition in error in this court. They raise two principal questions in this court: (1) They claim that their said resolution of September 4, 1873, was and is void; (2) but, if it is not void, then they claim that it has no application to the employment or services of Prof. Mudge. Some other questions are suggested by briefs of counsel, but they are not of sufficient importance to require any separate consideration. We think we must decide both of the principal questions against the plaintiff in error.

1. The act relating to the agricultural college (Gen. St. 75) provides, among other things, as follows:

"Sec. 2. The government of such college is vested in a board of regents," etc.

"Sec. 3. The board of regents shall constitute a body corporate, with the right, as such, to sue and be sued, to use a common seal, and to alter the same at pleasure.

"Sec. 4. The regents shall have power to enact ordinances, by-laws, and regulations for the government of said college; to elect a president; to fix, increase, and diminish the regular *number of professors and teachers; and to appoint the same, and to determine the amount of their salaries. They shall have power to remove the president and any professor or teacher, whenever the interest of the college shall require.

*229

"Sec. 12. The board of regents shall have the general supervision of the college, and the direction and control of all expenditures."

It will be seen from the foregoing sections of the statute that the power reposed in the board of regents is very extensive. They are a corporation having the entire control of all departments of the college,—educational, financial, and administrative. They have the power to appoint and discharge the president, and all the professors and teachers, and to fix and increase or diminish their several salaries. But, with all these powers, they are not supreme, nor irresponsible. They may "sue and be sued," just as the managing officers of other public corporations, such as cities, towns, counties, townships, and school-districts, may. While their powers are extensive, still they may render their board liable by the wrongful exercise of such power. Thus they have the unquestioned and the continuing power of employing a president and professors and teachers whenever they may choose, and of discharging any of them whenever they may choose; but if they agree to employ a president or professor or teacher for a period of three months, and then wrongfully discharge him before the three months have elapsed, they will leave their board responsible for the whole amount of the salary for such three months, notwithstanding such discharge. While the legislature unquestionably intended to confer upon the board of regents extensive powers, yet it did not intend to confer upon them the irresponsible power of trifling with other men's rights with impunity; and making the regents responsible for their acts does not in the least abridge their powers. It only tends to make them more cautious and circumspect in the exercise of their powers.

But the plaintiff in error claims, in substance, that the board has no legal power to make a contract to employ a president or a pro-
*230   fessor or a teacher for any particular period of time,—not *even for a day or an hour,—and therefore that an agreement to employ a president or a professor or a teacher for three months, or for any other definite period of time, would be an absolute nullity. Now, we cannot think that this is correct. There is no express limitation upon the power of the board to make a contract to employ a president or a professor or a teacher for any period of time, and we know of no implied limitation that would prevent the board from employing, or agreeing to employ, a president or a professor or a teacher for three months, or for even a longer period of time, provided it were not unreasonably long. We would think that the board has the power to make a valid contract, in advance, to employ a president or a professor or teacher for some short but definite time,—say three months,—and especially so where the board reserves the right to discharge such president, professor, or teacher at any time for misconduct. It would certainly be for the interest of the college that the board should have such power. No man of spirit, of self-respect, and of capability would want to hold an office or position at the whim or caprice of a body of men with whom he might have but little if any personal acquaintance. No man of spirit, of self-respect, and of capability would accept an office unless he felt that he was reasonably certain to hold the same for some reasonable period of time. The shorter and more precarious the tenure of the office, the less attractive, important, and valuable it would be; and generally, men of only inferior talent could be found to accept it or to perform its functions with such a precarious tenure, and even then a higher rate of compensation would be required than where the tenure is more stable and certain. In the present case, the contract may be considered as a continuing contract with each professor for his services for the next three succeeding months; that is, the services of each professor are continually contracted for, for three months in advance, until after he gives or receives notice that his services are to be terminated at the expiration of such three months; and
*231   his employment will still continue for three months after such *notice is given. Now, we know of no sufficient reason why such a contract should not be valid. We think it is eminently reasonable, and for the best interests of the college.

2. But the plaintiff in error claims that even if the board of regents had the power to pass said resolution of September 4, 1873, still, that the facts of this case do not constitute a contract under the resolution. We think they do. The board passed a resolution tendering said professorship to Prof. Mudge. The board passed another resolution "that each professor shall give and receive three months' notice of resignation or discharge, except in case of gross misconduct." Prof. Mudge had knowledge of these resolutions, and, having such knowledge, entered upon the discharge of the duties of his professorship. Now, we think that

these facts are sufficient to constitute a contract between the regents and Prof. Mudge that he should receive three months' notice before he should be discharged, except in case of gross misconduct; or, rather, these facts (in the absence of any express contract) are sufficient to authorize a find-finding of an implied contract to that effect. The question was fairly submitted to the jury, under proper instructions. The court also instructed the jury that if Prof. Mudge was guilty of gross misconduct, and was discharged for that reason, he could not recover, and the jury found in his favor.

The judgment of the court below will be affirmed.

(All the justices concurring.)

PEOPLE ex rel. KELSEY v.
NEW YORK POSTGRADUATE
MEDICAL SCHOOL AND HOSPITAL

PEOPLE ex rel. KELSEY v. NEW YORK POSTGRADUATE MEDICAL
SOHOOL AND HOSPITAL.

(Supreme Court, Appellate Division, First Department. May 6, 1898.)

1. COLLEGES—REMOVAL OF PROFESSOR.

In a mandamus proceeding to compel the defendant, a medical college, to
rescind a resolution of its board of directors which had revoked the relator's
appointment as a professor in the college, it appeared that its by-laws provided that professors should hold office "during the pleasure of the board,"
while by another provision the chair of any professor might be declared
vacant by a three-fourths vote of the board, after notice and a hearing
upon charges. *Held*, that the two provisions were distinct, and that under
the first it was competent for the board, in the exercise of its absolute discretion, to remove a professor without charges or hearing.

2. MANDAMUS—EVIDENCE.

Where, upon a motion for a peremptory mandamus, the undisputed facts
are, upon their face, plainly against the relator, it is not competent to go
below the surface, and grant the writ upon debatable inferences drawn
therefrom.

3. SAME—WHEN GRANTED.

If a professor in a medical college, which is a private corporation, is removed, his remedy is not mandamus, but, if his relation with the college
is contractual, he may sue for his salary or other emolument, while, if it
is purely honorary, its continuance or discontinuance must be mutually optional.

Appeal from special term, New York county.

Application by the people of the state of New York, on the relation of Charles B. Kelsey, for a writ of mandamus against the New
York Postgraduate Medical School and Hospital. From an order
granting the writ, defendant appeals. Reversed.

Argued before VAN BRUNT, P. J., and BARRETT, RUMSEY,
McLAUGHLIN, and INGRAHAM, JJ.

John E. Parsons, for appellant.

Jordan J. Rollins, for respondent.

BARRETT, J. This is an appeal from an order granting to the
relator a peremptory mandamus commanding the defendant to rescind a resolution of its board of directors which revoked the relat-
or's appointment as one of its professors of surgery, and as a
member of its faculty, and further commanding the defendant to
restore the relator to these positions, and to all the rights, franchises, and privileges lawfully incident thereto. The relator was
removed from the positions in question, by a majority vote of the
board of directors, upon the 28th day of January, 1898. Prior to
the latter date, charges had been preferred against him by the faculty of the college. The relator had been notified that these charges
would be considered by the board on the 31st day of January, 1898.

Upon the 27th of that month the faculty passed a resolution requesting the directors to return to them, unacted upon, their previous
resolution asking an investigation of these charges.   In response
to this request the directors, at a meeting held upon the same day,
returned to the faculty, unacted upon, the latter's resolution requesting such investigation.   The relator was present when the
directors passed the resolution for the return of the charges to the
faculty, and he voted upon that resolution.   After this action was
had, the directors passed the resolution which the court below
directed the defendant to rescind.   The relator again voted upon
this resolution.   The question is, was the latter resolution valid?
The relator claims that it was invalid, for two reasons: First, because, as he contends, he could be lawfully removed, under the defendant's by-laws, only by an affirmative vote of three-fourths of the
entire board of directors, after a hearing upon preferred charges;
second, because, as he also contends, the attempted amotion of the
defendant was really an amotion upon the charges which had been
previously preferred by the faculty.   The court below sustained
both of these contentions, and directed the relator's reinstatement.
    The first question depends upon the construction of the by-laws.
These by-laws formulated a carefully devised and symmetrical system upon the subject of appointments and removals.   Nominations
for professors are, in the first instance, to be made by the faculty.
These nominations can only be rejected by a three-fourths affirmative vote of the entire board of directors.   If not so rejected, the
board appoints the nominated professor.   The second subdivision
of the twelfth article then provides that professors shall hold office
during the pleasure of the board of directors.   This subdivision is
entitled "Appointments."   We find in this second subdivision a
different regulation with regard to the tenure of "instructors."   The
provision on that head is as follows:

"The term of office of an instructor shall expire on June —— of each year,
unless reappointed by the board of directors."

    Then follows a third subdivision, entitled "Removals," which reads
as follows:

"The chair of any professor may be declared vacant by a three-fourths vote
of the board of directors, upon at least two weeks' notice, together with a copy
of the charges having been given to said professor of the time of which such
action is to be taken, when said professor may have the opportunity of being
heard in his own behalf."

    The learned judge below held that the provision of the second
subdivision, that professors should hold office during the pleasure
of the board of directors, is qualified by this third subdivision, and
that thus the power of the board is limited to removal under the
latter subdivision; in other words, that the board could only express its pleasure under the second subdivision by acting upon the
charges in the manner provided in the third.   We are unable to
concur in this view.   It creates an incongruity where none is apparent.   By a forced construction, and apparently without reason,
it deprives the language used in the second subdivision of its nat-
ural import.   The system contemplated by the two subdivisions is

entirely harmonious, and the subdivisions may co-exist, as they literally read, without inconvenience or injustice. The one calls for an exercise of discretion; the other, for an exercise of judgment. The decision of a board upon charges, after a hearing, cannot in any proper sense be deemed a manifestation of its pleasure. The power in the one case is absolute; in the other, judicial. It seems quite reasonable, too, that these alternative powers should thus have been conferred. It seems equally reasonable that a majority vote should have been deemed sufficient for removal at pleasure, while a three-fourths vote should have been required for a removal upon charges. When a professor is removed at pleasure, no stigma attaches to the act of removal. His services are no longer required, and he is told so. That is what, in substance, such a removal amounts to. When he is removed upon charges, however, he is sent out into the professional world with a stain upon his record. The distinction here is obvious, and the intention to discriminate just. If a professor misconducts himself, he may be disciplined. The college in that case deems it improper to give him an honorable discharge, or to permit him to depart with the impunity attached to a mere causeless dismissal. If, however, its relations with him are severed merely because he is not liked, or because some one else is preferred, dismissal "at pleasure" is provided for. In the latter case it is reasonable that the majority, in the usual way, should govern and act. In the former, it is just that the stigma should not be fastened upon the professor without a hearing, and a substantial preponderance in the vote. The intention of these alternative by-laws was indeed quite within the line of the defendant's duty, both to the public and the profession. It has a certain responsibility, present and prospective, with regard to the occupants of its chairs. The fact that a professional man is deemed worthy to fill one of them cannot but be an important factor in the public estimate of his standing. Upon the other hand, the college should not be tied to a particular person, who, however able and worthy, happens to be afflicted with temperamental qualities which render association with him disagreeable. There can be no good reason why such a person should be permanently inflicted upon his associates so long as he does nothing which renders him amenable to charges. Relations with such a man may properly be severed at pleasure. Not so, however, as to a guilty man. It would be a practical condonation of his offense to remove such a man at pleasure. He should not be permitted to escape by that easy process, and the duty is thus imposed upon the directors, in such a case, to act in the manner specified in the third subdivision. This is the true construction, as it is the plain reading, of these by-laws. Then, too, upon any other construction the professor's tenure would be practically for life, or during good behavior. This, clearly, was not the intention. The appointment of a professor is not an appointment to office in the corporation, any more than is the appointment of an instructor. It is an appointment which implies contractual relations in some form, of which the by-law is the foundation. The professor may leave at his pleasure. The board may terminate his professorship at its pleas ure.   If the relator's view be correct, the "pleasure" is his, and his alone.   It would follow that he has an appointment which constitutes a unilateral contract of retention, at his own pleasure, for life or during good behavior; in other words, a contract which he alone can specifically enforce, and which is entirely dependent upon his individual will.   We think this theory is entirely unfounded. The by-laws are clear and explicit, both as to the professors and the instructors.   The tenure of the instructor is one year.   He must then be reappointed.   The tenure of the professor is at the pleasure of the board.   If, however, the latter misconducts himself, then another and different provision is made, calling for the exercise of judicial judgment upon charges made, and an explanation thereof given.   We think, therefore, that the removal of the relator by a majority vote of the board was lawful.

As to the second point, the record shows that when the board acted there were no charges against the relator actually pending before it.   The learned judge below has found that these charges, though formally returned to the faculty, unacted upon, were, in substance, pending before the board when the directors removed the relator, under the second subdivision of the twelfth article of the by-laws.   It was his opinion that, although the directors thus technically removed the relator at their pleasure, they essentially removed him upon the charges.   There is not a scintilla of direct evidence to support this conclusion.   It rests entirely upon the circumstances attendant upon the action of the board; in other words, upon inferences drawn from the facts established by the direct evidence.   The direct evidence proved that the charges were, at the request of the faculty, returned to the latter body, unacted upon, and that almost immediately thereafter the directors removed the relator under the second subdivision of the twelfth article; that is, at their pleasure.   We think the inference drawn from these facts by the learned judge below was unwarranted,—at least, upon the present application.   It was not competent, upon a motion for a peremptory mandamus, to go below the surface of the facts presented, and draw debatable inferences therefrom.   Such a writ can only be granted upon questions of law; never where there is a dispute as to the material facts.   The undisputed facts here are, upon their face, plainly conclusive against the relator.   The dispute arises only upon the just inferences to be drawn from these facts.   The court went behind the direct evidence, and attached to it a force and meaning which were not apparent upon its face.   It was weighed in the light of antecedent and surrounding circumstances, and when thus weighed the inference of bad faith on the part of the directors was drawn therefrom.   The difficulty at this point is obvious.   To say the least, two inferences might have been drawn from the evidence as thus weighed.   A jury, for instance, might have inferred, as did the learned judge, that what transpired was a subterfuge to enable the directors to effect the same purpose as the removal of the relator upon the charges.   Such a jury might, however, have drawn the opposite inference from precisely the same evidence.   They might have inferred therefrom that the board acted in good faith, that it honestly believed that the faculty no longer desired to press the charges, and that these charges were not again to be presented to them. Indeed, we think the latter the fairer inference. It certainly is more in consonance with the general principle that fraud is not to be lightly presumed, upon mere surmise or suspicion, and that it must be proved either by direct or circumstantial evidence of a convincing and satisfactory character. We have no doubt that the removal here resulted from the antagonisms engendered by these charges, and by the unpleasant criticisms which preceded them. Indeed, these antagonisms probably precipitated the final action of the board. The relator, whether right or wrong in the position which he had taken throughout, had become persona non grata with the directors, and these gentlemen thought proper to terminate their relations with him. That is the sum and substance of the whole matter. They had a right to their likes and their dislikes, and they had an equal right to express them in a lawful manner. The removal of the relator at their pleasure was within their power, under the by-law, and consequently such removal was legal and effective.

It follows that the relator was not entitled to the peremptory mandamus which was awarded him. Nor was he entitled to an alternative writ, even for the purpose of settling the question of good or bad faith, according to the inferences which a jury might draw from all the facts. Mandamus, in our judgment, was not the relator's proper remedy. The facts stated in the moving papers failed to show that he had not an adequate remedy at law. His application, so far as the remedy by mandamus is concerned, seems to be based upon the notion that the position of a professor in the defendant's college is in the nature of an office, and that it is the province of a mandamus to reinduct him into that office, and keep him there. This is an erroneous view, both of the relator's true position, and of the office of the writ. The college is a private corporation, and its professors and instructors are simply professional men appointed to serve the institution in a particular manner. They either hold contract or honorary relations with the college; but which, the papers here do not clearly disclose. If the former, the relator can sue for his salary, or for any other emolument to which he is entitled. If, however, the relation is honorary, its continuance or discontinuance must be mutually optional. A different rule applies where one is deprived of membership in a corporation. There he can be restored to membership, if improperly expelled. This was done in People v. New York Ben. Soc., 3 Hun, 361. It is also the proper remedy to compel a medical society to admit to membership one who is properly entitled thereto. People v. Erie Medical Soc., 32 N. Y. 187. The only case in this state, to which we have been referred, extending this principle to college professors in medical colleges, is People v. Albany Medical College, 62 How. Prac. 222. This case, however, was reversed upon appeal (26 Hun, 348), and the reversal was subsequently affirmed in the court of appeals (89 N. Y. 635). It is true that the reversal was upon the merits, and that nothing was said above as to the remedy. Even at special term, however, the question of the remedy was not fully considered. Judge Westbrook merely said that he did not deem it necessary to discuss the remedy by mandamus, adding a few words, to the effect that "where a court has jurisdiction of the subject-matter and the parties, by any of the modes known to the law, there is no reason why it should not exercise its powers to undo a wrong." This doctrine would include substantially all wrongs redressable by action, and would extend mandamus indefinitely. We are unable to concur in the reasoning of that case, or in the conclusion which was there arrived at as to the remedy. We are also referred to People v. Steele, 2 Barb. 397. This, however, was not a case of a college professor. It was that of a minister of the Gospel, and it was decided upon considerations specially applicable to ministers of religious sects. We need not, therefore, express an opinion as to its authority. It was decided by a learned judge, who subsequently expressed doubt as to the propriety of mandamus to reinstate a member of a college, and a candidate for the degree of medicine. People v. College of Physicians and Surgeons, 7 How. Prac. 290. In the latter case this learned judge cited with evident approval Dr. Goddard's Case, 1 Lev. 19, where it was held that a person entitled to a fellowship in a college could not obtain restoration thereto by mandamus. We think it quite clear upon principle, and the principle is not shaken by authority, that the relator in the case at bar held no office in the college corporation, that the defendant could not be compelled by mandamus to restore him to the professorship, and that his remedy for the unlawful deprivation of any right which the professorship conferred upon him was by action.

Upon both points, therefore, the order should be reversed, and the application for a mandamus denied, with $50 costs, and disbursements of this appeal. All concur.

COBB
v.
HOWARD UNIVERSITY

It is common knowledge that teachers, in seeking academic connections at the collegiate level, lay increasingly greater emphasis on provisions for tenure and retirement.

————◆— —

Appeal from the District Court of the United States for the District of Columbia.

Suit by James A. Cobb against Howard University for a mandatory injunction directing defendant to reinstate plaintiff as a part-time professor of law and accord him permanent tenure as such. From a final judgment dismissing the bill, plaintiff appeals.

Affirmed.

Geo. D. Horning, Jr., Wm. E. Leahy, and Geo. A. Parker, all of Washington, D. C., for appellant.

Spencer Gordon, of Washington, D. C., for appellee.

Before EDGERTON, VINSON, and RUTLEDGE, Associate Justices.

COBB v. HOWARD UNIVERSITY.

No. 7315.

United States Court of Appeals for the
District of Columbia.

Decided July 10, 1939.

The provision of act of incorporation of Howard University authorizing board of trustees to remove any professor or tutor or other officer when in their judgment the interests of the university should require removal became part of any contract which may have existed between university and part-time law professor whose services were terminated. Act March 2, 1867, § 7, 14 Stat. 439.

RUTLEDGE, Associate Justice.

This suit was brought by appellant, Cobb, for a mandatory injunction which, so far as it can be effective now, would direct appellee, Howard University, to reinstate him as a part-time professor of law and accord him permanent tenure as such. The case comes here on appeal from a final judgment below dismissing the bill after hearing on the merits. The parties will be referred to in this opinion according to their respective positions in the trial court.

Plaintiff was a part-time teacher in defendant's law school from 1917 to June 30, 1938.[1] He was also vice-dean of the

[1] There were frequent changes, by mutual agreement, in plaintiff's teaching load, salary and subjects taught. His teaching schedule was one hour per week until 1922, and thereafter varied from two to four hours per week. His salary ranged from $250 per annum the first year to $1,700 per annum during 1933–34. From 1934 to 1938 he received $1,100 per annum. His salary as judge of the Municipal Court was $8,000 per annum.

school from 1923 to 1931. During the entire period of his connection with defendant, he has practiced law as his principal occupation and source of livelihood, except from 1926 to 1935 when he was a judge of the Municipal Court. His original appointment was as "lecturer on negotiable instruments for one year" at a salary of $250. He claims, and testified to the fact, that it was made on oral assurances by the then dean of the school and other officials of defendant that his first year of service would be on probation after which, if the service was satisfactory, his employment would be indefinite in tenure. Plaintiff was retained during the following year and succeeding ones, with duties and compensations which were changed from time to time. He asserts and testified that during his second year he was notified verbally by the dean and by the secretary that he was appointed for an indefinite tenure, his work having been satisfactory.

Various formal actions were taken by defendant's Board of Trustees from 1917 to 1931 relating to his work and status as teacher or professor of law, but only on occasions when some change, such as an increase in salary, was involved. During this period there is no entry in the corporate records of any action of the Board or of any of its committees appointing or reappointing plaintiff annually as a teacher.[2] During the period from 1917 to 1930 or 1931, the defendant's law school was a part-time evening school and the officers and teachers were part-time officials, principally practicing lawyers and judges. Plaintiff was thus a typical member of the law faculty during this period.

Beginning about 1930 (perhaps a year earlier), the law school was reorganized radically by conversion into a full-time day school with full-time teachers as the principal staff, although plaintiff and one other were retained from the previous faculty as two of four part-time teachers. As a part of the reorganization, the Board of Trustees adopted a resolution, in 1929 or 1930, placing the entire faculty and administrative staff of the law school on year-to-year tenure. Apparently notice of this general resolution was not communicated to the faculty; but on June 27, 1931, the Executive Committee of the Board adopted a resolution making all appointments to the law faculty for 1931-1932 to be "for the duration of one year", including that of plaintiff as a part-time teacher with the rank of professor at a salary of $1,600. Except in respect to tenure, there was no attempt at this time to change any term of plaintiff's contract. Plaintiff was notified formally of this action by a letter from the secretary of defendant dated June 30, 1931.[3] After some colloquy with various officials of defendant, including the secretary, the acting dean of the law school and Mr. Crawford, a trustee and chairman of the law school committee of the Board, the defendant wrote a letter under date of July 14, 1931, to the secretary, in reply to his letter of June 30, "accepting reappointment".[4]

---

[2] Entries do appear in the Board's minutes for 1923 appointing him as vice-dean of the law school, and for the years 1924 and 1925 reappointing him as such. There are no similar entries from 1925 to 1930.

[3] The letter was as follows:
"Dear Judge Cobb:
"The Board of Trustees at its meeting held April 14, 1931, delegated the Trustee Committee on the School of Law, full authority in the matter of appointments to the Howard University School of Law Faculty and Administrative Staff for the school year 1931–1932.
"I write to officially convey to you the following vote of the Law School Committee of the Board of Trustees of Howard University, at its meeting held Saturday, June 28, 1931.
"*Extract from Minutes*
"'Voted, that James A. Cobb be reappointed as Professor, part-time, in the school of law, Howard University, for the school year 1931-1932, at a salary of $1600 for the year.'
"It gives me great pleasure to convey to you on behalf of the President and the members of the Law School Committee of the Board of Trustees, this renewed expression of confidence.
"I will very much appreciate acknowledgment of this communication at your convenience, so that your reply may be filed with the records of the Board of Trustees.
"Attest:
"Emmett J. Scott,
"Secretary-Treasurer."

[4] The letter was as follows:
"Dear Doctor Scott:
"I am duly in receipt of your letter of June 30th informing me of my re-appointment as Professor in the School of Law, part time, for the year 1931-1932, at a salary of $1600 for the year. In ac-

From 1931 to 1938, resolutions were adopted annually by the Board "reappointing" plaintiff as "Professor of Law for one year", all except that for 1932 stating the appointment would "expire automatically on June 30" of the following year. In each of these years, except 1936, plaintiff was duly notified in writing of the action taken by the Board. He did not reply in writing to these letters, but protested orally on many occasions to various officials of defendant and by letter dated September 14, 1937, addressed to the acting dean of the law school, against the attempt so to limit his tenure, asserting a contract right to tenure during good behavior extending back to 1923. Without going into further detail, the evidence shows clearly that from 1931 on defendant maintained, so far as its formal records and written notices go,[5] that plaintiff was on tenure from year to year, and plaintiff, except for his letter of July 14, 1931, consistently maintained that his contract with the university was for tenure during good behavior.

On March 23, 1938, plaintiff was called by telephone from the office of Senator Carter Glass to appear before a subcommittee of the Senate Committee on Appropriations to testify in connection with its consideration of the appropriation bill for the university, and made before the Committee the statement set out in the margin.[6] On April 12, following, defendant's Board of Trustees adopted the following resolution:

"Upon motion, it was voted that Judge Cobb be not reappointed and that his services terminate as of June 30, 1938, with an explanation to Judge Cobb that because of his action in appearing before a congressional committee in opposition to University Appropriations, his services are terminated." [7]

Plaintiff was duly notified of this action, protested in person and by attorney, and receiving no reply, instituted this suit on May 27, 1938. He continued to teach until June 30, 1938, and has not been permitted to do so thereafter.

On April 28, 1933, defendant's Board of Trustees formally adopted a statement of "Policy Concerning Tenure", which we do not regard as applicable to plaintiff.[8]

Plaintiff's basic claim is that prior to 1931 he acquired rank under contract with

cepting re-appointment, this being my 16th year of service in the Law School, I wish to thank you for conveying the above information and through you to thank the Board of Trustees and the Law School Committee for their confidence in me which is manifested by their re-appointment and to assure you and them of my appreciation for the same.

"Very sincerely yours,
"James A. Cobb."

[5] There were, however, statements made orally to plaintiff by various officials of the university, including Mr. Crawford, chairman of the Board's committee on the law school, which were not entirely consistent with the resolutions.

[6] "Mr. Cobb. Mr. Chairman and gentlemen of the committee, I am a teacher and have been since 1917 in Howard University. I want to say, Mr. Chairman, that it is not a question of the size of the appropriation. We would appreciate it if we had more. The only question is about this $3,000 item. We have had a field agent, and had one for a number of years, and upon the recommendation of Mordecai Johnson, the president, that field agent was eliminated on the ground that we did not need him, and the salary was abolished.

"He comes back now and asks for $3,-000 for a field agent. That field agent,

in the opinion of those who are closely connected and associated with the university, would be used to build up Mordecai Johnson and not be used for the development of Howard University. We feel that his services would be utilized to try to build up Mordecai Johnson, and we are firmly convinced that the item should be eliminated."

It should be added that the item was opposed also by Mr. Eugene Davidson, in his capacity as Secretary of the Alumni Association of the University.

[7] This action was taken upon a recommendation of the law school committee of the Board that plaintiff be "reappointed".

[8] The regulations contain some evidence of contractual intention upon their face, but they specifically provide that after a satisfactory probationary period a teacher "may *normally* expect further or permanent appointment" [italics supplied], thus reserving the right to withhold such appointment in individual cases. In our view, the annual resolutions of "reappointment" and the letters of notice thereof from 1931 forward were effective to prevent the tenure regulations from becoming applicable to plaintiff. This would be true, we believe, regardless of their effect or lack of it upon any contract for tenure made prior to 1931.

defendant as a full professor of law, though for only part-time service and pay, with tenure as such which is described variously as "indefinite", "without term", "during good behavior" and "permanent"; that this status remained unaltered by any subsequent occurrence; that the resolution of defendant's Board terminating his services and defendant's refusal, pursuant to it, to permit him to teach after June 30, 1938, are in violation of his rights under the contract; and that, having no plain, adequate and complete remedy at law, he is entitled to the equitable relief prayed in the bill. Some claim appears to be based also, though we think ineffectively,[9] upon the tenure regulations of 1933. Subordinate claims are based upon alleged removal without prior notice or hearing.

Defendant answered, hearing on the merits was had, and on October 25, 1938, the court made findings of fact and conclusions of law which sustained defendant's contentions fully on all issues. These, summarized, were to the effect that plaintiff's tenure was not at any time permanent, but was only from year to year; that his employment expired June 30, 1938; that he had no right to notice or hearing; that if, as contended, he acquired permanent tenure prior to 1931, he lost it in that year by accepting appointment on an annual basis; that defendant's tenure regulations of 1933 were not binding contractually upon it, or in any event applicable or applied to plaintiff; that, if plaintiff's contract had been for permanent tenure, his statements before the subcommittee of the Senate Committee on Appropriations constituted cause justifying his dismissal; and that the court could not decree "specific performance of a personal service contract of the kind alleged", or "order that plaintiff be allowed to teach certain subjects, certain hours each week, at a certain salary, when the details of the alleged contract of employment have been changed in those respects on numerous occasions." On the same day judgment was entered pursuant to these findings dismissing the bill.

Plaintiff contends that the court erred, not only in making the findings and conclusions summarized above and in rendering judgment thereon as stated, but also in excluding evidence tendered by him to show the existence, prior to 1931, of an established custom of the university giving permanent tenure to full professors and that this custom became a part of his contract with defendant.

We do not find it necessary to pass upon the validity of the trial court's rulings on many of the important and interesting issues involved in the case. We express no opinion as to whether there was error in the exclusion of the evidence tendered by plaintiff to show the existence of a general and established custom or practice of the defendant and its applicability to plaintiff. Nor do we determine the effect of his letter of July 14, 1931 upon relations existing previously between the parties, or indicate any opinion as to whether the appearance and statements of plaintiff before the Congressional committee constituted cause justifying removal. On another and controlling ground we think the plaintiff is not entitled to the only relief he seeks in this suit.

[1] Howard University is a private corporation,[10] organized and existing under an Act of Congress[11] and acts amendatory thereto, which vest the government and management of its affairs in a Board of Trustees, give it power to appoint instructors and determine their salaries, and confer upon it the usual corporate powers of acquiring and holding property and of suing and being sued. Section 7 of the original act of incorporation provides:

"That the board of trustees shall have power to remove any professor or tutor or other officers connected with the institution, when, in their judgment, the interest of the university shall require it."

We think this provision precludes the plaintiff from having the relief he seeks in this proceeding. The law is clear that it became a part of any contract which may have existed between the plaintiff and the defendant.[12] Its effect remains to be determined.

There is authority for the view that such a provision as Section 7 incapacitates the corporation to make any contract with a teacher which is not terminable at the

9 For the reason stated in the preceding note.

10 Maintico Construction Co. v. United States, 1935, 65 App.D.C. 62, 79 F.2d 418.

11 March 2, 1867, 14 Stat. 438, 439.

12 See the cases cited in notes 13 and 16, infra.

arbitrary will of the trustees or governing body.[13] In each of the cases cited there was a clear agreement either that the teacher's employment should be for a specified term which had not expired when he was discharged, or for what is in effect the same thing, namely, that notice should be given a specified time in advance of dismissal, which was not done. In none of the cases, with possibly a single exception, was there any showing of cause justifying dismissal prior to the end of the term. The view taken was that the statutory provision deprived the governing board of power to make a contract with a teacher for any definite term, however minute, and that attempts by it to do so were wholly nugatory in a legal sense.

Thus in Devol v. Board of Regents, 1899, 6 Ariz. 259, 56 P. 737, 738, the court said:

"They [the legislature] gave them [the Board of Regents] no power to fix times of notice for the discharge of employés. If the board could fix such time at three months, to bind themselves or their successors, they could fix it at six months, or nine months, or a year, which would be in direct violation of the interests of the institution as the legislature had created it."[14]

In Gillan v. Board of Regents of Normal Schools, 1894, 88 Wis. 7, 58 N.W. 1042, 1044, 24 L.R.A. 336, the court asserted:

"An emergency might arise when the continuance of an objectionable teacher, *even for a day,* in his employment, might be very injurious to the school." [Italics supplied] [15]

This interpretation, if the proper one, goes to the root of the plaintiff's case and in effect renders the university incapable of making a contract such as he claims existed and such as is essential to the giving of any relief.

On the other hand, there are decisions which give the statutory provision a less drastic effect. They take the view that, though the provision empowers the governing board to remove the instructor at any time, nevertheless it does not disable the board to contract effectively that it will not exercise the power arbitrarily or unreasonably, or, in other words, to make reasonable agreements for the tenure of teachers.[16] In Board of Regents v. Mudge, 1878, 21 Dass.Ed. 169, 21 Kan. 223, the court rejects the argument, under a statutory provision practically identical with the one before us, that "the board has no legal power to make a contract * * * for any particular period of time—not even for a day or an hour," saying:

"There is no express limitation upon the power of the board to make a contract to employ a president or a professor or a teacher for any period of time, and we know of no implied limitation that would

---

13 Hyslop v. Board of Regents, 1913, 23 Idaho 341, 129 P. 1073; Devol v. Board of Regents, 1899, 6 Ariz. 259, 56 P. 737; Gillan v. Board of Regents of Normal Schools, 1894, 88 Wis. 7, 58 N. W. 1042, 24 L.R.A. 336; State ex rel. Hunsicker v. Board of Regents of Normal Schools, 1932, 209 Wis. 83, 244 N. W. 618; Ward v. Board of Regents, 1905, 8 Cir., 138 F. 372. Cf. People ex rel. Kelsey v. New York Post Graduate Medical School & Hospital, 1898, 29 App.Div. 244, 51 N.Y.S. 420. This view is said to go back to Queen v. Darlington School [1844], 6 Q.B. 682, which, however, was a proceeding in mandamus, not an action for damages. The court, in 6 Q.B. at page 715, specifically stated: "The governors would be guilty of misconduct, might perhaps render themselves liable to a criminal prosecution, if they exercised their discretion of removal in an oppressive manner, or from any corrupt or indirect motive." The instructor was regarded as an "officer".

The principle has been applied to a superintendent of public schools [Farley v. Board of Education, 1917, 62 Okl. 181, 162 P. 797, where the statute prescribed holding office "during the pleasure of the board"], and the medical superintendent of a state hospital for insane persons [Smith v. Directors of Insane Asylum of New Mexico, 1914, 19 N.M. 137, 141 P. 608].

14 6 Ariz. 259, 56 Pac. at page 738.

15 88 Wis. 7, 58 N.W. at page 1044, 24 L.R.A. 336.

16 Board of Regents v. Mudge, 1878, 21 Dass.Ed. 169, 21 Kan. 223; State Board of Agriculture v. Meyers, 1904, 20 Colo.App. 139, 77 P. 372; Board of Education v. Cook, 1896, 3 Kan.App. 269, 45 P. 119. In the case last cited, a regulation of the board, "unless sooner removed by vote of the board", rather than a statute, was held to enter into and become part of the contract for a year's employment, but not effective to deprive the board of power to make a contract for a fixed term.

prevent the board from employing, or agreeing to employ, a president or a professor or a teacher for three months, or for even a longer period of time, provided it were not unreasonably long. * * * It would certainly be for the interest of the college that the board should have such power. No man of spirit, of self-respect, and of capability, would want to hold an office or position at the whim or caprice of a body of men with whom he might have but little if any personal acquaintance * * * would accept an office unless he felt that he was reasonably certain to hold the same for some reasonable period of time. The shorter and more precarious the tenure of the office, the less attractive, important, and valuable it would be; and generally, men of only inferior talent could be found to accept it or to perform its functions with such a precarious tenure, and even then a higher rate of compensation would be required than where the tenure is more stable and certain."[17]

The judgment of the trial court awarding damages to the plaintiff for breach of the contract was affirmed.

State Board of Agriculture v. Meyers, 1904, 20 Colo.App. 139, 77 P. 372, reached a similar result, both on principle and on the authority of the Mudge case and Board of Education v. Cook, 1896, 3 Kan.App. 269, 45 P. 119. The court said [20 Colo. App. 139, 77 P. 373]:

"In making such contracts [for the employment of teachers], the length of time for which they should run depends upon what is for the best interest of the college. We think the statute has left the determination of this question * * * largely to the judgment of the board, and that such lodgment * * * is wisely made. * * *

"This action is to recover damages for the wrongful discharge of appellee. It is not a proceeding to prevent the removal of appellee * * * nor to reinstate him * * *. To hold that appellant is liable in damages for a breach of its contract with appellee is not to hold that it cannot remove him. * * *

"* * * While section 76, supra, gives to appellant the power to remove appellee, it does not absolve it from responsibility in damages if the discharge be wrongful.[18]

The court refused to follow the result and the reasoning in the Devol case. In reply to the assertion made in that case that interpreting the statute to permit the board to contract for a definite term, however short, would deprive it of power to discharge, "when, in its judgment, it was to the interest of the university to do so," the court said:

"The lack of power to discharge does not follow from the exercise of the power to employ for a definite time. * * * The existence of the contract no more deprives the board of the power to discharge than a contract of employment deprives a private corporation of the power to discharge an employé. The effect of the contract made under the power is not to prevent a discharge, but to create responsibility in damages for a wrongful discharge."[19]

[2] We are neither required nor clearly asked[20] to hold in this case, nor did the trial court rule, that Howard University, under the statute, has no power to make a contract of employment other than one terminable at will. Such a decision would, in effect, determine the rights of other teachers and employees of the defendant, render legally ineffective the tenure regulations of 1933, and perhaps seriously handicap the university in its effort to secure men of competence to carry on its educational work.[21] In advance of the final necessity for making such a decision,

---

[17] 21 Dass.Ed. at page 174, 21 Kan. at page 230.

[18] 20 Colo.App. 139, 77 P. at pages 373, 374.

[19] 20 Colo.App. 139, 77 P. at page 376.

[20] While defendant's brief cites the Hunsicker, Devol and Darlington School cases and suggests that "It is reasonable to assume that the Board of Trustees had in mind that they could not bind their successors *not to remove* members of the faculty" [italics supplied] when they adopted the tenure regulations of 1933, and that the appointment of a pro-

106 F.2d—55

fessor "without term", as indicated in the tenure policy, "did not result in a contract" for employment until the age of retirement, emphasis in defendant's argument is placed upon the contention that plaintiff did not, rather than that he could not, secure permanent tenure from defendant.

[21] It is common knowledge that teachers, in seeking academic connections at the collegiate level, lay increasingly greater emphasis upon provisions for tenure and retirement. The American Association of University Professors, com-

and in view of the divided state of the authorities, we are unwilling to make it. The issues in this case do not require us to do more than decide that plaintiff is not entitled to reinstatement, as we must do if the language of Section 7 of the Act incorporating the defendant is to be given any effect.

The cases relied upon by appellant as sustaining his right to the relief here prayed are distinguishable, either by the ab-

sence of a statute such as is present here, or by the presence of a specific statutory provision investing public school teachers with the right of permanent tenure.[22]

It becomes unnecessary, therefore, for us to pass upon the other interesting and important issues, both of substantive and of remedial law, which were presented below and in argument here. For the reason given, the judgment is

Affirmed.

---

posed on January 1, 1939, of 14,595 members, devotes much of its effort toward promotion and protection of teachers' rights of tenure.

[22] See, for example, State of Indiana ex rel. Anderson v. ·Brand, 1938, 303 U. S. 95, 58 S.Ct. 443, 82 L.Ed. 685, 113 A. L.R. 1482; Blair v. United States ex

rel. Hellmann, 1916, 45 App.D.C. 353; Whitwell v. United States ex rel. Selden, 1932, 61 App.D.C. 169, 58 F.2d 895; Gerritt v. Fullerton Union High School, 1938, 24 Cal.App.2d 482, 75 P.2d 627; Brumfield v. State ex rel. Wallace, 1934, 206 Ind. 647, 190 N.E. 863; State ex rel. Nyberg v. Board of School Directors, 1926, 190 Wis. 570, 209 N.W. 683.

W. W. WORZELLA, Plaintiff and Appellant, v.
THE BOARD OF REGENTS
OF EDUCATION
OF THE
STATE OF SOUTH DAKOTA, *et al.*

W. W. WORZELLA, Plaintiff and
Appellant,

v.

The BOARD OF REGENTS OF EDUCA-
TION OF THE STATE of South Dakota,
and Harry J. Eggen, Frank Gellerman,
Eric Heidepriem, Byron Helgerson, Lem
Overpeck, Maylou Amunson, Dona S.
Brown, as Members of said Board, and H.
M. Crothers, Acting President of South
Dakota State College, Defendants and Re-
spondents.

No. 9722–a.

Supreme Court of South Dakota.

Dec. 10, 1958.

Petition for writ of mandamus to compel state board of regents to reinstate petitioner as professor or head of a department at state college. The Circuit Court
of Brookings County, R. F. Manson, J.,
denied relief, and petitioner appealed. The
Supreme Court, Hanson, J., held that tenure
policy at state college, under which board
of regents could not remove a faculty
member for any reason or cause without
prior action and approval of president and
tenure committee, constituted an unlawful
encroachment upon board's constitutional
and statutory power of control over state
college.

Affirmed.

1. Colleges and Universities ⊕8

Statutory provisions, confirming and
clarifying power of board of regents under
constitution to employ and dismiss all officers, instructors, and employees at all institutions under board's control, become a
part of every contract of employment entered into by the board. SDC 15.0709,
15.0714; Const. art. 14, § 3.

2. Colleges and Universities ⊕7

Power of board of regents under constitution and statutes to employ and dismiss all officers, instructors, and employees
at all institutions under board's control
cannot be restricted, surrendered, or delegated away. SDC 15.0709, 15.0714; Const.
art. 14, § 3.

3. Colleges and Universities ⊕7

Under section of statute providing
that board of regents shall have power to
enact and enforce rules and regulations
necessary for management of institutions
under its control and government of students and employees therein and authorizing board to delegate provisionally so much
of authority conferred by the section as in
its judgment seems proper and in accordance with usual custom in such cases,
board has only limited power to delegate
the authority conferred on it by the same
section and is not empowered to delegate
away all of its powers or its constitutional
duty of control. SDC 15.0714; Const. art.
14, § 3.

4. Colleges and Universities ⊕8

Tenure policy at state college, under
which board of regents could not remove a
faculty member for any reason or cause
without prior action and approval of president and tenure committee, constituted an
unlawful encroachment upon board's constitutional and statutory power of control
over state college. SDC 15.0709, 15.0714;
Const. art. 14, § 3.

5. Mandamus ⊜79

A member of faculty of state college, summarily dismissed by board of regents after investigation on ground that his retention was incompatible with best interests of college, its students, and the state, was not entitled to writ of mandamus requiring board to reinstate him as professor or head of a department at college, regardless of whether dismissal was made in compliance with tenure policy at state college. SDC 15.0709, 15.0714; Const. art. 14, § 3.

M. T. Woods, Sioux Falls, for plaintiff and appellant.

Phil Saunders, Atty. Gen., George Wuest, Val Higgins, Asst. Attys. Gen., for defendants and respondents.

HANSON, Judge.

The petitioner, Dr. W. W. Worzella, seeks a writ of mandamus compelling the State Board of Regents to reinstate him as professor of agronomy or as head of the agronomy department at South Dakota State College. The circuit court refused relief and he appeals.

Dr. Worzella was first employed as a professor of agronomy at State College on October 1, 1943. Thereafter he served continuously on that faculty until discharged by the Board of Regents on January 11, 1958. He was dismissed after an extensive investigation into the personnel and administrative affairs of State College by the Board. After the investigation the Board prepared a written report. With reference to Dr. Worzella the Board found he " * * * wittingly or unwittingly, permitted himself and his name to become involved in serious personal disputes and activities in the many years above referred to, and has * * * been guilty of insubordination; that by virtue of the controversial character he has become, it would not be to the best interests of South Dakota

State College for him to be retained." The Board concluded "the retention of Dr. W. W. Worzella as head of the Department of Agronomy is incompatible to the best interest and welfare of State College, its students, and the State of South Dakota as a whole, and that he should be summarily dismissed and relieved from all further duties under his current contract; his compensation, however, to continue as therein provided during the remainder of this fiscal year." His summary dismissal followed.

Dr. Worzella contends he has permanent tenure under a tenure policy approved by the Board of Regents and could be dismissed only in compliance with its substantive and procedural provisions. It is conceded that no complaint was filed, notice given, or hearing held pursuant thereto. However, the Board maintains the tenure policy did not, and could not, abrogate its constitutional and statutory power to dismiss all officers, instructors, and employees under its control.

The advisability of establishing and the merits of academic tenure are not involved. We are concerned only with the validity and enforceability of the tenure policy approved for State College by the Board of Regents.

The exact meaning and intent of this so-called tenure policy eludes us. Its vaporous objectives, purposes, and procedures are lost in a fog of nebulous verbiage. We gather from it, in general, that a faculty member who is retained on the staff at State College for over three years gains permanent tenure. He cannot thereafter be divested of tenure unless a complaint against him is filed by the president of the college. He is then entitled to have notice of hearing, and a hearing before a Tenure Committee consisting of seven faculty members. It further provides that "since the final decision must be made by the President" it is desirable that he sit with the Tenure Committee during the formal hearing as an auditor. At the conclusion of the hearing the committee makes its recommendations to the president. The president must then decide whether to recommend the dismissal of the accused faculty member to the Board of Regents. The faculty member whose dismissal is recommended may appeal for a hearing before the Board. The concluding paragraph states that the tenure policy is based "upon good faith between the college administration and the individual faculty member".

The policy statement is silent as to the Board of Regents' authority. By inference we may assume the Board would have power to discharge a faculty member having tenure when recommended by the Tenure Committee and President. Otherwise the Board would have no authority to act. Apparently the Board could not discharge or remove a faculty member with tenure for any reason if the President failed or refused to file a complaint, or if the Tenure Committee and President failed or refused to recommend dismissal. We believe this to be an unlawful abdication of the Board's exclusive prerogative and power.

The Board of Regents is a constitutionally created administrative body charged with the control of all institutions of higher learning "under such rules and restrictions as the legislature shall provide". § 3, art. XIV. With reference to the issue involved the legislature has provided:

"The Board of Regents is authorized to employ and dismiss all officers, instructors, and employees of such institutions, necessary to the proper management thereof, to determine their number, qualifications, and duties, fix the term of their employment, and rate and manner of their compensation, and provide for sabbatical leave on part pay; provided, that no person shall be employed or dismissed by reason of any sectarian or political opinions held." SDC 15.0709.

"The Board of Regents shall have power to enact and enforce all rules and regulations, not in conflict with any law, and deemed necessary by it for the wise and successful management of the institutions under its control and for the government of students and employees therein.

"The Board may delegate provisionally to the president, dean, principal, or faculty of any school under its control, so much of the authority conferred by this section as in its judgment seems proper and in accordance with the usual custom in such cases." SDC 15.0714.

[1, 2] The above statutory provisions merely confirm and clarify the Board of Regents' constitutional power to employ and dismiss all officers, instructors, and employees at all institutions under its control. These provisions become a part of every contract of employment entered into by the Board. Gillan v. Board of Regents of Normal Schools, 88 Wis. 7, 58 N.W. 1042, 24 L.R.A. 336. It cannot be restricted, surrendered, or delegated away. Our constitution prescribes that our state university and colleges "shall be under the control" of the Board of Regents. Without the right to employ, and the power to discharge, its employees the Board loses its constitutional right of control. The same result was reached in a recent comparable case in North Dakota involving similar constitutional and statutory provisions. See Posin v. State Board of Higher Education, N.D., 86 N.W.2d 31.

[3] Under SDC 15.0714 the Board of Regents "may delegate provisionally to the president, dean, principal, or faculty of any school under its control, so much of the authority conferred by this section as in its judgment seems proper * * *." This is a limited power. It does not empower the Board to delegate away all of its powers or its constitutional duty of control. Under its provisions the Board may only delegate the limited authority conferred on it by the same section.

In support of his contentions petitioner cites, and largely relies on, the cases of State ex rel. Keeney v. Ayers, 108 Mont. 547, 92 P.2d 306, and State ex rel. Richardson v. Board of Regents of University of Nevada, 70 Nev. 144, 261 P.2d 515. Neither case involves comparable facts. Both are readily distinguishable. In Montana the state university and colleges are under the control of the State Board of Education. In Nevada they are under the control of the State Board of Regents. The tenure regulations in both states provide for the removal of a faculty member after a hearing before the governing board itself. In Nevada apparently no provision whatsoever is made for a preliminary hearing before a faculty committee. In Montana the recommendation of the faculty service committee is advisory only. Its recommendation is not binding on the Board. Neither case involves the question of delegated, surrendered, or diminished authority to dismiss or discharge faculty members. In both Montana and Nevada the governing boards reserve the ultimate power to remove any faculty member on tenure. Their power of dismissal is not dependent upon the prior action or recommendation of any subordinate body, committee, or person. The distinction is of vital importance.

[4, 5] In South Dakota, under the present tenure policy at State College, the Board of Regents cannot remove a faculty member for any reason or cause on its own volition. Without the prior action and approval of the President and Tenure Committee the Board is powerless to act. The President and Tenure Committee do not serve in an advisory capacity only. Their action and approval are conditions precedent to any dismissal of college personnel by the Board. Such delegation of authority to subordinates is an unlawful encroachment upon the Board of Regents' constitutional and statutory power of control over such college. A writ of mandamus was, therefore, properly denied by the trial court.

Affirmed.

All the Judges concur.

BOARD OF REGENTS
OF STATE COLLEGES et al.
v. ROTH

BOARD OF REGENTS OF STATE COLLEGES
ET AL. *v.* ROTH

CERTIORARI TO THE UNITED STATES COURT OF APPEALS FOR
THE SEVENTH CIRCUIT

No. 71–162. Argued January 18, 1972—Decided June 29, 1972

Respondent, hired for a fixed term of one academic year to teach at
a state university, was informed without explanation that he
would not be rehired for the ensuing year. A statute provided
that all state university teachers would be employed initially on
probation and that only after four years' continuous service would
teachers achieve permanent employment "during efficiency and
good behavior," with procedural protection against separation.
University rules gave a nontenured teacher "dismissed" before the
end of the year some opportunity for review of the "dismissal,"
but provided that no reason need be given for nonretention of
a nontenured teacher, and no standards were specified for re-
employment. Respondent brought this action claiming deprivation of his Fourteenth Amendment rights, alleging infringement
of (1) his free speech right because the true reason for his nonretention was his criticism of the university administration, and
(2) his procedural due process right because of the university's
failure to advise him of the reason for its decision. The District
Court granted summary judgment for the respondent on the procedural issue. The Court of Appeals affirmed. *Held:* The Fourteenth Amendment does not require opportunity for a hearing
prior to the nonrenewal of a nontenured state teacher's contract,
unless he can show that the nonrenewal deprived him of an interest
in "liberty" or that he had a "property" interest in continued
employment, despite the lack of tenure or a formal contract.
Here the nonretention of respondent, absent any charges against
him or stigma or disability foreclosing other employment, is not
tantamount to a deprivation of "liberty," and the terms of respondent's employment accorded him no "property" interest protected by procedural due process. The courts below therefore
erred in granting summary judgment for the respondent on the
procedural due process issue. Pp. 569–579.

446 F. 2d 806, reversed and remanded.

STEWART, J., delivered the opinion of the Court, in which BURGER, C. J., and WHITE, BLACKMUN, and REHNQUIST, JJ., joined. BURGER, C. J., filed a concurring opinion, *post*, p. 603. DOUGLAS, J., filed a dissenting opinion, *post*, p. 579. BRENNAN, J., filed a dissenting opinion, in which DOUGLAS, J., joined, *post*, p. 604. MARSHALL, J., filed a dissenting opinion, *post*, p. 587. POWELL, J., took no part in the decision of the case.

Charles A. Bleck, Assistant Attorney General of Wisconsin, argued the cause for petitioners. With him on the brief were *Robert W. Warren,* Attorney General, and *Robert D. Martinson,* Assistant Attorney General.

Steven H. Steinglass argued the cause for respondent. With him on the brief were *Robert L. Reynolds, Jr., Richard Perry,* and *Richard M. Klein.*

Briefs of *amici curiae* urging reversal were filed by *Robert H. Quinn,* Attorney General, *Walter H. Mayo III,* Assistant Attorney General, and *Morris M. Goldings* for the Commonwealth of Massachusetts; by *Evelle J. Younger,* Attorney General of California, *Elizabeth Palmer,* Acting Assistant Attorney General, and *Donald B. Day,* Deputy Attorney General, for the Board of Trustees of the California State Colleges; by *J. Lee Rankin* and *Stanley Buchsbaum* for the City of New York; and by *Albert E. Jenner, Jr., Chester T. Kamin,* and *Richard T. Dunn* for the American Council on Education et al.

Briefs of *amici curiae* urging affirmance were filed by *David Rubin, Michael H. Gottesman, George H. Cohen,* and *Warren Burnett* for the National Education Association et al.; by *Herman I. Orentlicher* and *William W. Van Alstyne* for the American Association of University Professors; by *John Ligtenberg* and *Andrew J. Leahy* for the American Federation of Teachers; and by *Richard L. Cates* for the Wisconsin Education Association.

MR. JUSTICE STEWART delivered the opinion of the Court.

In 1968 the respondent, David Roth, was hired for his first teaching job as assistant professor of political science at Wisconsin State University-Oshkosh. He was hired for a fixed term of one academic year. The notice of his faculty appointment specified that his employ-ment would begin on September 1, 1968, and would end on June 30, 1969.[1] The respondent completed that term. But he was informed that he would not be re-hired for the next academic year.

The respondent had no tenure rights to continued employment. Under Wisconsin statutory law a state university teacher can acquire tenure as a "permanent" employee only after four years of year-to-year em-ployment. Having acquired tenure, a teacher is entitled to continued employment "during efficiency and good behavior." A relatively new teacher without tenure, however, is under Wisconsin law entitled to nothing beyond his one-year appointment.[2] There are no statu-

---

[1] The respondent had no contract of employment. Rather, his formal notice of appointment was the equivalent of an employment contract.

The notice of his appointment provided that: *"David F. Roth* is hereby appointed to the faculty of the Wisconsin State University Position number 0262. (Location:) *Oshkosh* as (Rank:) *Assistant Professor* of (Department:) *Political Science* this (Date:) *first* day of (Month:) *September* (Year:) *1968."* The notice went on to specify that the respondent's "appointment basis" was for the "academic year." And it provided that "[r]egulations governing tenure are in accord with Chapter 37.31, Wisconsin Statutes. The employment of any staff member for an academic year shall not be for a term beyond June 30th of the fiscal year in which the appoint-ment is made." See n. 2, *infra.*

[2] Wis. Stat. § 37.31 (1) (1967), in force at the time, provided in pertinent part that:

"All teachers in. any state university shall initially be employed

tory or administrative standards defining eligibility for re-employment. State law thus clearly leaves the decision whether to rehire a nontenured teacher for another year to the unfettered discretion of university officials.

The procedural protection afforded a Wisconsin State University teacher before he is separated from the University corresponds to his job security. As a matter of statutory law, a tenured teacher cannot be "discharged except for cause upon written charges" and pursuant to certain procedures.[3] A nontenured teacher, similarly, is protected to some extent *during* his one-year term. Rules promulgated by the Board of Regents provide that a nontenured teacher "dismissed" before the end of the year may have some opportunity for review of the "dismissal." But the Rules provide no real protection for a nontenured teacher who simply is not re-employed for the next year. He must be informed by February 1 "concerning retention or non-retention for the ensuing year." But "no reason for non-retention need be given. No review or appeal is provided in such case."[4]

---

on probation. The employment shall be permanent, during efficiency and good behavior after 4 years of continuous service in the state university system as a teacher."

[3] Wis. Stat. § 37.31 (1) further provided that:

"No teacher who has become permanently employed as herein provided shall be discharged except for cause upon written charges. Within 30 days of receiving the written charges, such teacher may appeal the discharge by a written notice to the president of the board of regents of state colleges. The board shall cause the charges to be investigated, hear the case and provide such teacher with a written statement as to their decision."

[4] The Rules, promulgated by the Board of Regents in 1967, provide:

"RULE I—February first is established throughout the State University system as the deadline for written notification of non-tenured

In conformance with these Rules, the President of Wisconsin State University-Oshkosh informed the respondent before February 1, 1969, that he would not be rehired for the 1969–1970 academic year. He gave the respondent no reason for the decision and no opportunity to challenge it at any sort of hearing.

The respondent then brought this action in Federal District Court alleging that the decision not to rehire him for the next year infringed his Fourteenth Amendment rights. He attacked the decision both in substance and procedure. First, he alleged that the true reason for the decision was to punish him for certain statements critical of the University administration, and that it therefore violated his right to freedom of speech.[5]

---

faculty concerning retention or non-retention for the ensuing year. The President of each University shall give such notice each year on or before this date."

"RULE II—During the time a faculty member is on probation, no reason for non-retention need be given. No review or appeal is provided in such case.

"RULE III—'Dismissal' as opposed to 'Non-Retention' means termination of responsibilities during an academic year. When a non-tenure faculty member is dismissed he has no right under Wisconsin Statutes to a review of his case or to appeal. The President may, however, in his discretion, grant a request for a review within the institution, either by a faculty committee or by the President, or both. Any such review would be informal in nature and would be advisory only.

"RULE IV—When a non-tenure faculty member is dismissed he may request a review by or hearing before the Board of Regents. Each such request will be considered separately and the Board will, in its discretion, grant or deny same in each individual case."

[5] While the respondent alleged that he was not rehired because of his exercise of free speech, the petitioners insisted that the non-retention decision was based on other, constitutionally valid grounds. The District Court came to no conclusion whatever regarding the true reason for the University President's decision. "In the pres-

Second, he alleged that the failure of University officials
to give him notice of any reason for nonretention and
an opportunity for a hearing violated his right to procedural due process of law.

The District Court granted summary judgment for the
respondent on the procedural issue, ordering the University officials to provide him with reasons and a hearing.
310 F. Supp. 972. The Court of Appeals, with one judge
dissenting, affirmed this partial summary judgment. 446
F. 2d 806. We granted certiorari. 404 U. S. 909. The
only question presented to us at this stage in the case is
whether the respondent had a constitutional right to a
statement of reasons and a hearing on the University's
decision not to rehire him for another year.[6] We hold
that he did not.

I

The requirements of procedural due process apply only
to the deprivation of interests encompassed by the
Fourteenth Amendment's protection of liberty and property. When protected interests are implicated, the right

---

ent case," it stated, "it appears that a determination as to the
actual bases of [the] decision must await amplification of the facts
at trial. . . . Summary judgment is inappropriate." 310 F. Supp.
972, 982.

[6] The courts that have had to decide whether a nontenured public
employee has a right to a statement of reasons or a hearing upon
nonrenewal of his contract have come to varying conclusions. Some
have held that neither procedural safeguard is required. *E. g., Orr*
v. *Trinter*, 444 F. 2d 128 (CA6); *Jones* v. *Hopper*, 410 F. 2d 1323
(CA10); *Freeman* v. *Gould Special School District*, 405 F. 2d 1153
(CA8). At least one court has held that there is a right to a
statement of reasons but not a hearing. *Drown* v. *Portsmouth School
District*, 435 F. 2d 1182 (CA1). And another has held that both
requirements depend on whether the employee has an "expectancy"
of continued employment. *Ferguson* v. *Thomas*, 430 F. 2d 852,
856 (CA5).

to some kind of prior hearing is paramount.[7] But the range of interests protected by procedural due process is not infinite.

The District Court decided that procedural due process guarantees apply in this case by assessing and balancing the weights of the particular interests involved. It concluded that the respondent's interest in re-employment at Wisconsin State University-Oshkosh outweighed the University's interest in denying him re-employment summarily. 310 F. Supp., at 977–979. Undeniably, the respondent's re-employment prospects were of major concern to him—concern that we surely cannot say was insignificant. And a weighing processs has long been a part of any determination of the *form* of hearing required in particular situations by procedural due process.[8] But, to determine whether

---

[7] Before a person is deprived of a protected interest, he must be afforded opportunity for some kind of a hearing, "except for extraordinary situations where some valid governmental interest is at stake that justifies postponing the hearing until after the event." *Boddie* v. *Connecticut*, 401 U. S. 371, 379. "While '[m]any controversies have raged about . . . the Due Process Clause,' . . . it is fundamental that except in emergency situations (and this is not one) due process requires that when a State seeks to terminate [a protected] interest . . . , it must afford 'notice and opportunity for hearing appropriate to the nature of the case' *before* the termination becomes effective." *Bell* v. *Burson*, 402 U. S. 535, 542. For the rare and extraordinary situations in which we have held that deprivation of a protected interest need not be preceded by opportunity for some kind of hearing, see, *e. g., Central Union Trust Co.* v. *Garvan*, 254 U. S. 554, 566; *Phillips* v. *Commissioner*, 283 U. S. 589, 597; *Ewing* v. *Mytinger & Casselberry, Inc.*, 339 U. S. 594.

[8] "The formality and procedural requisites for the hearing can vary, depending upon the importance of the interests involved and the nature of the subsequent proceedings." *Boddie* v. *Connecticut*, *supra*, at 378. See, *e. g., Goldberg* v. *Kelly*, 397 U. S. 254, 263; *Hannah* v. *Larche*, 363 U. S. 420. The constitutional requirement

due process requirements apply in the first place, we
must look not to the "weight" but to the *nature* of
the interest at stake. See *Morrissey* v. *Brewer, ante,*
at 481. We must look to see if the interest is within
the Fourteenth Amendment's protection of liberty and
property.

"Liberty" and "property" are broad and majestic
terms. They are among the "[g]reat [constitutional]
concepts . . . purposely left to gather meaning from
experience. . . . [T]hey relate to the whole domain
of social and economic fact, and the statesmen who
founded this Nation knew too well that only a stagnant
society remains unchanged." *National Ins. Co.* v. *Tide-
water Co.,* 337 U. S. 582, 646 (Frankfurter, J., dissenting). For that reason, the Court has fully and finally
rejected the wooden distinction between "rights" and
"privileges" that once seemed to govern the applicability of procedural due process rights.[9] The Court has
also made clear that the property interests protected by

of opportunity for *some* form of hearing before deprivation of a
protected interest, of course, does not depend upon such a narrow
balancing process. See n. 7, *supra.*

[9] In a leading case decided many years ago, the Court of Appeals
for the District of Columbia Circuit held that public employment in
general was a "privilege," not a "right," and that procedural due process guarantees therefore were inapplicable. *Bailey* v. *Richardson,* 86
U. S. App. D. C. 248, 182 F. 2d 46, aff'd by an equally divided Court,
341 U. S. 918. The basis of this holding has been thoroughly undermined in the ensuing years. For, as MR. JUSTICE BLACKMUN wrote
for the Court only last year, "this Court now has rejected the concept that constitutional rights turn upon whether a governmental
benefit is characterized as a 'right' or as a 'privilege.'" *Graham* v.
Richardson, 403 U. S. 365, 374. See, *e. g., Morrissey* v. *Brewer,
ante,* at 482; *Bell* v. *Burson, supra,* at 539; *Goldberg* v. *Kelly,
supra,* at 262; *Shapiro* v. *Thompson,* 394 U. S. 618, 627 n. 6;
Pickering v. *Board of Education,* 391 U. S. 563, 568; *Sherbert* v.
Verner, 374 U. S. 398, 404.

procedural due process extend well beyond actual ownership of real estate, chattels, or money.[10] By the
same token, the Court has required due process protection for deprivations of liberty beyond the sort of formal
constraints imposed by the criminal process.[11]

Yet, while the Court has eschewed rigid or formalistic
limitations on the protection of procedural due process,
it has at the same time observed certain boundaries.
For the words "liberty" and "property" in the Due
Process Clause of the Fourteenth Amendment must be
given some meaning.

II

"While this Court has not attempted to define with
exactness the liberty . . . guaranteed [by the Fourteenth
Amendment], the term has received much consideration
and some of the included things have been definitely
stated. Without doubt, it denotes not merely freedom
from bodily restraint but also the right of the individual
to contract, to engage in any of the common occupations of life, to acquire useful knowledge, to marry,
establish a home and bring up children, to worship God
according to the dictates of his own conscience, and
generally to enjoy those privileges long recognized . . .
as essential to the orderly pursuit of happiness by free
men." *Meyer* v. *Nebraska,* 262 U. S. 390, 399. In
a Constitution for a free people, there can be no doubt
that the meaning of "liberty" must be broad indeed.
See, *e. g., Bolling* v. *Sharpe,* 347 U. S. 497, 499–500;
Stanley v. *Illinois,* 405 U. S. 645.

---

[10] See, *e. g., Connell* v. *Higginbotham,* 403 U. S. 207, 208; *Bell*
v. *Burson, supra; Goldberg* v. *Kelly, supra.*

[11] "Although the Court has not assumed to define 'liberty' [in
the Fifth Amendment's Due Process Clause] with any great precision, that term is not confined to mere freedom from bodily restraint." *Bolling* v. *Sharpe,* 347 U. S. 497, 499. See, *e. g., Stanley*
v. *Illinois,* 405 U. S. 645.

There might be cases in which a State refused to re-employ a person under such circumstances that interests in liberty would be implicated. But this is not such a case.

The State, in declining to rehire the respondent, did not make any charge against him that might seriously damage his standing and associations in his community. It did not base the nonrenewal of his contract on a charge, for example, that he had been guilty of dishonesty, or immorality. Had it done so, this would be a different case. For "[w]here a person's good name, reputation, honor, or integrity is at stake because of what the government is doing to him, notice and an opportunity to be heard are essential." *Wisconsin* v. *Constantineau,* 400 U. S. 433, 437. *Wieman* v. *Updegraff,* 344 U. S. 183, 191; *Joint Anti-Fascist Refugee Committee* v. *McGrath,* 341 U. S. 123; *United States* v. *Lovett,* 328 U. S. 303, 316–317; *Peters* v. *Hobby,* 349 U. S. 331, 352 (DOUGLAS, J., concurring). See *Cafeteria Workers* v. *McElroy,* 367 U. S. 886, 898. In such a case, due process would accord an opportunity to refute the charge before University officials.[12] In the present case, however, there is no suggestion whatever that the respondent's "good name, reputation, honor, or integrity" is at stake.

Similarly, there is no suggestion that the State, in declining to re-employ the respondent, imposed on him a stigma or other disability that foreclosed his freedom to take advantage of other employment opportunities. The State, for example, did not invoke any regulations to bar the respondent from all other public employment in state universities. Had it done so, this, again, would

---

[12] The purpose of such notice and hearing is to provide the person an opportunity to clear his name. Once a person has cleared his name at a hearing, his employer, of course, may remain free to deny him future employment for other reasons.

be a different case. For "[t]o be deprived not only of
present government employment but of future opportunity for it certainly is no small injury . . . ." *Joint
Anti-Fascist Refugee Committee* v. *McGrath, supra,* at
185 (Jackson, J., concurring). See *Truax* v. *Raich,* 239
U. S. 33, 41. The Court has held, for example, that a
State, in regulating eligibility for a type of professional
employment, cannot foreclose a range of opportunities "in
a manner . . . that contravene[s] . . . Due Process,"
Schware v. *Board of Bar Examiners,* 353 U. S. 232, 238,
and, specifically, in a manner that denies the right to a
full prior hearing. *Willner* v. *Committee on Character,*
373 U. S. 96, 103. See *Cafeteria Workers* v. *McElroy,*
supra, at 898. In the present case, however, this principle does not come into play.[13]

To be sure, the respondent has alleged that the nonrenewal of his contract was based on his exercise of his
right to freedom of speech. But this allegation is not
now before us. The District Court stayed proceedings
on this issue, and the respondent has yet to prove that

---

[13] The District Court made an *assumption* "that non-retention by
one university or college creates concrete and practical difficulties for
a professor in his subsequent academic career." 310 F. Supp., at
979. And the Court of Appeals based its affirmance of the summary
judgment largely on the premise that "the substantial adverse effect
non-retention is likely to have upon the career interests of an individual professor" amounts to a limitation on future employment opportunities sufficient to invoke procedural due process guarantees.
446 F. 2d, at 809. But even assuming, *arguendo,* that such a "substantial adverse effect" under these circumstances would constitute a
state-imposed restriction on liberty, the record contains no support
for these assumptions. There is no suggestion of how nonretention
might affect the respondent's future employment prospects. Mere
proof, for example, that his record of nonretention in one job, taken
alone, might make him somewhat less attractive to some other employers would hardly establish the kind of foreclosure of opportunities
amounting to a deprivation of "liberty." Cf. *Schware* v. *Board of
Bar Examiners,* 353 U. S. 232.

the decision not to rehire him was, in fact, based on his free speech activities.[14]

Hence, on the record before us, all that clearly appears is that the respondent was not rehired for one year at one university.   It stretches the concept too far to suggest that a person is deprived of "liberty" when he simply is not rehired in one job but remains as free as before to seek another. *Cafeteria Workers* v. *McElroy, supra,* at 895–896.

---

[14] See n. 5, *supra.*   The Court of Appeals, nonetheless, argued that opportunity for a hearing and a statement of reasons were required here "as a *prophylactic* against non-retention decisions improperly motivated by exercise of protected rights." 446 F. 2d, at 810 (emphasis supplied).   While the Court of Appeals recognized the lack of a finding that the respondent's nonretention was based on exercise of the right of free speech, it felt that the respondent's interest in liberty was sufficiently implicated here because the decision not to rehire him was made "with a background of controversy and unwelcome expressions of opinion." *Ibid.*

When a State would directly impinge upon interests in free speech or free press, this Court has on occasion held that opportunity for a fair adversary hearing must precede the action, whether or not the speech or press interest is clearly protected under substantive First Amendment standards.   Thus, we have required fair notice and opportunity for an adversary hearing before an injunction is issued against the holding of rallies and public meetings. *Carroll* v. *Princess Anne,* 393 U. S. 175.   Similarly, we have indicated the necessity of procedural safeguards before a State makes a large-scale seizure of a person's allegedly obscene books, magazines, and so forth. *A Quantity of Books* v. *Kansas,* 378 U. S. 205; *Marcus* v. *Search Warrant,* 367 U. S. 717.   See *Freedman* v. *Maryland,* 380 U. S. 51; *Bantam Books* v. *Sullivan,* 372 U. S. 58.   See generally Monaghan, First Amendment "Due Process," 83 Harv. L. Rev. 518.

In the respondent's case, however, the State has not directly impinged upon interests in free speech or free press in any way comparable to a seizure of books or an injunction against meetings. Whatever may be a teacher's rights of free speech, the interest in holding a teaching job at a state university, *simpliciter,* is not itself a free speech interest.

III

The Fourteenth Amendment's procedural protection of property is a safeguard of the security of interests that a person has already acquired in specific benefits. These interests—property interests—may take many forms.

Thus, the Court has held that a person receiving welfare benefits under statutory and administrative standards defining eligibility for them has an interest in continued receipt of those benefits that is safeguarded by procedural due process. *Goldberg* v. *Kelly,* 397 U. S. 254.[15] See *Flemming* v. *Nestor,* 363 U. S. 603, 611. Similarly, in the area of public employment, the Court has held that a public college professor dismissed from an office held under tenure provisions, *Slochower* v. *Board of Education,* 350 U. S. 551, and college professors and

---

[15] *Goldsmith* v. *Board of Tax Appeals,* 270 U. S. 117, is a related case. There, the petitioner was a lawyer who had been refused admission to practice before the Board of Tax Appeals. The Board had "published rules for admission of persons entitled to practice before it, by which attorneys at law admitted to courts of the United States and the States, and the District of Columbia, as well as certified public accountants duly qualified under the law of any State or the District, are made eligible. . . . The rules further provide that the Board may in its discretion deny admission to any applicant, or suspend or disbar any person after admission." *Id.,* at 119. The Board denied admission to the petitioner under its discretionary power, without a prior hearing and a statement of the reasons for the denial. Although this Court disposed of the case on other grounds, it stated, in an opinion by Mr. Chief Justice Taft, that the existence of the Board's eligibility rules gave the petitioner an interest and claim to practice before the Board to which procedural due process requirements applied. It said that the Board's discretionary power "must be construed to mean the exercise of a discretion to be exercised after fair investigation, with such a notice, hearing and opportunity to answer for the applicant as would constitute due process." *Id.,* at 123.

staff members dismissed during the terms of their contracts, *Wieman* v. *Updegraff*, 344 U. S. 183, have interests in continued employment that are safeguarded by due process. Only last year, the Court held that this principle "proscribing summary dismissal from public employment without hearing or inquiry required by due process" also applied to a teacher recently hired without tenure or a formal contract, but nonetheless with a clearly implied promise of continued employment. *Connell* v. *Higginbotham*, 403 U. S. 207, 208.

Certain attributes of "property" interests protected by procedural due process emerge from these decisions. To have a property interest in a benefit, a person clearly must have more than an abstract need or desire for it. He must have more than a unilateral expectation of it. He must, instead, have a legitimate claim of entitlement to it. It is a purpose of the ancient institution of property to protect those claims upon which people rely in their daily lives, reliance that must not be arbitrarily undermined. It is a purpose of the constitutional right to a hearing to provide an opportunity for a person to vindicate those claims.

Property interests, of course, are not created by the Constitution. Rather, they are created and their dimensions are defined by existing rules or understandings that stem from an independent source such as state law—rules or understandings that secure certain benefits and that support claims of entitlement to those benefits. Thus, the welfare recipients in *Goldberg* v. *Kelly, supra,* had a claim of entitlement to welfare payments that was grounded in the statute defining eligibility for them. The recipients had not yet shown that they were, in fact, within the statutory terms of eligibility. But we held that they had a right to a hearing at which they might attempt to do so.

Just as the welfare recipients' "property" interest in welfare payments was created and defined by statutory terms, so the respondent's "property" interest in employment at Wisconsin State University-Oshkosh was created and defined by the terms of his appointment. Those terms secured his interest in employment up to June 30, 1969. But the important fact in this case is that they specifically provided that the respondent's employment was to terminate on June 30. They did not provide for contract renewal absent "sufficient cause." Indeed, they made no provision for renewal whatsoever.

Thus, the terms of the respondent's appointment secured absolutely no interest in re-employment for the next year. They supported absolutely no possible claim of entitlement to re-employment. Nor, significantly, was there any state statute or University rule or policy that secured his interest in re-employment or that created any legitimate claim to it.[16] In these circumstances, the respondent surely had an abstract concern in being rehired, but he did not have a *property* interest sufficient to require the University authorities to give him a hearing when they declined to renew his contract of employment.

IV

Our analysis of the respondent's constitutional rights in this case in no way indicates a view that an opportunity for a hearing or a statement of reasons for nonretention would, or would not, be appropriate or wise in public

---

[16] To be sure, the respondent does suggest that most teachers hired on a year-to-year basis by Wisconsin State University-Oshkosh are, in fact, rehired. But the District Court has not found that there is anything approaching a "common law" of re-employment, see *Perry* v. *Sindermann, post,* at 602, so strong as to require University officials to give the respondent a statement of reasons and a hearing on their decision not to rehire him.

colleges and universities.[17]   For it is a written Constitution that we apply.   Our role is confined to interpretation of that Constitution.

We must conclude that the summary judgment for the respondent should not have been granted, since the respondent has not shown that he was deprived of liberty or property protected by the Fourteenth Amendment. The judgment of the Court of Appeals, accordingly, is reversed and the case is remanded for further proceedings consistent with this opinion.

It is so ordered.

Mr. Justice Powell took no part in the decision of this case.

[For concurring opinion of Mr. Chief Justice Burger, see *post*, p. 603.]

[For dissenting opinion of Mr. Justice Brennan, see *post*, p. 604.]

Mr. Justice Douglas, dissenting.

Respondent Roth, like Sindermann in the companion case, had no tenure under Wisconsin law and, unlike Sindermann, he had had only one year of teaching at Wisconsin State University-Oshkosh—where during 1968–1969 he had been Assistant Professor of Political Science and International Studies. Though Roth was rated by the faculty as an excellent teacher, he had publicly criticized the administration for suspending an entire group of 94 black students without determining individual guilt. He also criticized the university's regime as being authoritarian and autocratic. He used his classroom to discuss what was being done about the

---

[17] See, *e. g.*, Report of Committee A on Academic Freedom and Tenure, Procedural Standards in the Renewal or Nonrenewal of Faculty Appointments, 56 AAUP Bulletin No. 1, p. 21 (Spring 1970).

black episode; and one day, instead of meeting his class, he went to the meeting of the Board of Regents.

In this case, as in *Sindermann,* an action was started in Federal District Court under 42 U. S. C. § 1983 [1] claiming in part that the decision of the school authorities not to rehire was in retaliation for his expression of opinion. The District Court, in partially granting Roth's motion for summary judgment, held that the Fourteenth Amendment required the university to give a hearing to teachers whose contracts were not to be renewed and to give reasons for its action. 310 F. Supp. 972, 983. The Court of Appeals affirmed. 446 F. 2d 806.

Professor Will Herberg, of Drew University, in writing of "academic freedom" recently said:

> "[I]t is sometimes conceived as a basic constitutional right guaranteed and protected under the First Amendment.
>
> "But, of course, this is not the case. Whereas a man's right to speak out on this or that may be guaranteed and protected, he can have no imaginable human or constitutional right to remain a member of a university faculty. Clearly, the right to academic freedom is an acquired one, yet an acquired right of such value to society that in the minds of many it has verged upon the constitutional." Washington Sunday Star, Jan. 23, 1972, B-3, col. 1.

---

[1] Section 1983 reads as follows:

"Every person who, under color of any statute, ordinance, regulation, custom, or usage, of any State or Territory, subjects, or causes to be subjected, any citizen of the United States or other person within the jurisdiction thereof to the deprivation of any rights, privileges, or immunities secured by the Constitution and laws, shall be liable to the party injured in an action at law, suit in equity, or other proper proceeding for redress."

There may not be a constitutional right to continued employment if private schools and colleges are involved. But Prof. Herberg's view is not correct when public schools move against faculty members. For the First Amendment, applicable to the States by reason of the Fourteenth Amendment, protects the individual against state action when it comes to freedom of speech and of press and the related freedoms guaranteed by the First Amendment; and the Fourteenth protects "liberty" and "property" as stated by the Court in *Sindermann.*

No more direct assault on academic freedom can be imagined than for the school authorities to be allowed to discharge a teacher because of his or her philosophical, political, or ideological beliefs. The same may well be true of private schools, if through the device of financing or other umbilical cords they become instrumentalities of the State. Mr. Justice Frankfurter stated the constitutional theory in *Sweezy* v. *New Hampshire,* 354 U. S. 234, 261–262 (concurring in result):

> "Progress in the natural sciences is not remotely confined to findings made in the laboratory. Insights into the mysteries of nature are born of hypothesis and speculation. The more so is this true in the pursuit of understanding in the groping endeavors of what are called the social sciences, the concern of which is man and society. The problems that are the respective preoccupations of anthropology, economics, law, psychology, sociology and related areas of scholarship are merely departmentalized dealing, by way of manageable division of analysis, with interpenetrating aspects of holistic perplexities. For society's good—if understanding be an essential need of society—inquiries into these problems, speculations about them, stimulation in others of reflection upon them, must be left as unfettered

as possible. Political power must abstain from intrusion into this activity of freedom, pursued in the interest of wise government and the people's well-being, except for reasons that are exigent and obviously compelling."

We repeated that warning in *Keyishian* v. *Board of Regents,* 385 U. S. 589, 603:

"Our Nation is deeply committed to safeguarding academic freedom, which is of transcendent value to all of us and not merely to the teachers concerned. That freedom is therefore a special concern of the First Amendment, which does not tolerate laws that cast a pall of orthodoxy over the classroom."

When a violation of First Amendment rights is alleged, the reasons for dismissal or for nonrenewal of an employment contract must be examined to see if the reasons given are only a cloak for activity or attitudes protected by the Constitution. A statutory analogy is present under the National Labor Relations Act, 29 U. S. C. § 151 *et seq.* While discharges of employees for "cause" are permissible (*Fibreboard Corp.* v. *NLRB,* 379 U. S. 203, 217), discharges because of an employee's union activities are banned by § 8 (a)(3), 29 U. S. C. § 158 (a)(3). So the search is to ascertain whether the stated ground was the real one or only a pretext. See *J. P. Stevens & Co.* v. *NLRB,* 380 F. 2d 292, 300.

In the case of teachers whose contracts are not renewed, tenure is not the critical issue. In the *Sweezy* case, the teacher, whose First Amendment rights we honored, had no tenure but was only a guest lecturer. In the *Keyishian* case, one of the petitioners (Keyishian himself) had only a "one-year-term contract" that was not renewed. 385 U. S., at 592. In *Shelton* v. *Tucker,* 364 U. S. 479, one of the petitioners was a teacher whose "contract for the ensuing school year was not renewed" (*id.*, at 483) and two others who refused to comply were advised that it made "impossible their re-employment as teachers for the following school year." *Id.*, at 484. The oath required in *Keyishian* and the affidavit listing memberships required in *Shelton* were both, in our view, in violation of First Amendment rights. Those cases mean that conditioning renewal of a teacher's contract upon surrender of First Amendment rights is beyond the power of a State.

There is sometimes a conflict between a claim for First Amendment protection and the need for orderly administration of the school system, as we noted in *Pickering* v. *Board of Education*, 391 U. S. 563, 569. That is one reason why summary judgments in this class of cases are seldom appropriate. Another reason is that careful factfinding is often necessary to know whether the given reason for nonrenewal of a teacher's contract is the real reason or a feigned one.

It is said that since teaching in a public school is a privilege, the State can grant it or withhold it on conditions. We have, however, rejected that thesis in numerous cases, *e. g.*, *Graham* v. *Richardson*, 403 U. S. 365, 374. See Van Alstyne, The Demise of the Right-Privilege Distinction in Constitutional Law, 81 Harv. L. Rev. 1439 (1968). In *Hannegan* v. *Esquire, Inc.*, 327 U. S. 146, 156, we said that Congress may not by withdrawal of mailing privileges place limitations on freedom of speech which it could not do constitutionally if done directly. We said in *American Communications Assn.* v. *Douds*, 339 U. S. 382, 402, that freedom of speech was abridged when the only restraint on its exercise was withdrawal of the privilege to invoke the facilities of the National Labor Relations Board. In *Wieman* v. *Updegraff*, 344 U. S. 183, we held that an applicant could not be denied the opportunity

for public employment because he had exercised his
First Amendment rights. And in *Speiser* v. *Randall*, 357 U. S. 513, we held that a denial of a tax
exemption unless one gave up his First Amendment
rights was an abridgment of Fourteenth Amendment
rights.

As we held in *Speiser* v. *Randall, supra,* when a State
proposes to deny a privilege to one who it alleges has
engaged in unprotected speech, Due Process requires
that the State bear the burden of proving that the
speech was not protected. "[T]he 'protection of the individual against arbitrary action' . . . [is] the very
essence of due process," *Slochower* v. *Board of Education*, 350 U. S. 551, 559, but where the State is
allowed to act secretly behind closed doors and without
any notice to those who are affected by its actions, there
is no check against the possibility of such "arbitrary
action."

Moreover, where "important interests" of the citizen
are implicated (*Bell* v. *Burson*, 402 U. S. 535, 539) they
are not to be denied or taken away without due process.
Ibid. *Bell* v. *Burson* involved a driver's license.
But also included are disqualification for unemployment compensation (*Sherbert* v. *Verner*, 374 U. S.
398), discharge from public employment (*Slochower*
v. *Board of Education, supra*), denial of tax exemption (*Speiser* v. *Randall, supra*), and withdrawal of welfare benefits (*Goldberg* v. *Kelly*, 397 U. S. 254). And
see *Wisconsin* v. *Constantineau*, 400 U. S. 433. We
should now add that nonrenewal of a teacher's contract,
whether or not he has tenure, is an entitlement of the
same importance and dignity.

Cafeteria Workers v. *McElroy*, 367 U. S. 886, is not
opposed. It held that a cook employed in a cafeteria in
a military installation was not entitled to a hearing prior

to the withdrawal of her access to the facility. Her employer was prepared to employ her at another of its restaurants, the withdrawal was not likely to injure her reputation, and her employment opportunities elsewhere were not impaired. The Court held that the very limited individual interest in this one job did not outweigh the Government's authority over an important federal military establishment. Nonrenewal of a teacher's contract is tantamount in effect to a dismissal and the consequences may be enormous. Nonrenewal can be a blemish that turns into a permanent scar and effectively limits any chance the teacher has of being rehired as a teacher, at least in his State.

If this nonrenewal implicated the First Amendment, then Roth was deprived of constitutional rights because his employment was conditioned on a surrender of First Amendment rights; and, apart from the First Amendment, he was denied due process when he received no notice and hearing of the adverse action contemplated against him. Without a statement of the reasons for the discharge and an opportunity to rebut those reasons—both of which were refused by petitioners—there is no means short of a lawsuit to safeguard the right not to be discharged for the exercise of First Amendment guarantees.

The District Court held, 310 F. Supp., at 979–980:

"Substantive constitutional protection for a university professor against non-retention in violation of his First Amendment rights or arbitrary non-retention is useless without procedural safeguards. I hold that minimal procedural due process includes a statement of the reasons why the university intends not to retain the professor, notice of a hearing at which he may respond to the stated reasons, and a hearing if the professor appears at the appointed time and place. At such a hearing the professor must have a reasonable opportunity to submit evidence relevant to the stated reasons. The burden of going forward and the burden of proof rests with the professor. Only if he makes a reasonable showing that the stated reasons are wholly inappropriate as a basis for decision or that they are wholly without basis in fact would the university administration become obliged to show that the stated reasons are not inappropriate or that they have a basis in fact."

It was that procedure that the Court of Appeals approved. 446 F. 2d, at 809–810. The Court of Appeals also concluded that though the § 1983 action was pending in court, the court should stay its hand until the academic procedures had been completed.[2] As stated by the Court of Appeals in *Sindermann* v. *Perry*, 430 F. 2d 939 (CA5):

"School-constituted review bodies are the most appropriate forums for initially determining issues of this type, both for the convenience of the parties and in order to bring academic expertise to bear in resolving the nice issues of administrative discipline, teacher competence and school policy, which so frequently must be balanced in reaching a proper determination." *Id.*, at 944–945.

That is a permissible course for district courts to take, though it does not relieve them of the final determination

---

[2] Such a procedure would not be contrary to the well-settled rule that § 1983 actions do not require exhaustion of other remedies. See, *e. g., Wilwarding* v. *Swenson*, 404 U. S. 249 (1971); *Damico* v. *California*, 389 U. S. 416 (1967); *McNeese* v. *Board of Education*, 373 U. S. 668 (1963); *Monroe* v. *Pape*, 365 U. S. 167 (1961). One of the allegations in the complaint was that respondent was denied any effective state remedy, and the District Court's staying its hand thus furthered rather than thwarted the purposes of § 1983.

whether nonrenewal of the teacher's contract was in retaliation for the exercise of First Amendment rights or a
denial of due process.

Accordingly I would affirm the judgment of the Court
of Appeals.

MR. JUSTICE MARSHALL, dissenting.

Respondent was hired as an assistant professor of
political science at Wisconsin State University-Oshkosh
for the 1968–1969 academic year. During the course of
that year he was told that he would not be rehired for
the next academic term, but he was never told why.
In this case, he asserts that the Due Process Clause of
the Fourteenth Amendment to the United States Constitution entitled him to a statement of reasons and a
hearing on the University's decision not to rehire him
for another year.[1] This claim was sustained by the
District Court, which granted respondent summary judgment, 310 F. Supp. 972, and by the Court of Appeals
which affirmed the judgment of the District Court. 446
F. 2d 806. This Court today reverses the judgment of
the Court of Appeals and rejects respondent's claim.
I dissent.

While I agree with Part I of the Court's opinion, setting forth the proper framework for consideration of the
issue presented, and also with those portions of Parts
II and III of the Court's opinion that assert that a
public employee is entitled to procedural due process
whenever a State stigmatizes him by denying employment, or injures his future employment prospects severely, or whenever the State deprives him of a prop-

---

[1] Respondent has also alleged that the true reason for the decision
not to rehire him was to punish him for certain statements critical
of the University. As the Court points out, this issue is not before
us at the present time.

erty interest, I would go further than the Court does in defining the terms "liberty" and "property."

The prior decisions of this Court, discussed at length in the opinion of the Court, establish a principle that is as obvious as it is compelling—*i. e.*, federal and state governments and governmental agencies are restrained by the Constitution from acting arbitrarily with respect to employment opportunities that they either offer or control. Hence, it is now firmly established that whether or not a private employer is free to act capriciously or unreasonably with respect to employment practices, at least absent statutory [2] or contractual [3] controls, a government employer is different. The government may only act fairly and reasonably.

This Court has long maintained that "the right to work for a living in the common occupations of the community is of the very essence of the personal freedom and opportunity that it was the purpose of the [Fourteenth] Amendment to secure." *Truax* v. *Raich,* 239 U. S. 33, 41 (1915) (Hughes, J.). See also *Meyer* v. *Nebraska,* 262 U. S. 390, 399 (1923). It has also established that the fact that an employee has no contract guaranteeing work for a specific future period does not mean that as the result of action by the government he may be "discharged at any time for any reason or for no reason." *Truax* v. *Raich, supra,* at 38.

In my view, every citizen who applies for a government job is entitled to it unless the government can establish some reason for denying the employment. This is the "property" right that I believe is protected by the Fourteenth Amendment and that cannot be denied "without due process of law." And it is also liberty—

---

[2] See, *e. g., Griggs* v. *Duke Power Co.,* 401 U. S. 424 (1971); 42 U. S. C. § 2000e.

[3] Cf. Note, Procedural "Due Process" in Union Disciplinary Proceedings, 57 Yale L. J. 1302 (1948).

liberty to work—which is the "very essence of the personal freedom and opportunity" secured by the Fourteenth Amendment.

This Court has often had occasion to note that the denial of public employment is a serious blow to any citizen. See, *e. g., Joint Anti-Fascist Refugee Committee* v. *McGrath,* 341 U. S. 123, 185 (1951) (Jackson, J., concurring); *United States* v. *Lovett,* 328 U. S. 303, 316–317 (1946). Thus, when an application for public employment is denied or the contract of a government employee is not renewed, the government must say why, for it is only when the reasons underlying government action are known that citizens feel secure and protected against arbitrary government action.

Employment is one of the greatest, if not the greatest, benefits that governments offer in modern-day life. When something as valuable as the opportunity to work is at stake, the government may not reward some citizens and not others without demonstrating that its actions are fair and equitable. And it is procedural due process that is our fundamental guarantee of fairness, our protection against arbitrary, capricious, and unreasonable government action.

MR. JUSTICE DOUGLAS has written that:

> "It is not without significance that most of the provisions of the Bill of Rights are procedural. It is procedure that spells much of the difference between rule by law and rule by whim or caprice. Steadfast adherence to strict procedural safeguards is our main assurance that there will be equal justice under law." *Joint Anti-Fascist Refugee Committee* v. *McGrath, supra,* at 179 (concurring opinion).

And Mr. Justice Frankfurter has said that "[t]he history of American freedom is, in no small measure, the history of procedure." *Malinski* v. *New York,* 324 U. S. 401, 414 (1945) (separate opinion). With respect to occupations controlled by the government, one lower court has said that "[t]he public has the right to expect its officers . . . to make adjudications on the basis of merit. The first step toward insuring that these expectations are realized is to require adherence to the standards of due process; absolute and uncontrolled discretion invites abuse." *Hornsby* v. *Allen,* 326 F. 2d 605, 610 (CA5 1964).

We have often noted that procedural due process means many different things in the numerous contexts in which it applies. See, *e. g., Goldberg* v. *Kelly,* 397 U. S. 254 (1970); *Bell* v. *Burson,* 402 U. S. 535 (1971). Prior decisions have held that an applicant for admission to practice as an attorney before the United States Board of Tax Appeals may not be rejected without a statement of reasons and a chance for a hearing on disputed issues of fact; [4] that a tenured teacher could not be summarily dismissed without notice of the reasons and a hearing; [5] that an applicant for admission to a state bar could not be denied the opportunity to practice law without notice of the reasons for the rejection of his application and a hearing; [6] and even that a substitute teacher who had been employed only two months could not be dismissed merely because she refused to take a loyalty oath without an inquiry into the specific facts of her case and a hearing on those in dispute. [7] I would follow these cases and hold that respondent was denied due process when his contract was not renewed and he was not informed of the reasons and given an opportunity to respond.

---

[4] *Goldsmith* v. *Board of Tax Appeals,* 270 U. S. 117 (1926).

[5] *Slochower* v. *Board of Education,* 350 U. S. 551 (1956).

[6] *Willner* v. *Committee on Character,* 373 U. S. 96 (1963).

[7] *Connell* v. *Higginbotham,* 403 U. S. 207 (1971).

It may be argued that to provide procedural due process to all public employees or prospective employees would place an intolerable burden on the machinery of government. Cf. *Goldberg* v. *Kelly, supra.* The short answer to that argument is that it is not burdensome to give reasons when reasons exist. Whenever an application for employment is denied, an employee is discharged, or a decision not to rehire an employee is made, there should be some reason for the decision. It can scarcely be argued that government would be crippled by a requirement that the reason be communicated to the person most directly affected by the government's action.

Where there are numerous applicants for jobs, it is likely that few will choose to demand reasons for not being hired. But, if the demand for reasons is exceptionally great, summary procedures can be devised that would provide fair and adequate information to all persons. As long as the government has a good reason for its actions it need not fear disclosure. It is only where the government acts improperly that procedural due process is truly burdensome. And that is precisely when it is most necessary.

It might also be argued that to require a hearing and a statement of reasons is to require a useless act, because a government bent on denying employment to one or more persons will do so regardless of the procedural hurdles that are placed in its path. Perhaps this is so, but a requirement of procedural regularity at least renders arbitrary action more difficult. Moreover, proper procedures will surely eliminate some of the arbitrariness that results, not from malice, but from innocent error. "Experience teaches . . . that the affording of procedural safeguards, which by their nature serve to illuminate the underlying facts, in itself often operates to prevent erroneous decisions on the merits

from occurring." *Silver* v. *New York Stock Exchange,*
373 U. S. 341, 366 (1963). When the government knows
it may have to justify its decisions with sound reasons,
its conduct is likely to be more cautious, careful, and
correct.

Professor Gellhorn put the argument well:

> "In my judgment, there is no basic division of in-
> terest between the citizenry on the one hand and
> officialdom on the other. Both should be interested
> equally in the quest for procedural safeguards. I
> echo the late Justice JACKSON in saying: 'Let it
> not be overlooked that due process of law is not for
> the sole benefit of an accused. It is the best in-
> surance for the Government itself against those blun-
> ders which leave lasting stains on a system of
> justice'—blunders which are likely to occur when
> reasons need not be given and when the reasonable-
> ness and indeed legality of judgments need not
> be subjected to any appraisal other than one's
> own. . . ." Summary of Colloquy on Administra-
> tive Law, 6 J. Soc. Pub. Teachers of Law 70, 73
> (1961).

Accordingly, I dissent.

PERRY et al.
v.
SINDERMANN

PERRY ET AL. *v.* SINDERMANN

CERTIORARI TO THE UNITED STATES COURT OF APPEALS FOR
THE FIFTH CIRCUIT

No. 70–36. Argued January 18, 1972—Decided June 29, 1972

Respondent was employed in a state college system for 10 years, the last four as a junior college professor under a series of one-year written contracts. The Regents declined to renew his employment for the next year, without giving him an explanation or prior hearing. Respondent then brought this action in the District Court, alleging that the decision not to rehire him was based on respondent's public criticism of the college administration and thus infringed his free speech right, and that the Regents' failure to afford him a hearing violated his procedural due process right. The District Court granted summary judgment for petitioners, concluding that respondent's contract had terminated and the junior college had not adopted the tenure system. The Court of Appeals reversed on the grounds that, despite lack of tenure, nonrenewal of respondent's contract would violate the Fourteenth Amendment if it was in fact based on his protected free speech, and that if respondent could show that he had an "expectancy" of re-employment, the failure to allow him an opportunity for a hearing would violate the procedural due process guarantee. *Held:*

1. Lack of a contractual or tenure right to re-employment, taken alone, did not defeat respondent's claim that the nonrenewal of his contract violated his free speech right under the First and Fourteenth Amendments. The District Court therefore erred in foreclosing determination of the contested issue whether the decision not to renew was based on respondent's exercise of his right of free speech. Pp. 596–598.

2. Though a subjective "expectancy" of tenure is not protected by procedural due process, respondent's allegation that the college had a *de facto* tenure policy, arising from rules and understandings officially promulgated and fostered, entitled him to an opportunity of proving the legitimacy of his claim to job tenure. Such proof would obligate the college to afford him a requested hearing where he could be informed of the grounds for his nonretention and challenge their sufficiency. Pp. 599–603.

430 F. 2d 939, affirmed.

STEWART, J., delivered the opinion of the Court, in which BURGER, C. J., and WHITE, BLACKMUN, and REHNQUIST, JJ., joined. BURGER, C. J., filed a concurring opinion, *post*, p. 603. BRENNAN, J., filed an opinion dissenting in part, in which DOUGLAS, J., joined, *post*, p. 604. MARSHALL, J., filed an opinion dissenting in part, *post*, p. 605. POWELL, J., took no part in the decision of the case.

W. O. Shafer argued the cause for petitioners. With him on the brief was *Lucius D. Bunton.*

Michael H. Gottesman argued the cause for respondent. With him on the brief were *George H. Cohen* and *Warren Burnett.*

Briefs of *amici curiae* urging affirmance were filed by *David Rubin* and *Richard J. Medalie* for the National Education Association; by *John Ligtenberg* and *Andrew J. Leahy* for the American Federation of Teachers; and by *Herman I. Orentlicher* and *William W. Van Alstyne* for the American Association of University Professors.

MR. JUSTICE STEWART delivered the opinion of the Court.

From 1959 to 1969 the respondent, Robert Sindermann, was a teacher in the state college system of the State of Texas. After teaching for two years at the University of Texas and for four years at San Antonio Junior College, he became a professor of Government and Social Science at Odessa Junior College in 1965. He was employed at the college for four successive years, under a series of one-year contracts. He was successful enough to be appointed, for a time, the cochairman of his department.

During the 1968–1969 academic year, however, controversy arose between the respondent and the college administration. The respondent was elected president of the Texas Junior College Teachers Association. In this capacity, he left his teaching duties on several occasions to testify before committees of the Texas Legislature, and he became involved in public disagreements with the policies of the college's Board of Regents. In particular, he aligned himself with a group advocating the elevation of the college to four-year status—a change opposed by the Regents. And, on one occasion, a newspaper advertisement appeared over his name that was highly critical of the Regents.

Finally, in May 1969, the respondent's one-year employment contract terminated and the Board of Regents voted not to offer him a new contract for the next academic year. The Regents issued a press release setting forth allegations of the respondent's insubordination.[1] But they provided him no official statement of the reasons for the nonrenewal of his contract. And they allowed him no opportunity for a hearing to challenge the basis of the nonrenewal.

The respondent then brought this action in Federal District Court. He alleged primarily that the Regents' decision not to rehire him was based on his public criticism of the policies of the college administration and thus infringed his right to freedom of speech. He also alleged that their failure to provide him an opportunity for a hearing violated the Fourteenth Amendment's guarantee of procedural due process. The petitioners— members of the Board of Regents and the president of the college—denied that their decision was made in retaliation for the respondent's public criticism and argued that they had no obligation to provide a hearing.[2] On the basis of these bare pleadings and three

---

[1] The press release stated, for example, that the respondent had defied his superiors by attending legislative committee meetings when college officials had specifically refused to permit him to leave his classes for that purpose.

[2] The petitioners claimed, in their motion for summary judgment, that the decision not to retain the respondent was really based on his insubordinate conduct. See n. 1, *supra.*

brief affidavits filed by the respondent,[3] the District Court granted summary judgment for the petitioners. It concluded that the respondent had "no cause of action against the [petitioners] since his contract of employment terminated May 31, 1969, and Odessa Junior College has not adopted the tenure system."[4]

The Court of Appeals reversed the judgment of the District Court. 430 F. 2d 939. First, it held that, despite the respondent's lack of tenure, the nonrenewal of his contract would violate the Fourteenth Amendment if it in fact was based on his protected free speech. Since the actual reason for the Regents' decision was "in total dispute" in the pleadings, the court remanded the case for a full hearing on this contested issue of fact. *Id.*, at 942–943. Second, the Court of Appeals held that, despite the respondent's lack of tenure, the failure to allow him an opportunity for a hearing would violate the constitutional guarantee of procedural due process if the respondent could show that he had an "expectancy" of re-employment. It, therefore, ordered that this issue of fact also be aired upon remand. *Id.*, at 943–944. We granted a writ of certiorari, 403 U. S. 917, and we have considered this case along with *Board of Regents* v. *Roth, ante,* p. 564.

I

The first question presented is whether the respondent's lack of a contractual or tenure right to re-employment, taken alone, defeats his claim that the nonrenewal of his contract violated the First and Fourteenth Amendments. We hold that it does not.

---

[3] The petitioners, for whom summary judgment was granted, submitted no affidavits whatever. The respondent's affidavits were very short and essentially repeated the general allegations of his complaint.

[4] The findings and conclusions of the District Court—only several lines long—are not officially reported.

For at least a quarter-century, this Court has made clear that even though a person has no "right" to a valuable governmental benefit and even though the government may deny him the benefit for any number of reasons, there are some reasons upon which the government may not rely. It may not deny a benefit to a person on a basis that infringes his constitutionally protected interests—especially, his interest in freedom of speech. For if the government could deny a benefit to a person because of his constitutionally protected speech or associations, his exercise of those freedoms would in effect be penalized and inhibited. This would allow the government to "produce a result which [it] could not command directly." *Speiser* v. *Randall*, 357 U. S. 513, 526. Such interference with constitutional rights is impermissible.

We have applied this general principle to denials of tax exemptions, *Speiser* v. *Randall, supra,* unemployment benefits, *Sherbert* v. *Verner*, 374 U. S. 398, 404–405, and welfare payments, *Shapiro* v. *Thompson*, 394 U. S. 618, 627 n. 6; *Graham* v. *Richardson*, 403 U. S. 365, 374. But, most often, we have applied the principle to denials of public employment. *United Public Workers* v. *Mitchell*, 330 U. S. 75, 100; *Wieman* v. *Updegraff*, 344 U. S. 183, 192; *Shelton* v. *Tucker*, 364 U. S. 479, 485–486; *Torcaso* v. *Watkins*, 367 U. S. 488, 495–496; *Cafeteria Workers* v. *McElroy*, 367 U. S. 886, 894; *Cramp* v. *Board of Public Instruction*, 368 U. S. 278, 288; *Baggett* v. *Bullitt*, 377 U. S. 360; *Elfbrandt* v. *Russell*, 384 U. S. 11, 17; *Keyishian* v. *Board of Regents*, 385 U. S. 589, 605–606; *Whitehill* v. *Elkins*, 389 U. S. 54; *United States* v. *Robel*, 389 U. S. 258; *Pickering* v. *Board of Education*, 391 U. S. 563, 568. We have applied the principle regardless of the public employee's contractual or other claim to a job. Compare *Pickering* v. *Board of Education, supra,* with *Shelton* v. *Tucker, supra.*

Thus, the respondent's lack of a contractual or tenure

"right" to re-employment for the 1969–1970 academic year is immaterial to his free speech claim. Indeed, twice before, this Court has specifically held that the nonrenewal of a nontenured public school teacher's one-year contract may not be predicated on his exercise of First and Fourteenth Amendment rights. *Shelton* v. *Tucker, supra; Keyishian* v. *Board of Regents, supra.* We reaffirm those holdings here.

In this case, of course, the respondent has yet to show that the decision not to renew his contract was, in fact, made in retaliation for his exercise of the constitutional right of free speech. The District Court foreclosed any opportunity to make this showing when it granted summary judgment. Hence, we cannot now hold that the Board of Regents' action was invalid.

But we agree with the Court of Appeals that there is a genuine dispute as to "whether the college refused to renew the teaching contract on an impermissible basis—as a reprisal for the exercise of constitutionally protected rights." 430 F. 2d, at 943. The respondent has alleged that his nonretention was based on his testimony before legislative committees and his other public statements critical of the Regents' policies. And he has alleged that this public criticism was within the First and Fourteenth Amendments' protection of freedom of speech. Plainly, these allegations present a bona fide constitutional claim. For this Court has held that a teacher's public criticism of his superiors on matters of public concern may be constitutionally protected and may, therefore, be an impermissible basis for termination of his employment. *Pickering* v. *Board of Education, supra.*

For this reason we hold that the grant of summary judgment against the respondent, without full exploration of this issue, was improper.

II

The respondent's lack of formal contractual or tenure security in continued employment at Odessa Junior College, though irrelevant to his free speech claim, is highly relevant to his procedural due process claim. But it may not be entirely dispositive.

We have held today in *Board of Regents* v. *Roth, ante,* p. 564, that the Constitution does not require opportunity for a hearing before the nonrenewal of a nontenured teacher's contract, unless he can show that the decision not to rehire him somehow deprived him of an interest in "liberty" or that he had a "property" interest in continued employment, despite the lack of tenure or a formal contract. In *Roth* the teacher had not made a showing on either point to justify summary judgment in his favor.

Similarly, the respondent here has yet to show that he has been deprived of an interest that could invoke procedural due process protection. As in *Roth,* the mere showing that he was not rehired in one particular job, without more, did not amount to a showing of a loss of liberty.[5] Nor did it amount to a showing of a loss of property.

But the respondent's allegations—which we must construe most favorably to the respondent at this stage of the litigation—do raise a genuine issue as to his interest in continued employment at Odessa Junior College. He alleged that this interest, though not secured by a formal contractual tenure provision, was secured by a no less binding understanding fostered by the college administra-

---

[5] The Court of Appeals suggested that the respondent might have a due process right to some kind of hearing simply if he *asserts* to college officials that their decision was based on his constitutionally protected conduct. 430 F. 2d, at 944. We have rejected this approach in *Board of Regents* v. *Roth, ante,* at 575 n. 14.

tion.   In particular, the respondent alleged that the college had a *de facto* tenure program, and that he had tenure under that program.   He claimed that he and others legitimately relied upon an unusual provision that had been in the college's official Faculty Guide for many years:

> "*Teacher Tenure:* Odessa College has no tenure system.   The Administration of the College wishes the faculty member to feel that he has permanent tenure as long as his teaching services are satisfactory and as long as he displays a cooperative attitude toward his co-workers and his superiors, and as long as he is happy in his work."

Moreover, the respondent claimed legitimate reliance upon guidelines promulgated by the Coordinating Board of the Texas College and University System that provided that a person, like himself, who had been employed as a teacher in the state college and university system for seven years or more has some form of job tenure.[6]

---

[6] The relevant portion of the guidelines, adopted as "Policy Paper 1" by the Coordinating Board on October 16, 1967, reads:

"A. Tenure

"Tenure means assurance to an experienced faculty member that he may expect to continue in his academic position unless adequate cause for dismissal is demonstrated in a fair hearing, following established procedures of due process.

"A specific system of faculty tenure undergirds the integrity of each academic institution.   In the Texas public colleges and universities, this tenure system should have these components:

"(1) Beginning with appointment to the rank of full-time instructor or a higher rank, the probationary period for a faculty member shall not exceed seven years, including within this period appropriate full-time service in all institutions of higher education. This is subject to the provision that when, after a term of probationary service of more than three years in one or more institutions, a faculty member is employed by another institution, it may be agreed in writing that his new appointment is for a probationary period

Thus, the respondent offered to prove that a teacher with his long period of service at this particular State College had no less a "property" interest in continued employment than a formally tenured teacher at other colleges, and had no less a procedural due process right to a statement of reasons and a hearing before college officials upon their decision not to retain him.

We have made clear in *Roth, supra,* at 571–572, that "property" interests subject to procedural due process protection are not limited by a few rigid, technical forms. Rather, "property" denotes a broad range of interests that are secured by "existing rules or understandings." *Id.,* at 577. A person's interest in a benefit is a "property" interest for due process purposes if there are such rules or mutually explicit understandings that support his claim of entitlement to the benefit and that he may invoke at a hearing. *Ibid.*

A written contract with an explicit tenure provision clearly is evidence of a formal understanding that supports a teacher's claim of entitlement to continued employment unless sufficient "cause" is shown. Yet absence of such an explicit contractual provision may not always foreclose the possibility that a teacher has a "property" interest in re-employment. For example, the law of contracts in most, if not all, jurisdictions long has employed

---

of not more than four years (even though thereby the person's total probationary period in the academic profession is extended beyond the normal maximum of seven years).

.   .   .   .   .

"(3) Adequate cause for dismissal for a faculty member with tenure may be established by demonstrating professional incompetence, moral turpitude, or gross neglect of professional responsibilities."

The respondent alleges that, because he has been employed as a "full-time instructor" or professor within the Texas College and University System for 10 years, he should have "tenure" under these provisions.

a process by which agreements, though not formalized in writing, may be "implied." 3 A. Corbin on Contracts §§ 561–572A (1960). Explicit contractual provisions may be supplemented by other agreements implied from "the promisor's words and conduct in the light of the surrounding circumstances." *Id.*, at § 562. And, "[t]he meaning of [the promisor's] words and acts is found by relating them to the usage of the past." *Ibid.*

A teacher, like the respondent, who has held his position for a number of years, might be able to show from the circumstances of this service—and from other relevant facts—that he has a legitimate claim of entitlement to job tenure. Just as this Court has found there to be a "common law of a particular industry or of a particular plant" that may supplement a collective-bargaining agreement, *Steelworkers* v. *Warrior & Gulf Co.*, 363 U. S. 574, 579, so there may be an unwritten "common law" in a particular university that certain employees shall have the equivalent of tenure. This is particularly likely in a college or university, like Odessa Junior College, that has no explicit tenure system even for senior members of its faculty, but that nonetheless may have created such a system in practice. See C. Byse & L. Joughin, Tenure in American Higher Education 17–28 (1959).[7]

In this case, the respondent has alleged the existence of rules and understandings, promulgated and fostered by state officials, that may justify his legitimate claim of entitlement to continued employment absent "suf-

---

[7] We do not now hold that the respondent has any such legitimate claim of entitlement to job tenure. For "[p]roperty interests . . . are not created by the Constitution. Rather, they are created and their dimensions are defined by existing rules or understandings that stem from an independent source such as state law . . . ." *Board of Regents* v. *Roth, supra*, at 577. If it is the law of Texas that a teacher in the respondent's position has no contractual or other claim to job tenure, the respondent's claim would be defeated.

ficient cause." We disagree with the Court of Appeals insofar as it held that a mere subjective "expectancy" is protected by procedural due process, but we agree that the respondent must be given an opportunity to prove the legitimacy of his claim of such entitlement in light of "the policies and practices of the institution." 430 F. 2d, at 943. Proof of such a property interest would not, of course, entitle him to reinstatement. But such proof would obligate college officials to grant a hearing at his request, where he could be informed of the grounds for his nonretention and challenge their sufficiency.

Therefore, while we do not wholly agree with the opinion of the Court of Appeals, its judgment remanding this case to the District Court is

Affirmed.

MR. JUSTICE POWELL took no part in the decision of this case.

MR. CHIEF JUSTICE BURGER, concurring.*

I concur in the Court's judgments and opinions in *Sindermann* and *Roth,* but there is one central point in both decisions that I would like to underscore since it may have been obscured in the comprehensive discussion of the cases. That point is that the relationship between a state institution and one of its teachers is essentially a matter of state concern and state law. The Court holds today only that a state-employed teacher who has a right to re-employment under state law, arising from either an express or implied contract, has, in turn, a right guaranteed by the Fourteenth Amendment to some form of prior administrative or academic hearing on the cause

---

*This opinion applies also to No. 71–162, *Board of Regents of State Colleges et al.* v. *Roth, ante,* p. 564.

for nonrenewal of his contract. Thus, whether a particular teacher in a particular context has any right to such administrative hearing hinges on a question of state law. The Court's opinion makes this point very sharply:

> "Property interests . . . are created and their dimensions are defined by existing rules or understandings that stem from an independent source such as state law . . . ." *Board of Regents* v. *Roth, ante,* at 577.

Because the availability of the Fourteenth Amendment right to a prior administrative hearing turns in each case on a question of state law, the issue of abstention will arise in future cases contesting whether a particular teacher is entitled to a hearing prior to nonrenewal of his contract. If relevant state contract law is unclear, a federal court should, in my view, abstain from deciding whether he is constitutionally entitled to a prior hearing, and the teacher should be left to resort to state courts on the questions arising under state law.

MR. JUSTICE BRENNAN, with whom MR. JUSTICE DOUGLAS joins, dissenting in No. 71–162, *ante,* p. 564, and dissenting in part in No. 70–36.

Although I agree with Part I of the Court's opinion in No. 70–36, I also agree with my Brother MARSHALL that "respondent[s] [were] denied due process when [their] contract[s] [were] not renewed and [they were] not informed of the reasons and given an opportunity to respond." *Ante,* at 590. Since respondents were entitled to summary judgment on that issue, I would affirm the judgment of the Court of Appeals in No. 71–162, and, to the extent indicated by my Brother MARSHALL, I would modify the judgment of the Court of Appeals in No. 70–36.

MR. JUSTICE MARSHALL, dissenting in part.

Respondent was a teacher in the state college system of the State of Texas for a decade before the Board of Regents of Odessa Junior College decided not to renew his contract. He brought this suit in Federal District Court claiming that the decision not to rehire him was in retaliation for his public criticism of the policies of the college administration in violation of the First Amendment, and that because the decision was made without giving him a statement of reasons and a hearing, it denied him the due process of law guaranteed by the Fourteenth Amendment. The District Court granted summary judgment for petitioners, but the Court of Appeals reversed and remanded the case for further proceedings. This Court affirms the judgment of the Court of Appeals.

I agree with Part I of the Court's opinion holding that respondent has presented a bona fide First Amendment claim that should be considered fully by the District Court. But, for the reasons stated in my dissenting opinion in *Board of Regents* v. *Roth,* No. 71–162, *ante,* p. 587, I would modify the judgment of the Court of Appeals to direct the District Court to enter summary judgment for respondent entitling him to a statement of reasons why his contract was not renewed and a hearing on disputed issues of fact.

ARNETT, DIRECTOR, OFFICE
OF ECONOMIC OPPORTUNITY, et al.
v. KENNEDY et al.

ARNETT, DIRECTOR, OFFICE OF ECONOMIC OPPORTUNITY, ET AL. *v.* KENNEDY ET AL.

APPEAL FROM THE UNITED STATES DISTRICT COURT FOR THE NORTHERN DISTRICT OF ILLINOIS

No. 72–1118.   Argued November 7, 1973—Decided April 16, 1974

Appellee, a nonprobationary employee in the competitive Civil Service, was dismissed from his position in the Office of Economic Opportunity (OEO) for allegedly having made recklessly false and defamatory statements about other OEO employees. Though previously advised of his right under OEO and Civil Service Commission (CSC) regulations to reply to the charges and that the material on which the dismissal notice was based was available for his inspection, he did not respond to the substance of the charges but brought this suit for injunctive and declaratory relief, contending that the standards and procedures established by and under the Lloyd-La Follette Act, 5 U. S. C. § 7501, for the removal of nonprobationary employees from the federal service unwarrantedly interfere with such employees' freedom of expression and deny them procedural due process. A three-judge District Court held that the Act and attendant regulations denied appellee due process because they failed to provide for a trial-type preremoval hearing before an impartial official and were unconstitutionally vague because they failed to furnish sufficiently precise guidelines as to what kind of speech might be made the basis for removal action. Section 7501 of the Act provides for removal of nonprobationary federal employees "only for such cause as will promote the efficiency of the service" and prescribes that the employing agency must furnish the employee with written notice of the proposed removal action and a copy of the charges; give him a reasonable time for a written answer and supporting affidavits; and promptly furnish him with the agency's decision. The Act further provides, however, that "[e]xamination of witnesses, trial, or hearing is not required," but is discretionary with the individual directing the removal. CSC and OEO regulations enlarge the statutory provisions by requiring 30 days' advance notice before removal and in other respects, and entitle the employee to a post-removal evidentiary trial-type hearing at the appeal stage. If the employee is reinstated on appeal, he receives full backpay. In addi-

tion to his First Amendment claims, appellee contends that, absent
a full adversary hearing before removal, he could not consistently
with due process requirements be divested of his property interest
or expectancy in employment or be deprived of his "liberty" to
refute the charges of dishonesty on which he asserts his dismissal
was based. *Held:* The judgment is reversed and the case remanded.
Pp. 148–171.

349 F. Supp. 863, reversed and remanded.

MR. JUSTICE REHNQUIST, joined by THE CHIEF JUSTICE and
MR. JUSTICE STEWART, concluded that:

1. In conferring upon nonprobationary federal employees the
right not to be discharged except for "cause" and at the same
time conditioning the grant of that right by procedural limitations,
the Act did not create and the Due Process Clause does not
require any additional expectancy of job retention. Cf. *Board of
Regents* v. *Roth*, 408 U. S. 564, 577. Pp. 148–155.

2. The CSC and OEO post-termination hearing procedures adequately protect the liberty interest of federal employees, recognized
in *Roth, supra,* in not being wrongfully stigmatized by untrue
and unsupported administrative charges. Pp. 156–158.

3. The Act's standard of employment protection, which describes
as explicitly as is feasible in view of the wide variety of factual
situations where employees' statements might justify dismissal for
"cause" the conduct that is ground for removal, is not impermissibly vague or overbroad in regulating federal employees'
speech. *CSC* v. *Letter Carriers*, 413 U. S. 548, 578–579. Pp.
158–163.

MR. JUSTICE POWELL, joined by MR. JUSTICE BLACKMUN, while
agreeing that 5 U. S. C. § 7501 (a) is not unconstitutionally vague
or overbroad, concluded with respect to the due process issue that
appellee, as a nonprobationary federal employee who could be
discharged only for "cause," had a legitimate claim of entitlement
to a property interest under the Fifth Amendment and his employment could not be terminated without notice and a full
evidentiary hearing. On the other hand, the Government as an
employer must have discretion expeditiously to remove employees
who hinder efficient operation. Since the procedures under the
Act and regulations minimize the risk of error in the initial
removal decision and provide for a post-removal evidentiary hearing with reinstatement and backpay should that decision be
wrongful, a reasonable accommodation comporting with due proc-

ess is provided between the competing interests of the employee
and the Government as employer. Pp. 164–171.

Rehnquist, J., announced the Court's judgment and delivered
an opinion, in which Burger, C. J., and Stewart, J., joined.
Powell, J., filed an opinion concurring in part and concurring in
the result in part, in which Blackmun, J., joined, *post,* p. 164.
White, J., filed an opinion concurring in part and dissenting in part,
post, p. 171. Douglas, J., filed a dissenting opinion, *post,* p. 203.
Marshall, J., filed a dissenting opinion, in which Douglas and
Brennan, JJ., joined, *post,* p. 206.

Daniel M. Friedman argued the cause for appellants.
On the brief were *Solicitor General Bork, Assistant Attorney General Wood, Keith A. Jones, Walter H. Fleischer,* and *William Kanter.*

Charles Barnhill, Jr., argued the cause for appellees.
With him on the brief were *Judson H. Miner* and *Leo
Pellerzi.**

Mr. Justice Rehnquist announced the judgment of
the Court in an opinion in which The Chief Justice and
Mr. Justice Stewart join.

Prior to the events leading to his discharge, appellee
Wayne Kennedy [1] was a nonprobationary federal em-

Mozart G. Ratner and *Jerry D. Anker* filed a brief for the National Association of Letter Carriers, AFL–CIO, et al. as *amici
curiae* urging affirmance.

[1] "Appellee" refers to appellee Wayne Kennedy, the named
plaintiff in the original complaint. The participation of the 18
other named plaintiffs, who were added in the amended complaint,
see n. 3, *infra,* appears to have been little more than nominal. The
amended complaint alleged that the added named plaintiffs' exercise
of their rights of free speech were chilled because they feared that
any off-duty public comments made by them would constitute
grounds for discharge or punishment under the Lloyd-La Follette
Act. Two conclusory affidavits supporting that bare allegation (one
signed by one of the added named plaintiffs, the other by the

ployee in the competitive Civil Service. He was a field
representative in the Chicago Regional Office of the
Office of Economic Opportunity (OEO). In March
1972, he was removed from the federal service pursuant
to the provisions of the Lloyd-La Follette Act, 5 U. S. C.
§ 7501, after Wendell Verduin, the Regional Director of
the OEO, upheld written administrative charges made in
the form of a "Notification of Proposed Adverse Action"
against appellee. The charges listed five events occurring
in November and December 1971; the most serious of
the charges was that appellee "without any proof whatsoever and in reckless disregard of the actual facts"
known to him or reasonably discoverable by him had
publicly stated that Verduin and his administrative
assistant had attempted to bribe a representative of a
community action organization with which the OEO had
dealings. The alleged bribe consisted of an offer of a
$100,000 grant of OEO funds if the representative
would sign a statement against appellee and another
OEO employee.

Appellee was advised of his right under regulations
promulgated by the Civil Service Commission and the
OEO to reply to the charges orally and in writing, and
to submit affidavits to Verduin. He was also advised
that the material on which the notice was based was
available for his inspection in the Regional Office, and
that a copy of the material was attached to the notice of
proposed adverse action.

Appellee did not respond to the substance of the
charges against him, but instead asserted that the charges
were unlawful because he had a right to a trial-type hearing before an impartial hearing officer before he could
be removed from his employment, and because state-

---

remaining 17) were filed in connection with plaintiffs' motion for
summary judgment or temporary injunctive relief.

ments made by him were protected by the First Amendment to the United States Constitution.[2]   On March 20, 1972, Verduin notified appellee in writing that he would be removed from his position at the close of business on March 27, 1972.   Appellee was also notified of his right to appeal Verduin's decision either to the OEO or to the Civil Service Commission.

Appellee then instituted this suit in the United States District Court for the Northern District of Illinois on behalf of himself and others similarly situated, seeking both injunctive and declaratory relief.   In his amended complaint,[3] appellee contended that the standards and procedures established by and under the Lloyd-La Follette Act for the removal of nonprobationary em-

---

[2] Appellee's response to the "Notification of Proposed Adverse Action," made through counsel, set forth briefly his position that the charges against him were unlawful under the Fifth and First Amendments.   One of the three sentences devoted to his First Amendment claim noted parenthetically that the "conversations . . . with union members and the public" for which he was being punished were "inaccurately set forth in the adverse action."   Appellee's response did not explain in what respects the charges against him were inaccurate, nor did it offer any alternative version of the events described in the charges.

[3] Appellee's original complaint, filed March 27, 1972, contained two counts.   In the first count appellee sought, on behalf of himself and others similarly situated, to enjoin his removal pending a full, trial-type hearing before an impartial hearing officer.   In the second count appellee sought to enjoin his removal for the exercise of his rights of free speech.   The single-judge court referred the constitutional question presented in the first count to a three-judge court, and dismissed the second count pending appellee's exhaustion of available administrative remedies before the Civil Service Commission.   Appellee then amended the second count of his complaint to allege, on behalf of himself, 18 added named plaintiffs, see n. 1, supra, and others similarly situated, that the Lloyd-La Follette Act's removal standard was unconstitutionally vague and overbroad and violated the plaintiffs' First Amendment rights.

ployees from the federal service unwarrantedly interfere with those employees' freedom of expression and deny them procedural due process of law. The three-judge District Court, convened pursuant to 28 U. S. C. §§ 2282 and 2284, granted summary judgment for appellee. 349 F. Supp. 863. The court held that the discharge procedures authorized by the Act and attendant Civil Service Commission and OEO regulations denied appellee due process of law because they failed to provide for a trial-type hearing before an impartial agency official prior to removal; the court also held the Act and implementing regulations unconstitutionally vague because they failed to furnish sufficiently precise guidelines as to what kind of speech may be made the basis of a removal action. The court ordered that appellee be reinstated in his former position with backpay, and that he be accorded a hearing prior to removal in any future removal proceedings. Appellants were also enjoined from further enforcement of the Lloyd-La Follette Act, and implementing rules, as "construed to regulate the speech of competitive service employees." [4]

I

The numerous affidavits submitted to the District Court by both parties not unexpectedly portray two widely differing versions of the facts which gave rise to this lawsuit. Since the District Court granted summary judgment to appellee, it was required to resolve all genuine disputes as to any material facts in favor of appellants, and we therefore take as true for purposes

---

[4] The court ordered appellee's reinstatement but deferred determination whether the suit was maintainable as a class action. Appellee's appeal to the Civil Service Commission was first delayed as a result of the pendency of this suit, then "terminated" because of appellee's reinstatement following the decision of the District Court.

of this opinion the material particulars of appellee's conduct which were set forth in the notification of proposed adverse action dated February 18, 1972. The District Court's holding necessarily embodies the legal conclusions that, even though all of these factual statements were true, the procedure which the Government proposed to follow in this case was constitutionally insufficient to accomplish appellee's discharge, and the standard by which his conduct was to be judged in the course of those procedures infringed his right of free speech protected by the First Amendment.

The statutory provisions which the District Court held invalid are found in 5 U. S. C. § 7501. Subsection (a) of that section provides that "[a]n individual in the competitive service may be removed or suspended without pay only for such cause as will promote the efficiency of the service."

Subsection (b) establishes the administrative procedures by which an employee's rights under subsection (a) are to be determined, providing:

"(b) An individual in the competitive service whose removal or suspension without pay is sought is entitled to reasons in writing and to—

"(1) notice of the action sought and of any charges preferred against him;

"(2) a copy of the charges;

"(3) a reasonable time for filing a written answer to the charges, with affidavits; and

"(4) a written decision on the answer at the earliest practicable date.

"Examination of witnesses, trial, or hearing is not required but may be provided in the discretion of the individual directing the removal or suspension without pay. Copies of the charges, the notice of hearing, the answer, the reasons for and the order of removal or suspension without pay, and also the reasons for reduction in grade or pay, shall be made a part of the records of the employing agency, and, on request, shall be furnished to the individual affected and to the Civil Service Commission."

This codification of the Lloyd-La Follette Act is now supplemented by the regulations of the Civil Service Commission, and, with respect to the OEO, by the regulations and instructions of that agency. Both the Commission and the OEO have by regulation given further specific content to the general removal standard in subsection (a) of the Act. The regulations of the Commission [5] and the OEO,[6] in nearly identical language, re-

---

[5] 5 CFR §§ 735.201a, 735.209. Section 735.201a provides:

"An employee shall avoid any action, whether or not specifically prohibited by this subpart, which might result in, or create the appearance of:

"(a) Using public office for private gain;

"(b) Giving preferential treatment to any person;

"(c) Impeding Government efficiency or economy;

"(d) Losing complete independence or impartiality;

"(e) Making a Government decision outside official channels; or

"(f) Affecting adversely the confidence of the public in the integrity of the Government."

Section 735.209 provides:

"An employee shall not engage in criminal, infamous, dishonest, immoral, or notoriously disgraceful conduct, or other conduct prejudicial to the Government."

[6] 45 CFR §§ 1015.735–1, 1015.735–24. Section 1015.735–1 provides:

"The purpose of this part is to guide OEO employees toward maintaining the high standard of integrity expected of all Government employees. It is intended to require that employees avoid any action which might result in, or create the appearance of:

"(a) Using public office for private gain;

"(b) Giving preferential treatment to any organization or person;

"(c) Impeding Government efficiency or economy;

"(d) Making a Government decision outside official channels;

"(e) Losing complete independence or impartiality of action; or

quire that employees "avoid any action . . . which might result in, or create the appearance of . . . [a]ffecting adversely the confidence of the public in the integrity of [OEO and] the Government," and that employees not "engage in criminal, infamous, dishonest, immoral, or notoriously disgraceful or other conduct prejudicial to the Government." The OEO further provides by regulation that its Office of General Counsel is available to supply counseling on the interpretation of the laws and regulations relevant to the conduct of OEO employees.[7]

Both the Commission and the OEO also follow regulations enlarging the procedural protections accorded by the Act itself.[8] The Commission's regulations provide,

_____

"(f) Affecting adversely the confidence of the public in the integrity of OEO and the Government."

Section 1015.735–24 provides:

"No employee shall engage in criminal, infamous, dishonest, immoral, or notoriously disgraceful conduct or other conduct prejudicial to the Government."

[7] 45 CFR § 1015.735–4. Section 1015.735–4 provides:

"The Office of General Counsel of OEO is available to advise on the interpretation of the provisions of this part and the other laws and regulations relevant to the conduct of OEO employees. The General Counsel is designated as OEO counselor for this purpose."

[8] The Civil Service Commission regulations governing procedures for adverse actions implement, in addition to the Lloyd-La Follette Act, the Veterans' Preference Act of 1944 and Executive Order No. 11491. The Veterans' Preference Act, Act of June 27, 1944, c. 287, 58 Stat. 387, imposed procedural requirements for processing adverse actions in addition to those imposed by the Lloyd-La Follette Act. Those additional requirements include an opportunity for the employee to respond orally or in writing to the charges on which his dismissal is based; the Veterans' Preference Act also authorizes Civil Service Commission appeals from adverse agency decisions. See 5 U. S. C. § 7701. The Act itself applies only to veterans of military service, 5 U. S. C. §§ 2108, 7511, but Executive Order No. 11491, printed in note following 5 U. S. C. § 7301, extends the Act's protections to all nonpreference eligible employees in the classified service.

inter alia, that the employing agency must give 30 days' advance written notice to the employee prior to removal, and make available to him the material on which the notice is based.[9] They also provide that the employee shall have an opportunity to appear before the official vested with authority to make the removal decision in order to answer the charges against him,[10]

---

[9] 5 CFR § 752.202 (a). Section 752.202 (a) provides:

"(a) *Notice of proposed adverse action.* (1) Except as provided in paragraph (c) of this section, an employee against whom adverse action is sought is entitled to at least 30 full days' advance written notice stating any and all reasons, specifically and in detail, for the proposed action.

"(2) Subject to the provisions of subparagraph (3) of this paragraph, the material on which the notice is based and which is relied on to support the reasons in that notice, including statements of witnesses, documents, and investigative reports or extracts therefrom, shall be assembled and made available to the employee for his review. The notice shall inform the employee where he may review that material.

"(3) Material which cannot be disclosed to the employee, or to his designated physician under § 294.401 of this chapter, may not be used by an agency to support the reasons in the notice."

[10] 5 CFR § 752.202 (b). Section 752.202 (b) provides:

"(b) *Employee's answer.* Except as provided in paragraph (c) of this section, an employee is entitled to a reasonable time for answering a notice of proposed adverse action and for furnishing affidavits in support of his answer. The time to be allowed depends on the facts and circumstances of the case, and shall be sufficient to afford the employee ample opportunity to review the material relied on by the agency to support the reasons in the notice and to prepare an answer and secure affidavits. The agency shall provide the employee a reasonable amount of official time for these purposes if he is otherwise in an active duty status. If the employee answers, the agency shall consider his answer in reaching its decision. The employee is entitled to answer personally, or in writing, or both personally and in writing. The right to answer personally includes the right to answer orally in person by being given a reasonable opportunity to make any representations which the employee believes might sway the final decision on his case, but does

that the employee must receive notice of an adverse decision on or before its effective date, and that the employee may appeal from an adverse decision.[11] This appeal may be either to a reviewing authority within the employing agency,[12] or directly to the Commis-

not include the right to a trial or formal hearing with examination of witnesses. When the employee requests an opportunity to answer personally, the agency shall make a representative or representatives available to hear his answer. The representative or representatives designated to hear the answer shall be persons who have authority either to make a final decision on the proposed adverse action or to recommend what final decision should be made."

[11] 5 CFR § 752.202 (f). Section 752.202 (f) provides:

"(f) *Notice of adverse decision.* The employee is entitled to notice of the agency's decision at the earliest practicable date. The agency shall deliver the notice of decision to the employee at or before the time the action will be made effective. The notice shall be in writing, be dated, and inform the employee:

"(1) Which of the reasons in the notice of proposed adverse action have been found sustained and which have been found not sustained;

"(2) Of his right of appeal to the appropriate office of the Commission;

"(3) Of any right of appeal to the agency under Subpart B of Part 771 of this chapter, including the person with whom, or the office with which, such an appeal shall be filed;

"(4) Of the time limit for appealing as provided in § 752.204;

"(5) Of the restrictions on the use of appeal rights as provided in § 752.205; and

"(6) Where he may obtain information on how to pursue an appeal."

[12] 5 CFR §§ 771.205, 771.208. Section 771.205 provides:

"An employee is entitled to appeal under the agency appeals system from the original decision. The agency shall accept and process a properly filed appeal in accordance with its appeals system."

Section 771.208 provides:

"(a) *Entitlement.* Except as provided in paragraph (b) of this section, an employee is entitled to a hearing on his appeal before an examiner. The employee is entitled to appear at the hearing personally or through or accompanied by his representative. The

sion,[13] and the employee is entitled to an evidentiary trial-type hearing at the appeal stage of the proceeding.[14] The only trial-type hearing available within the OEO is, by

hearing may precede either the original decision or the appellate decision, at the agency's option. Only one hearing shall be held unless the agency determines that unusual circumstances require a second hearing.

"(b) *Denial of hearing.* The agency may deny an employee a hearing on his appeal only (1) when a hearing is impracticable by reason of unusual location or other extraordinary circumstance, or (2) when the employee failed to request a hearing offered before the original decision.

"(c) *Notice.* The agency shall notify an employee in writing before the original decision or before the appellate decision of (1) his right to a hearing, or (2) the reasons for the denial of a hearing."

[13] 5 CFR § 752.203. Section 752.203 provides:

"An employee is entitled to appeal to the Commission from an adverse action covered by this subpart. The appeal shall be in writing and shall set forth the employee's reasons for contesting the adverse action, with such offer of proof and pertinent documents as he is able to submit."

Appeals to both the discharging agency and the Commission from an original adverse action will not be processed concurrently, 5 CFR § 752.205 (a), and a direct appeal to the Commission from an initial removal decision constitutes a waiver of appeal rights within the employing agency. 5 CFR § 752.205 (b). However, if the employee first appeals within the employing agency, he is entitled, if necessary, to an appeal to the Commission. 5 CFR § 752.205 (c).

[14] 5 CFR §§ 771.208, 771.210–771.212, 772.305 (c). Sections 771.210–771.212 govern the conduct of hearings by the discharging agency. Those sections provide:

"§ 771.210   Conduct of hearing.

"(a) The hearing is not open to the public or the press. Except as provided in paragraph (h) of this section, attendance at a hearing is limited to persons determined by the examiner to have a direct connection with the appeal.

"(b) The hearing is conducted so as to bring out pertinent facts, including the production of pertinent records.

[*Footnote 14 is continued on p. 146*]

virtue of its regulations and practice, typically held after actual removal;[15] but if the employee is reinstated on appeal, he receives full backpay, less any amounts earned by him through other employment during that period.[16]

"(c) Rules of evidence are not applied strictly, but the examiner shall exclude irrelevant or unduly repetitious testimony.

"(d) Decisions on the admissibility of evidence or testimony are made by the examiner.

"(e) Testimony is under oath or affirmation.

"(f) The examiner shall give the parties opportunity to cross-examine witnesses who appear and testify.

"(g) The examiner may exclude any person from the hearing for contumacious conduct or misbehavior that obstructs the hearing.

"(h) An agency may provide through a negotiated agreement with a labor organization holding exclusive recognition for the attendance at hearings under this subpart of an observer from that organization. When attendance is provided for, the agreement shall further provide that when the employee who requested the hearing objects to the attendance of an observer on grounds of privacy, the examiner shall determine the validity of the objection and make the decision on the question of attendance.

"§ 771.211 Witnesses.

"(a) Both parties are entitled to produce witnesses.

"(b) The agency shall make its employees available as witnesses before an examiner when requested by the examiner after consideration of a request by the employee or the agency.

"(c) If the agency determines that it is not administratively practicable to comply with the request of the examiner, it shall notify him in writing of the reasons for that determination. If, in the examiner's judgment, compliance with his request is essential to a full and fair hearing, he may postpone the hearing until such time as the agency complies with his request.

"(d) Employees of the agency are in a duty status during the time they are made available as witnesses.

"(e) The agency shall assure witnesses freedom from restraint, interference, coercion, discrimination, or reprisal in presenting their testimony.

"§ 771.212 Record of hearing.

"(a) The hearing shall be recorded and transcribed verbatim. All

[Footnotes 15 and 16 are on p. 148]

We must first decide whether these procedures established for the purpose of determining whether there is
"cause" under the Lloyd-La Follette Act for the dismissal

---

documents submitted to and accepted by the examiner at the hearing shall be made a part of the record of the hearing. If the
agency submits a document that is accepted, it shall furnish a copy
of the document to the employee. If the employee submits a
document that is accepted, he shall make the document available
to the agency representative for reproduction.

"(b) The employee is entitled to be furnished a copy of the
hearing record at or before the time he is furnished a copy of the
report of the examiner."

Section 772.305 (c) governs the conduct of hearings before
the Civil Service Commission. It provides:

"(c) *Hearing procedures.* (1) An appellant is entitled to appear
at the hearing on his appeal personally or through or accompanied
by his representative. The agency is also entitled to participate
in the hearing. Both parties are entitled to produce witnesses.
The Commission is not authorized to subpoena witnesses.

"(2) An agency shall make its employees available as witnesses at
the hearing when (i) requested by the Commission after consideration of a request by the appellant or the agency and (ii) it is
administratively practicable to comply with the request of the
Commission. If the agency determines that it is not administratively practicable to comply with the request of the Commission,
it shall submit to the Commission its written reasons for the
declination. Employees of the agency shall be in a duty status
during the time they are made available as witnesses. Employees
of the agency shall be free from restraint, interference, coercion,
discrimination, or reprisal in presenting their testimony.

"(3) Hearings are not open to the public or the press. Attendance at hearings is limited to persons determined by the Commission
to have a direct connection with the appeal.

"(4) A representative of the Commission shall conduct the hearing and shall afford the parties opportunity to introduce evidence
(including testimony and statements by the appellant, his representative, representatives of the agency, and witnesses), and to
cross-examine witnesses. Testimony is under oath or affirmation.
Rules of evidence are not applied strictly, but the representative

of a federal employee comport with procedural due
process, and then decide whether that standard of
"cause" for federal employee dismissals was within the
constitutional power of Congress to adopt.

II

For almost the first century of our national existence,
federal employment was regarded as an item of patron-
age, which could be granted, withheld, or withdrawn for
whatever reasons might appeal to the responsible executive hiring officer. Following the Civil War, grass-roots
sentiment for "Civil Service reform" began to grow, and
it was apparently brought to a head by the assassination
of President James A. Garfield on July 2, 1881. Garfield,
having then held office only four months, was accosted
in Washington's Union Station and shot by a dissatis-
fied office seeker who believed that the President had
been instrumental in refusing his request for appointment as United States Consul in Paris. During the

---

of the Commission shall exclude irrelevant or unduly repetitious
testimony.

"(5) The office of the Commission having initial jurisdiction of
the appeal shall determine how the hearing will be reported. When
the hearing is reported verbatim, that office shall make the transcript
a part of the record of the proceedings and shall furnish a copy
of the transcript to each party. When the hearing is not reported
verbatim, the representative of the Commission who conducts the
hearing shall make a suitable summary of the pertinent portions
of the testimony. When agreed to in writing by the parties, the
summary constitutes the report of the hearing and is made a part
of the record of the proceedings. Each party is entitled to be
furnished a copy of the report of the hearing. If the representative
of the Commission and the parties fail to agree on the summary,
the parties are entitled to submit written exceptions to any parts
of the summary which are made a part of the record of the
proceedings for consideration in deciding the appeal."

[15] OEO Staff Instruction No. 771–2 (1971).

[16] 5 U. S. C. § 5596.

summer, while President Garfield lingered prior to his death in September, delegates from 13 Civil Service reform associations met and formed the National Civil Service Reform League. Responding to public demand for reform led by this organization, Congress in January 1883 enacted the Pendleton Act.[17]

While the Pendleton Act is regarded as the keystone in the present arch of Civil Service legislation, by present-day standards it was quite limited in its application. It dealt almost exclusively with entry into the federal service, and hardly at all with tenure, promotion, removal, veterans' preference, pensions, and other subjects addressed by subsequent Civil Service legislation. The Pendleton Act provided for the creation of a classified Civil Service, and required competitive examination for entry into that service. Its only provision with respect to separation was to prohibit removal for the failure of an employee in the classified service to contribute to a political fund or to render any political service.[18]

For 16 years following the effective date of the Pendleton Act, this last-mentioned provision of that Act appears to have been the only statutory or regulatory limitation on the right of the Government to discharge classified employees. In 1897, President William McKinley promulgated Civil Service Rule II,[19] which provided that removal from the competitive classified service should not be made except for just cause and for

----

[17] Act of Jan. 16, 1883, c. 27, 22 Stat. 403.

[18] Id., § 2.

[19] Fifteenth Report of the Civil Service Commission 70 (1897-1898). Rule II, § 8, provided: "No removal shall be made from any position subject to competitive examination except for just cause and upon written charges filed with the head of the Department or other appointing officer, and of which the accused shall have full notice and an opportunity to make defense."

reasons given in writing. While job tenure was thereby accorded protection, there were no administrative appeal rights for action taken in violation of this rule, and the courts declined to judicially enforce it. Thus matters stood with respect to governmental authority to remove federal employees until the enactment of the Lloyd-La Follette Act.

The Lloyd-La Follette Act was enacted as one section of the Post Office Department appropriation bill for the fiscal year 1913. That Act guaranteed the right of federal employees to communicate with members of Congress, and to join employee organizations. It also substantially enacted and enlarged upon Civil Service Rule II in the following language:

> "[N]o person in the classified civil service of the United States shall be removed therefrom except for such cause as will promote the efficiency of said service and for reasons given in writing, and the person whose removal is sought shall have notice of the same and of any charges preferred against him, and be furnished with a copy thereof, and also be allowed a reasonable time for personally answering the same in writing; and affidavits in support thereof; but no examination of witnesses nor any trial or hearing shall be required except in the discretion of the officer making the removal; and copies of charges, notice of hearing, answer, reasons for removal, and of the order of removal shall be made a part of the records of the proper department or office, as shall also the reasons for reduction in rank or compensation; and copies of the same shall be furnished to the person affected upon request, and the Civil Service Commission also shall, upon request, be furnished copies of the same. . . ." [20]

---

[20] Act of Aug. 24, 1912, c. 389, § 6, 37 Stat. 555.

That Act, as now codified, 5 U. S. C. § 7501, together with the administrative regulations issued by the Civil Service Commission and the OEO, provided the statutory and administrative framework which the Government contends controlled the proceedings against appellee. The District Court, in its ruling on appellee's procedural contentions, in effect held that the Fifth Amendment to the United States Constitution prohibited Congress, in the Lloyd-La Follette Act, from granting protection against removal without cause and at the same time—indeed, in the same sentence—specifying that the determination of cause should be without the full panoply of rights which attend a trial-type adversary hearing. We do not believe that the Constitution so limits Congress in the manner in which benefits may be extended to federal employees.

Appellee recognizes that our recent decisions in *Board of Regents* v. *Roth,* 408 U. S. 564 (1972), and *Perry* v. *Sindermann,* 408 U. S. 593 (1972), are those most closely in point with respect to the procedural rights constitutionally guaranteed public employees in connection with their dismissal from employment. Appellee contends that he had a property interest or an expectancy of employment which could not be divested without first affording him a full adversary hearing.

In *Board of Regents* v. *Roth,* we said:

> "Property interests, of course, are not created by the Constitution. Rather, they are created and their dimensions are defined by existing rules or understandings that stem from an independent source such as state law—rules or understandings that secure certain benefits and that support claims of entitlement to those benefits." 408 U. S., at 577.

Here appellee did have a statutory expectancy that he not be removed other than for "such cause as will promote the efficiency of [the] service." But the very section of the statute which granted him that right, a right which had previously existed only by virtue of administrative regulation, expressly provided also for the procedure by which "cause" was to be determined, and expressly omitted the procedural guarantees which appellee insists are mandated by the Constitution. Only by bifurcating the very sentence of the Act of Congress which conferred upon appellee the right not to be removed save for cause could it be said that he had an expectancy of that substantive right without the procedural limitations which Congress attached to it. In the area of federal regulation of government employees, where in the absence of statutory limitation the governmental employer has had virtually uncontrolled latitude in decisions as to hiring and firing, *Cafeteria Workers* v. *McElroy,* 367 U. S. 886, 896–897 (1961), we do not believe that a statutory enactment such as the Lloyd-La Follette Act may be parsed as discretely as appellee urges. Congress was obviously intent on according a measure of statutory job security to governmental employees which they had not previously enjoyed, but was likewise intent on excluding more elaborate procedural requirements which it felt would make the operation of the new scheme unnecessarily burdensome in practice. Where the focus of legislation was thus strongly on the procedural mechanism for enforcing the substantive right which was simultaneously conferred, we decline to conclude that the substantive right may be viewed wholly apart from the procedure provided for its enforcement. The employee's statutorily defined right is not a guarantee against removal without cause in the abstract, but such a guarantee as enforced by the procedures which Congress has designated for the determination of cause.

The Court has previously viewed skeptically the action of a litigant in challenging the constitutionality of portions of a statute under which it has simultaneously claimed benefits. In *Fahey* v. *Mallonee,* 332 U. S. 245 (1947), it was observed:

> "In the name and right of the Association it is now being asked that the Act under which it has its existence be struck down in important particulars, hardly severable from those provisions which grant its right to exist. . . . It would be intolerable that the Congress should endow an association with the right to conduct a public banking business on certain limitations and that the Court at the behest of those who took advantage from the privilege should remove the limitations intended for public protection. It would be difficult to imagine a more appropriate situation in which to apply the doctrine that one who utilizes an Act to gain advantages of corporate existence is estopped from questioning the validity of its vital conditions." *Id.,* at 255–256.
>
> "It is an elementary rule of constitutional law that one may not 'retain the benefits of an Act while attacking the constitutionality of one of its important conditions.' *United States* v. *San Francisco,* 310 U. S. 16, 29. As formulated by Mr. Justice Brandeis, concurring in *Ashwander* v. *Tennessee Valley Authority,* 297 U. S. 288, 348, 'The Court will not pass upon the constitutionality of a statute at the instance of one who has availed himself of its benefits.' " *Id.,* at 255.

This doctrine has unquestionably been applied unevenly in the past, and observed as often as not in the breach. We believe that at the very least it gives added weight to our conclusion that where the grant of a substantive right is inextricably intertwined with the limitations on the procedures which are to be employed in determining that right, a litigant in the position of appellee must take the bitter with the sweet.

To conclude otherwise would require us to hold that although Congress chose to enact what was essentially a legislative compromise, and with unmistakable clarity granted governmental employees security against being dismissed without "cause," but refused to accord them a full adversary hearing for the determination of "cause," it was constitutionally disabled from making such a choice. We would be holding that federal employees had been granted, as a result of the enactment of the Lloyd-La Follette Act, not merely that which Congress had given them in the first part of a sentence, but that which Congress had expressly withheld from them in the latter part of the same sentence. Neither the language of the Due Process Clause of the Fifth Amendment nor our cases construing it require any such hobbling restrictions on legislative authority in this area.

Appellees urge that the judgment of the District Court must be sustained on the authority of cases such as *Goldberg* v. *Kelly,* 397 U. S. 254 (1970), *Fuentes* v. *Shevin,* 407 U. S. 67 (1972), *Bell* v. *Burson,* 402 U. S. 535 (1971), and *Sniadach* v. *Family Finance Corp.,* 395 U. S. 337 (1969). *Goldberg* held that welfare recipients are entitled under the Due Process Clause of the Fifth and Fourteenth Amendments to an adversary hearing before their benefits are terminated. *Fuentes* v. *Shevin* held that a hearing was generally required before one could have his property seized under a writ of replevin. In *Bell* v. *Burson* the Court held that due process required a procedure for determining whether there was a reasonable possibility of a judgment against a driver as a result of an accident before his license and vehicle registration could be suspended for failure to post security under Georgia's uninsured motorist statute. And in *Sniadach*

v. *Family Finance Corp.* a Wisconsin statute providing for prejudgment garnishment without notice to the debtor or prior hearing was struck down as violative of the principles of due process. These cases deal with areas of the law dissimilar to one another and dissimilar to the area of governmental employer-employee relationships with which we deal here. The types of "liberty" and "property" protected by the Due Process Clause vary widely, and what may be required under that Clause in dealing with one set of interests which it protects may not be required in dealing with another set of interests.

> "The very nature of due process negates any concept of inflexible procedures universally applicable to every imaginable situation." *Cafeteria Workers* v. *McElroy,* 367 U. S., at 895.

Here the property interest which appellee had in his employment was itself conditioned by the procedural limitations which had accompanied the grant of that interest. The Government might, then, under our holdings dealing with Government employees in *Roth, supra,* and *Sindermann, supra,* constitutionally deal with appellee's claims as it proposed to do here.[21]

---

[21] Our Brother WHITE would hold that Verduin himself might not make the initial decision as to removal on behalf of the agency, because he was the victim of the alleged slander which was one of the bases for appellee's removal. Because of our holding with respect to appellee's property-type expectations under *Roth* and *Sindermann,* we do not reach this question in its constitutional dimension. But since our Brother WHITE suggests that he reaches that conclusion as a matter of statutory construction, albeit because of constitutional emanations, we state our reasons for disagreeing with his conclusion. We, of course, find no constitutional overtones lurking in the statutory issue, because of our holding as to the nature of appellee's property interest in his employment. The reference in the Lloyd-La Follette Act itself to the discretion "of the officer making the removal" suggests rather strongly that he is likewise the

Appellee also contends in this Court that because of
the nature of the charges on which his dismissal was
based, he was in effect accused of dishonesty, and that
therefore a hearing was required before he could be
deprived of this element of his "liberty" protected by the
Fifth Amendment against deprivation without due
process. In *Board of Regents v. Roth*, 408 U. S., at 573,
we said:

> "The State, in declining to rehire the respondent,
> did not make any charge against him that might
> seriously damage his standing and associations in
> his community. It did not base the nonrenewal of

officer who will have brought the charges, and there is no indication
that during the 60 years' practice under the Act it has ever been
administratively construed to require the initial hearing on the discharge to be before any official other than the one making the charges.
And while our Brother WHITE's statement of his conclusion suggests
that it may be limited to facts similar to those presented here,
post, at 199, we doubt that in practice it could be so confined. The
decision of an employee's supervisor to dismiss an employee "for
such cause as will promote the efficiency of the service" will all
but invariably involve a somewhat subjective judgment on the part
of the supervisor that the employee's performance is not "up to snuff."
Employer-employee disputes of this sort can scarcely avoid involving
clashes of personalities, and while a charge that an employee has
defamed a supervisor may generate a maximum of personal involvement on the part of the latter, a statement of more typical charges
will necessarily engender some degree of personal involvement on
the part of the supervisor.

Additional difficulties in applying our Brother WHITE's standard
would surely be found if the official bringing the charges were himself the head of a department or an agency, for in that event none
of his subordinates could be assumed to have a reasonable degree
of detached neutrality, and the initial hearing would presumably
have to be conducted by someone wholly outside of the department
or agency. We do not believe that Congress, clearly indicating as
it did in the Lloyd-LaFollette Act its preference for relatively simple
procedures, contemplated or required the complexities which would
be injected into the Act by our Brother WHITE.

his contract on a charge, for example, that he had
been guilty of dishonesty, or immorality. . . .   In
such a case, due process would accord an opportunity
to refute the charge before university officials."[22]

The liberty here implicated by appellants' action is not
the elemental freedom from external restraint such as
was involved in *Morrissey* v. *Brewer,* 408 U. S. 471 (1972),
but is instead a subspecies of the right of the individual
"to enjoy those privileges long recognized . . . as essential
to the orderly pursuit of happiness by free men." *Meyer*
v. *Nebraska,* 262 U. S. 390, 399 (1923).   But that liberty is
not offended by dismissal from employment itself, but instead by dismissal based upon an unsupported charge
which could wrongfully injure the reputation of an employee.   Since the purpose of the hearing in such a case is
to provide the person "an opportunity to clear his name,"
a hearing afforded by administrative appeal procedures
after the actual dismissal is a sufficient compliance with
the requirements of the Due Process Clause.   Here
appellee chose not to rely on his administrative appeal,
which, if his factual contentions are correct, might well
have vindicated his reputation and removed any wrongful stigma from his reputation.

Appellee urges that the delays in processing agency
and Civil Service Commission appeals, amounting to
more than three months in over 50% of agency appeals,[23]
mean that the available administrative appeals do not

---

[22] The Court's footnote there stated:

"The purpose of such notice and hearing is to provide the person
an opportunity to clear his name.   Once a person has cleared his
name at a hearing, his employer, of course, may remain free to
deny him future employment for other reasons." 408 U. S., at
573 n. 12.

[23] See Merrill, Procedures for Adverse Actions Against Federal
Employees, 59 Va. L. Rev. 196, 206 (1973).

suffice to protect his liberty interest recognized in *Roth.*
During the pendency of his administrative appeals,
appellee asserts, a discharged employee suffers from both
the stigma and the consequent disadvantage in obtaining
a comparable job that result from dismissal for cause
from Government employment. We assume that some
delay attends vindication of an employee's reputation
throughout the hearing procedures provided on appeal,
and conclude that at least the delays cited here do not
entail any separate deprivation of a liberty interest
recognized in *Roth.*

III

Appellee also contends that the provisions of 5 U. S. C.
§ 7501 (a), authorizing removal or suspension without
pay "for such cause as will promote the efficiency of the
service," are vague and overbroad. The District Court
accepted this contention:

> "Because employees faced with the standard of 'such
> cause as will promote the efficiency of the service'
> can only guess as to what utterances may cost them
> their jobs, there can be little question that they will
> be deterred from exercising their First Amendment
> rights to the fullest extent." 349 F. Supp., at 866.

A certain anomaly attends appellee's substantive constitutional attack on the Lloyd-La Follette Act just as it
does his attack on its procedural provisions. Prior to
the enactment of this language in 1912, there was no
such statutory inhibition on the authority of the Government to discharge a federal employee, and an employee
could be discharged with or without cause for conduct which was not protected under the First Amendment. Yet under the District Court's holding, a federal
employee after the enactment of the Lloyd-La Follette
Act may not even be discharged for conduct which constitutes "cause" for discharge and which is not protected

by the First Amendment, because the guarantee of job
security which Congress chose to accord employees is
"vague" and "overbroad."

We hold the standard of "cause" set forth in the
Lloyd-La Follette Act as a limitation on the Government's authority to discharge federal employees is constitutionally sufficient against the charges both of
overbreadth and of vagueness. In *CSC* v. *Letter Carriers,* 413 U. S. 548, 578–579 (1973), we said:

> "[T]here are limitations in the English language with
> respect to being both specific and manageably brief,
> and it seems to us that although the prohibitions
> may not satisfy those intent on finding fault at any
> cost, they are set out in terms that the ordinary
> person exercising ordinary common sense can suffi-
> ciently understand and comply with, without sacri-
> fice to the public interest. '[T]he general class of
> offense to which . . . [the provisions are] directed
> is plainly within [their] terms . . . , [and they]
> will not be struck down as vague, even though
> marginal cases could be put where doubts might
> arise.' *United States* v. *Harriss,* 347 U. S. 612, 618
> (1954)."

Congress sought to lay down an admittedly general
standard, not for the purpose of defining criminal conduct, but in order to give myriad different federal
employees performing widely disparate tasks a common
standard of job protection. We do not believe that Congress was confined to the choice of enacting a detailed
code of employee conduct, or else granting no job protection at all. As we said in *Colten* v. *Kentucky,* 407
U. S. 104 (1972):

> "The root of the vagueness doctrine is a rough idea
> of fairness. It is not a principle designed to convert
> into a constitutional dilemma the practical difficul-

ties in drawing criminal statutes both general enough
to take into account a variety of human conduct and
sufficiently specific to provide fair warning that certain kinds of conduct are prohibited." *Id.*, at 110.

Here the language "such cause as will promote the efficiency of the service" was not written upon a clean slate
in 1912, and it does not appear on a clean slate now.
The Civil Service Commission has indicated that what
might be said to be longstanding principles of employer-
employee relationships, like those developed in the private sector, should be followed in interpreting the language
used by Congress.[24] Moreover, the OEO has provided by
regulation that its Office of General Counsel is available to
counsel employees who seek advice on the interpretation
of the Act and its regulations.[25] We found the similar
procedure offered by the Civil Service Commission important in rejecting the respondents' vagueness contentions
in *CSC* v. *Letter Carriers*, 413 U. S., at 580.

The phrase "such cause as will promote the efficiency
of the service" as a standard of employee job protection
is without doubt intended to authorize dismissal for
speech as well as other conduct. *Pickering* v. *Board of
Education*, 391 U. S. 563, 568 (1968), makes it clear that
in certain situations the discharge of a Government employee may be based on his speech without offending
guarantees of the First Amendment:

"At the same time it cannot be gainsaid that the
State has interests as an employer in regulating the

---

[24] The Federal Personnel Manual, Subchapter S3-1. a., states:
"Basically a 'cause' for disciplinary adverse action is a recognizable
offense against the employer-employee relationship. Causes for adverse action run the entire gamut of offenses against the employer-
employee relationship, including inadequate performance of duties
and improper conduct on or off the job. . . ." Supp. 752-1, Adverse
Action by Agencies, Feb. 1972.

[25] See n. 7, *supra.*

speech of its employees that differ significantly from
those it possesses in connection with regulation of
the speech of the citizenry in general. The problem in any case is to arrive at a balance between the
interests of the teacher, as a citizen, in commenting
upon matters of public concern and the interest of
the State, as an employer, in promoting the efficiency
of the public services it performs through its
employees."

Because of the infinite variety of factual situations in
which public statements by Government employees might
reasonably justify dismissal for "cause," we conclude that
the Act describes, as explicitly as is required, the
employee conduct which is ground for removal. The
essential fairness of this broad and general removal
standard, and the impracticability of greater specificity,
were recognized by Judge Leventhal, writing for a panel
of the United States Court of Appeals for the District
of Columbia Circuit in *Meehan* v. *Macy*, 129 U. S. App.
D. C. 217, 230, 392 F. 2d 822, 835 (1968), modified, 138
U. S. App. D. C. 38, 425 F. 2d 469, aff'd en banc, 138
U. S. App. D. C. 41, 425 F. 2d 472 (1969):

> "[I]t is not feasible or necessary for the Govern-
> ment to spell out in detail all that conduct which
> will result in retaliation. The most conscientious
> of codes that define prohibited conduct of employees
> include 'catchall' clauses prohibiting employee 'mis-
> conduct,' 'immorality,' or 'conduct unbecoming.'
> We think it is inherent in the employment relation-
> ship as a matter of common sense if not [of] com-
> mon law that [a Government] employee . . . cannot
> reasonably assert a right to keep his job while at
> the same time he inveighs against his superiors in
> public with intemperate and defamatory [car-
> toons]. . . . [Dismissal in such circumstances

neither] comes as an unfair surprise [nor] is so
unexpected as to chill . . . freedom to engage in
appropriate speech."

Since Congress when it enacted the Lloyd-La Follette
Act did so with the intention of conferring job protection rights on federal employees which they had not
previously had, it obviously did not intend to authorize
discharge under the Act's removal standard for speech
which is constitutionally protected. The Act proscribes
only that public speech which improperly damages and
impairs the reputation and efficiency of the employing
agency, and it thus imposes no greater controls on the
behavior of federal employees than are necessary for
the protection of the Government as an employer. Indeed the Act is not directed at speech as such, but
at employee behavior, including speech, which is detrimental to the efficiency of the employing agency. We
hold that the language "such cause as will promote the
efficiency of the service" in the Act excludes constitutionally protected speech, and that the statute is therefore not overbroad. *Colten* v. *Kentucky,* 407 U. S., at
111. We have observed previously that the Court has
a duty to construe a federal statute to avoid constitutional questions where such a construction is reasonably
possible. *United States* v. *12 200-ft. Reels of Film,*
413 U. S. 123, 130 n. 7 (1973); *United States* v. *Thirty-
seven Photographs,* 402 U. S. 363, 368–369 (1971).

We have no hesitation, as did the District Court, in
saying that on the facts alleged in the administrative
charges against appellee, the appropriate tribunal would
infringe no constitutional right of appellee in concluding that there was "cause" for his discharge. *Pickering*
v. *Board of Education,* 391 U. S., at 569. Nor have
we any doubt that satisfactory proof of these allegations
could constitute "such cause as will promote the effi-

ciency of the service" within the terms of 5 U. S. C.
§ 7501 (a). Appellee's contention then boils down to
the assertion that although no constitutionally protected
conduct of his own was the basis for his discharge on the
Government's version of the facts, the statutory language in question must be declared inoperative, and a
set of more particularized regulations substituted for it,
because the generality of its language might result in
marginal situations in which other persons seeking to engage ,in constitutionally protected conduct would be
deterred from doing so. But we have held that Congress in establishing a standard of "cause" for discharge
did not intend to include within that term any constitutionally protected conduct. We think that our
statement in *Colten* v. *Kentucky,* is a complete answer
to appellee's contention:

> "As we understand this case, appellant's own con-
> duct was not immune under the First Amendment
> and neither is his conviction vulnerable on the
> ground that the statute threatens constitutionally
> protected conduct of others." 407 U. S., at 111.

In sum, we hold that the Lloyd-La Follette Act, in
at once conferring upon nonprobationary federal employees the right not to be discharged except for "cause"
and prescribing the procedural means by which that
right was to be protected, did not create an expectancy
of job retention in those employees requiring procedural
protection under the Due Process Clause beyond that
afforded here by the statute and related agency regulations. We also conclude that the post-termination
hearing procedures provided by the Civil Service Commission and the OEO adequately protect those federal
employees' liberty interest, recognized in *Roth, supra,* in
not being wrongfully stigmatized by untrue and unsupported administrative charges. Finally, we hold that

the standard of employment protection imposed by Congress in the Lloyd-La Follette Act, is not impermissibly vague or overbroad in its regulation of the speech of federal employees and therefore unconstitutional on its face. Accordingly, we reverse the decision of the District Court on both grounds on which it granted summary judgment and remand for further proceedings not inconsistent with this opinion.

Reversed and remanded.

MR. JUSTICE POWELL, with whom MR. JUSTICE BLACKMUN joins, concurring in part and concurring in the result in part.

For the reasons stated by MR. JUSTICE REHNQUIST, I agree that the provisions of 5 U. S. C. § 7501 (a) are neither unconstitutionally vague nor overbroad. I also agree that appellee's discharge did not contravene the Fifth Amendment guarantee of procedural due process. Because I reach that conclusion on the basis of different reasoning, I state my views separately.

I

The applicability of the constitutional guarantee of procedural due process depends in the first instance on the presence of a legitimate "property" or "liberty" interest within the meaning of the Fifth or Fourteenth Amendment. Governmental deprivation of such an interest must be accompanied by minimum procedural safeguards, including some form of notice and a hearing.[1]

---

[1] As the Court stated in *Boddie* v. *Connecticut*, 401 U. S. 371, 378 (1971), "The formality and procedural requisites for [a due process] hearing can vary, depending upon the importance of the interests involved and the nature of the subsequent proceedings." In this case, we are concerned with an administrative hearing in the context of appellee's discharge from public employment.

The Court's decisions in *Board of Regents* v. *Roth*, 408 U. S. 564 (1972), and *Perry* v. *Sindermann*, 408 U. S. 593 (1972), provide the proper framework for analysis of whether appellee's employment constituted a "property" interest under the Fifth Amendment. In *Roth,* the Court stated:

> "To have a property interest in a benefit, a person clearly must have more than an abstract need or desire for it. He must have more than a unilateral expectation of it. He must, instead, have a legitimate claim of entitlement to it. It is a purpose of the ancient institution of property to protect those claims upon which people rely in their daily lives, reliance that must not be arbitrarily undermined. It is a purpose of the constitutional right to a hearing to provide an opportunity for a person to vindicate those claims.
>
> "Property interests, of course, are not created by the Constitution. Rather, they are created and their dimensions are defined by existing rules or understandings that stem from an independent source such as state law—rules or understandings that secure certain benefits and that support claims of entitlement to those benefits." 408 U. S., at 577.

The Court recognized that the "wooden distinction" between "rights" and "privileges" was not determinative of the applicability of procedural due process and that a property interest may be created by statute as well as by contract. *Id.,* at 571. In particular, the Court stated that a person may have a protected property interest in public employment if contractual or statutory provisions guarantee continued employment absent "sufficient cause" for discharge. *Id.,* at 576–578.

In *Sindermann,* the Court again emphasized that a person may have a protected property interest in continued public employment.   There, a state college teacher alleged that the college had established a *de facto* system of tenure and that he had obtained tenure under that system.   The Court stated that proof of these allegations would establish the teacher's legitimate claim of entitlement to continued employment absent "sufficient cause" for discharge.   In these circumstances, the teacher would have a property interest safeguarded by due process, and deprivation of that interest would have to be accompanied by some form of notice and a hearing.

Application of these precedents to the instant case makes plain that appellee is entitled to invoke the constitutional guarantee of procedural due process. Appellee was a nonprobationary federal employee, and as such he could be discharged only for "cause."   5 U. S. C. § 7501 (a).   The federal statute guaranteeing appellee continued employment absent "cause" for discharge conferred on him a legitimate claim of entitlement which constituted a "property" interest under the Fifth Amendment.   Thus termination of his employment requires notice and a hearing.

The plurality opinion evidently reasons that the nature of appellee's interest in continued federal employment is necessarily defined and limited by the statutory procedures for discharge and that the constitutional guarantee of procedural due process accords to appellee no procedural protections against arbitrary or erroneous discharge other than those expressly provided in the statute.   The plurality would thus conclude that the statute governing federal employment determines not only the nature of appellee's property interest, but also the extent of the procedural protections to which he may lay claim.   It seems to me that this approach is incompatible with the principles laid down in *Roth* and *Sindermann*.   Indeed, it would lead directly to the conclusion that whatever the nature

of an individual's statutorily created property interest,
deprivation of that interest could be accomplished
without notice or a hearing at any time.   This view
misconceives the origin of the right to procedural
due process. That right is conferred, not by legislative
grace, but by constitutional guarantee.   While the legislature may elect not to confer a property interest in
federal employment,[2] it may not constitutionally
authorize the deprivation of such an interest, once conferred, without appropriate procedural safeguards.   As
our cases have consistently recognized, the adequacy of
statutory procedures for deprivation of a statutorily
created property interest must be analyzed in constitutional terms.   *Goldberg* v. *Kelly,* 397 U. S. 254 (1970);[3]
Bell v. *Burson,* 402 U. S. 535 (1971); *Board of Regents*
v. *Roth, supra; Perry* v. *Sindermann, supra.*

II

Having determined that the constitutional guarantee
of procedural due process applies to appellee's discharge
from public employment, the question arises whether an
evidentiary hearing, including the right to present favorable witnesses and to confront and examine adverse witnesses, must be accorded *before* removal.   The resolution of this issue depends on a balancing process in
which the Government's interest in expeditious removal

---

[2] No property interest would be conferred, for example, where
the applicable statutory or contractual terms, either expressly or by
implication, did not provide for continued employment absent
"cause." See *Board of Regents* v. *Roth,* 408 U. S. 564, 578 (1972).

[3] In *Goldberg,* for example, the statutes and regulations defined
both eligibility for welfare benefits and the procedures for termination
of those benefits. The Court held that such benefits constituted a
statutory entitlement for persons qualified to receive them and that
the constitutional guarantee of procedural due process applied to
termination of benefits. 397 U. S., at 261–263.

of an unsatisfactory employee is weighed against the interest of the affected employee in continued public employment. *Goldberg* v. *Kelly, supra,* at 263–266. As the Court stated in *Cafeteria & Restaurant Workers* v. *McElroy,* 367 U. S. 886, 895 (1961), "consideration of what procedures due process may require under any given set of circumstances must begin with a determination of the precise nature of the government function involved as well as of the private interest that has been affected by governmental action."

In the present case, the Government's interest, and hence the public's interest, is the maintenance of employee efficiency and discipline. Such factors are essential if the Government is to perform its responsibilities effectively and economically. To this end, the Government, as an employer, must have wide discretion and control over the management of its personnel and internal affairs. This includes the prerogative to remove employees whose conduct hinders efficient operation and to do so with dispatch. Prolonged retention of a disruptive or otherwise unsatisfactory employee can adversely affect discipline and morale in the work place, foster disharmony, and ultimately impair the efficiency of an office or agency. Moreover, a requirement of a prior evidentiary hearing would impose additional administrative costs, create delay, and deter warranted discharges. Thus, the Government's interest in being able to act expeditiously to remove an unsatisfactory employee is substantial.[4]

---

[4] My Brother MARSHALL rejects the Government's interest in efficiency as insignificant, citing *Goldberg* v. *Kelly,* 397 U. S. 254, 266 (1970), and *Fuentes* v. *Shevin,* 407 U. S. 67, 90–91, n. 22 (1972). He also notes that nine federal agencies presently accord prior evidentiary hearings. *Post,* at 223, 224.

Neither *Goldberg* nor *Fuentes* involved the Government's substantial interest in maintaining the efficiency and discipline of its

Appellee's countervailing interest is the continuation of his public employment pending an evidentiary hearing. Since appellee would be reinstated and awarded backpay if he prevails on the merits of his claim, appellee's actual injury would consist of a temporary interruption of his income during the interim. To be sure, even a temporary interruption of income could constitute a serious loss in many instances. But the possible deprivation is considerably less severe than that involved in *Goldberg,* for example, where termination of welfare benefits to the recipient would have occurred in the face of "brutal need." 397 U. S., at 261. Indeed, as the Court stated in that case, "the crucial factor in this context—*a factor not present in the case of . . . the discharged government employee . . .*—is that termination of aid pending resolution of a controversy over eligibility may deprive an *eligible* recipient of *the very means by which to live while he waits." Id.,* at 264 (emphasis added). By contrast, a public employee may well have independent resources to overcome any temporary hardship, and he may be able to secure a job in the private sector. Alternatively, he will be eligible for welfare benefits.

own employees. Moreover, the fact that some federal agencies may have decided to hold prior evidentiary hearings cannot mean that such a procedure is constitutionally mandated. The Federal Government's general practice to the contrary argues that efficiency is in fact thought to be adversely affected by prior evidentiary hearings.

Nor do I agree with my Brother WHITE's argument that suspension with pay would obviate any problem posed by prolonged retention of a disruptive or unsatisfactory employee. Aside from the additional financial burden which would be imposed on the Government, this procedure would undoubtedly inhibit warranted discharges and weaken significantly the deterrent effect of immediate removal. In addition, it would create a strong incentive for the suspended employee to attempt to delay final resolution of the issues surrounding his discharge.

Appellee also argues that the absence of a prior evidentiary hearing increases the possibility of wrongful removal and that delay in conducting a post-termination evidentiary hearing further aggravates his loss. The present statute and regulations, however, already respond to these concerns. The affected employee is provided with 30 days' advance written notice of the reasons for his proposed discharge and the materials on which the notice is based. He is accorded the right to respond to the charges both orally and in writing, including the submission of affidavits. Upon request, he is entitled to an opportunity to appear personally before the official having the authority to make or recommend the final decision. Although an evidentiary hearing is not held, the employee may make any representations he believes relevant to his case. After removal, the employee receives a full evidentiary hearing, and is awarded backpay if reinstated. See 5 CFR §§ 771.208 and 772.305; 5 U. S. C. § 5596. These procedures minimize the risk of error in the initial removal decision and provide for compensation for the affected employee should that decision eventually prove wrongful.[5]

_____

[5] My Brother White argues that affirmance is required because the supervisory official who would have conducted the preremoval hearing was the "object of slander that was the basis for the employee's proposed discharge." Post, at 199. He would conclude that this violated the statutory requirement of an "impartial decisionmaker." I find no such requirement anywhere in the statute or the regulations. Nor do I believe that due process so mandates at the preremoval stage. In my view, the relevant fact is that an impartial decisionmaker is provided at the post-removal hearing where the employee's claims are finally resolved.

There are also significant practical considerations that argue against such a requirement. In most cases, the employee's supervisor is the official best informed about the "cause" for termination. If disqualification is required on the ground that the responsible supervisor could not be wholly impartial, the removal procedure

On balance, I would conclude that a prior evidentiary hearing is not required and that the present statute and regulations comport with due process by providing a reasonable accommodation of the competing interests.[6]

MR. JUSTICE WHITE, concurring in part and dissenting in part.

The Lloyd-La Follette Act, 5 U. S. C. § 7501 (a), provides that "[a]n individual in the competitive service may be removed or suspended without pay only for such cause as will promote the efficiency of the service."[1] The

---

would become increasingly complex. In effect, a "mini-trial" would be necessary to educate the impartial decisionmaker as to the basis for termination.

[6] Appellee also argues that the failure to provide a prior evidentiary hearing deprived him of his "liberty" interest in violation of the Fifth Amendment. For the reasons stated above, I find that the present statute comports with due process even with respect to appellee's liberty interest.

[1] The full text of the Act's pertinent provisions provides:

"(a) An individual in the competitive service may be removed or suspended without pay only for such cause as will promote the efficiency of the service.

"(b) An individual in the competitive service whose removal or suspension without pay is sought is entitled to reasons in writing and to—

"(1) notice of the action sought and of any charges preferred against him;

"(2) a copy of the charges;

"(3) a reasonable time for filing a written answer to the charges, with affidavits; and

"(4) a written decision on the answer at the earliest practicable date.

"Examination of witnesses, trial, or hearing is not required but may be provided in the discretion of the individual directing the removal or suspension without pay. Copies of the charges, the notice of hearing, the answer, the reasons for and the order of removal or suspension without pay, and also the reasons for reduction in grade or pay, shall be made a part of the records of the employing agency, and,

regulations of the Civil Service Commission and the Office of Economic Opportunity (OEO), at which appellee was employed, give content to "cause" by specifying grounds for removal which include "any action . . . which might result in . . . [a]ffecting adversely the confidence of the public in the integrity of [OEO and] the Government" and any "criminal, infamous, dishonest, immoral, or notoriously disgraceful conduct, or other conduct prejudicial to the Government." [2]

Aside from specifying the standards for discharges, Congress has also established the procedural framework in which the discharge determinations are to be made. The employee is to receive 30 days' advance written notice of the action sought and of any charges preferred against him, a copy of the charges, and a

---

on request, shall be furnished to the individual affected and to the Civil Service Commission.

"(c) This section applies to a preference eligible employee as defined by section 7511 of this title only if he so elects. This section does not apply to the suspension or removal of an employee under section 7532 of this title." 5 U. S. C. § 7501.

[2] The regulation of the Civil Service Commission as to "Proscribed actions," 5 CFR § 735.201a, provides:

"An employee shall avoid any action, whether or not specifically prohibited by this subpart, which might result in, or create the appearance of:

"(a) Using public office for private gain;

"(b) Giving preferential treatment to any person;

"(c) Impeding Government efficiency or economy;

"(d) Losing complete independence or impartiality;

"(e) Making a Government decision outside official channels; or

"(f) Affecting adversely the confidence of the public in the integrity of the Government."

The regulations, 5 CFR § 735.209, also provided:

"An employee shall not engage in criminal, infamous, dishonest, immoral, or notoriously disgraceful conduct, or other conduct prejudicial to the Government."

reasonable time for filing a written answer to the charges. Before being terminated he may also make a personal appearance before an agency official, and implementing Civil Service Commission regulations provide that "[t]he right to answer personally includes the right to answer orally in person by being given a reasonable opportunity to make any representations which the employee believes might sway the final decision on his case, but does not include the right to a trial or a formal hearing with examination of witnesses." The regulations further provide that the "representative or representatives designated to hear the answer shall be persons who have authority either to make a final decision on the proposed adverse action or to recommend what final decision should be made." The employee is entitled to notice of the agency's decision in writing, and the notice must inform the employee "[w]hich of the reasons in the notice of proposed adverse action have been found sustained and which have been found not sustained." [3] The employee

---

[3] The Civil Service Procedural Regulations, 5 CFR § 752.202, provide in relevant part:

"(a) *Notice of proposed adverse action.* (1) Except as provided in paragraph (c) of this section, an employee against whom adverse action is sought is entitled to at least 30 full days' advance written notice stating any and all reasons, specifically and in detail, for the proposed action.

"(2) Subject to the provisions of subparagraph (3) of this paragraph, the material on which the notice is based and which is relied on to support the reasons in that notice, including statements of witnesses, documents, and investigative reports or extracts therefrom, shall be assembled and made available to the employee for his review. The notice shall inform the employee where he may review that material.

"(3) Material which cannot be disclosed to the employee, or to his designated physician under § 294.401 of this chapter, may not be used by an agency to support the reasons in the notice.

"(b) *Employee's answer.* Except as provided in paragraph (c) of this section, an employee is entitled to a reasonable time for

may appeal from an adverse decision and is entitled to
an evidentiary trial-type hearing at this stage.[4] This
later hearing affords the employee certain rights not available within OEO at the pretermination stage, particu-

---

answering a notice of proposed adverse action and for furnishing
affidavits in support of his answer. The time to be allowed depends
on the facts and circumstances of the case, and shall be sufficient
to afford the employee ample opportunity to review the material
relied on by the agency to support the reasons in the notice and to
prepare an answer and secure affidavits. The agency shall provide
the employee a reasonable amount of official time for these purposes
if he is otherwise in an active duty status. If the employee answers,
the agency shall consider his answer in reaching its decision. The
employee is entitled to answer personally, or in writing, or both
personally and in writing. The right to answer personally includes
the right to answer orally in person by being given a reasonable
opportunity to make any representations which the employee believes
might sway the final decision on his case, but does not include
the right to a trial or formal hearing with examination of witnesses.
When the employee requests an opportunity to answer personally,
the agency shall make a representative or representatives available
to hear his answer. The representative or representatives designated to hear the answer shall be persons who have authority either
to make a final decision on the proposed adverse action or to recommend what final decision should be made.

.   .   .   .   .

"(f) *Notice of adverse decision.* The employee is entitled to
notice of the agency's decision at the earliest practicable date. The
agency shall deliver the notice of decision to the employee at or
before the time the action will be made effective. The notice shall
be in writing, be dated, and inform the employee:

"(1) Which of the reasons in the notice of proposed adverse
action have been found sustained and which have been found not
sustained . . . ."

[4] The Veterans' Preference Act of 1944 authorizes Civil Service Commission appeals from adverse agency decisions. See 5 U. S. C. § 7701.
The Act itself applies only to veterans of military service, 5 U. S. C.
§§ 2108, 7511, but Executive Order No. 11491, printed in note following 5 U. S. C. § 7301, extends the Act's protections to all nonpreference eligible employees in the classified service.

134   Opinion of WHITE, J.

larly the taking of testimony under oath and the cross-
examination of witnesses.

Appellee Kennedy was a nonprobationary federal employee in the competitive civil service and held the
position of field representative in the Chicago Regional
Office of OEO. As such, he was entitled to the protection of the statutes and regulations outlined above. On
February 18, 1972, Kennedy received a "Notification of
Proposed Adverse Action" from the Regional Director of
OEO, Wendell Verduin. The notice charged, among
other things, that Kennedy had made slanderous statements about Verduin and another coworker charging
them with bribing or attempting to bribe a potential
OEO grantee and had thereby caused disharmony in his
office by preventing its smooth functioning. Verduin
then ruled on March 20, 1972, after Kennedy had filed
a written answer objecting to the lack of certain procedures furnished at this pretermination hearing, but
had declined to appear personally, that Kennedy be removed from his job with OEO, effective March 27, 1972.[5]

---

[5] Appellee's response stated:

"The charges and proceedings brought against Mr. Kennedy are
invalid and, in fact, unlawful for the following two reasons among
others:

"*First,* Mr. Kennedy is entitled to a fair and impartial hearing
prior to any adverse action being taken against him. This means
a proceeding where there is a genuinely impartial hearing officer,
a proceeding where there is an opportunity to offer witnesses and
confront and cross examine those furnishing evidence against him,
a proceeding where he will have an opportunity to respond to all
evidence offered against him, a proceeding where a written record is
made of all evidence, testimony and argument, a proceeding where
the decision will be based exclusively on the record, a proceeding
where the decision will contain findings of fact and conclusions of law
with regard to all controverted issues, together with an analysis
indicating the manner in which the controversies were resolved.

"The present adverse action procedure fails in substantial ways
to provide all of these rudimentary elements required for a due

Kennedy then appealed directly to the Civil Service Commission and also instituted the present action. The first count of his complaint alleged that the discharge procedure of the Lloyd-La Follette Act, and the attendant Civil Service Commission regulations, deprived him of due process by failing to provide for a full hearing prior to termination. The second count alleged that he was discharged because of certain conversations, in violation of his rights under the First Amendment. The single judge who reviewed the complaint convened a three-judge court to hear the first count, and dismissed the second, without prejudice to refiling after the Civil Service Commission ruled on his appeal. It was the court's view that it should not act until the agency had the opportunity to review the merits of appellee's First Amendment claim.

After the convening of the three-judge court, appellee amended his complaint, then limited to the due process claim, to include a challenge to the Lloyd-La Follette Act on the grounds that it was vague and overbroad and violated the First Amendment.

The three-judge District Court, convened pursuant to 28 U. S. C. §§ 2282 and 2284, granted summary judgment for appellee. 349 F. Supp. 863. It held that the discharge procedures violated due process because "[t]here was no provision . . . for the decision on removal or suspension to be made by an impartial agency

---

process hearing. It therefore fails to meet the requirements of due process secured by the Fifth Amendment to the Constitution of the United States and is hence, invalid, null and void.

"*Second*, the charges brought against Mr. Kennedy are facially insufficient and illegal. As the adverse action makes clear, Mr. Kennedy is being punished for his conversations (inaccurately set forth in the adverse action) with union members and the public. Since the First Amendment protects such conversations these allegations are totally without merit." App. 62.

official, or for Kennedy (by his own means) to present witnesses; or for his right to confront adverse witnesses." *Id.*, at 865. The court also held that § 7501 was uncon- stitutional on vagueness and overbreadth grounds. The Government was ordered to reinstate Kennedy to his former position with backpay and to conduct any future removal proceedings with a hearing consistent with its opinion. Appellants were also enjoined from further en- forcement of the Lloyd-La Follette Act, and implement- ing regulations, as "construed to regulate the speech of competitive service employees." *Id.*, at 866.

I

In my view, three issues must be addressed in this case. First, does the Due Process Clause require that there be a full trial-type hearing *at some time* when a Federal Government employee in the competitive service is terminated? Secondly, if such be the case, must this hearing be held *prior* to the discharge of the employee, and, if so, was the process afforded in this case adequate? Third, and as an entirely separate matter, are the Lloyd- La Follette Act and its attendant regulations void for vagueness or overbreadth? I join the Court as to the third issue.

II

I differ basically with the plurality's view that "where the grant of a substantive right is inextricably inter- twined with the limitations on the procedures which are to be employed in determining that right, a litigant in the position of appellee must take the bitter with the sweet," and that "the property interest which appellee had in his employment was itself conditioned by the proce- dural limitations which had accompanied the grant of that interest." *Ante*, at 153–154, 155. The rationale of this position quickly leads to the conclusion that even though

the statute requires cause for discharge, the requisites
of due process could equally have been satisfied had the
law dispensed with any hearing at all, whether pretermination or post-termination.

The past cases of this Court uniformly indicate that
some kind of hearing is required at some time before a
person is finally deprived of his property interests.[6] The
principles of due process "come to us from the law of
England . . . and their requirement was there designed to
secure the subject against the arbitrary action of the crown
and place him under the protection of the law." *Dent
v. West Virginia*, 129 U. S. 114, 123 (1889). The "right
to be heard before being condemned to suffer grievous loss
of any kind, even though it may not involve the stigma
and hardships of a criminal conviction, is a principle
basic to our society." *Anti-Fascist Committee* v. *Mc-
Grath*, 341 U. S. 123, 168 (1951) (Frankfurter, J.,
concurring).

This basic principle has unwaveringly been applied
when private property has been taken by the State. A
fundamental requirement of due process is "the opportunity to be heard." *Grannis* v. *Ordean*, 234 U. S. 385, 394
(1914). "It is an opportunity which must be granted
at a meaningful time and in a meaningful manner."
Armstrong v. *Manzo*, 380 U. S. 545, 552 (1965). Where
the Court has rejected the need for a hearing prior to
the initial "taking," a principal rationale has been that
a hearing would be provided before the taking became
final. See *North American Cold Storage Co.* v. *Chicago*,
211 U. S. 306 (1908) (seizure of food unfit for consump-
tion); *Central Trust Co.* v. *Garvan*, 254 U. S.
554 (1921) (seizure of property under Trading with the

---

[6] My views as to the requirements of due process where property
interests are at stake does not deal with the entirely separate matter
and requirements of due process when a person is deprived of liberty.

Enemy Act); *Corn Exchange Bank* v. *Coler,* 280
U. S. 218 (1930) (seizure of assets of an absconding
husband); *Phillips* v. *Commissioner,* 283 U. S. 589 (1931)
(collection of a tax); *Bowles* v. *Willingham,* 321 U. S.
503 (1944) (setting of price regulations); *Fahey* v. *Mallonee,* 332 U. S. 245 (1947) (appointment of conservator
of assets of savings and loan association); *Ewing* v. *Mytinger & Casselberry,* 339 U. S. 594 (1950) (seizure of
misbranded articles in commerce). While these cases
indicate that the particular interests involved might not
have demanded a hearing immediately, they also reaffirm
the principle that property may not be taken without a
hearing at some time.

This principle has also been applied in situations where
the State has licensed certain activities. Where the
grant or denial of a license has been involved, and the
"right" to engage in business has been legitimately limited by the interest of the State in protecting its citizens
from inexpert or unfit performance, the decision of the
State to grant or deny a license has been subject to a
hearing requirement. See, *e. g., Dent* v. *West Virginia,
supra* (licensing of physicians); *Goldsmith* v. *United
States Board of Tax Appeals,* 270 U. S. 117 (1926) (licensing of accountant); *Willner* v. *Committee on Character and Fitness,* 373 U. S. 96 (1963) (admission to the
bar). The Court has put particular stress on the fact
that the absence of a hearing would allow the State to
be arbitrary in its grant or denial, and to make judgments on grounds other than the fitness of a particular
person to pursue his chosen profession. In the context
of admission to the bar, the Court has stated: "Obviously
an applicant could not be excluded merely because he
was a Republican or a Negro or a member of a particular
church. Even in applying permissible standards, officers
of a State cannot exclude an applicant when there is no

basis for their finding that he fails to meet these standards, or when their action is invidiously discriminatory."
Schware v. *Board of Bar Examiners,* 353 U. S. 232, 239
(1957). The hearing requirement has equally been applied when the license was to be removed, *In re Ruffalo,*
390 U. S. 544 (1968), or a licensee has been subject to
state regulation, *Ohio Bell Telephone Co.* v. *Public
Utilities Comm'n of Ohio,* 301 U. S. 292 (1937).

Similar principles prevail when the State affords its
process and mechanism of dispute settlement, its law
enforcement officers, and its courts, in aiding one person
to take property from another. Where there is a "taking" before a final determination of rights, as in some
cases when the State seizes property, to protect one of
the parties *pendente lite;* the Court has acted on the
assumption that at some time a full hearing will be
available, as when there is an attachment of property
preliminary to resolution of the merits of a dispute,
Ownbey v. *Morgan,* 256 U. S. 94 (1921); *Coffin Brothers*
v. *Bennett,* 277 U. S. 29 (1928); *McKay* v. *McInnes,*
279 U. S. 820 (1929). The opportunity to defend one's
property before it is finally taken is so basic that it hardly
bears repeating. Adequate notice of the court proceeding must be furnished, *Mullane* v. *Central Hanover Bank
& Trust Co.,* 339 U. S. 306 (1950), and there must be
jurisdiction over the person, *Pennoyer* v. *Neff,* 95 U. S.
714 (1878).

Since there is a need for some kind of hearing before
a person is finally deprived of his property, the argument
in the instant case, and that adopted in the plurality
opinion, is that there is something different about a final
taking from an individual of property rights which have
their origin in the public rather than the private sector
of the economy, and, as applied here, that there is no
need for any hearing at any time when the Government

discharges a person from his job, even though good cause
for the discharge is required.

In cases involving employment by the Government, the
earliest cases of this Court have distinguished between two
situations, where the entitlement to the job is conditioned
"at the pleasure" of the employer and where the job is to
be held subject to certain requirements being met by the
employee, as when discharge must be for "cause." The
Court has stated: "The inquiry is therefore whether there
were any causes of removal prescribed by law . . . . If
there were, then the rule would apply that where causes
of removal are specified by constitution or statute, as
also where the term of office is for a fixed period, notice
and hearing are essential. If there were not, the appointing power could remove at pleasure or for such
cause as it deemed sufficient." *Reagan* v. *United States,*
182 U. S. 419, 425 (1901); *Shurtleff* v. *United States,*
189 U. S. 311, 314 (1903). The Court has thus made
clear that Congress may limit the total discretion of the
Executive in firing an employee, by providing that terminations be for cause, and only for cause, and, if it
does so, notice and a hearing are "essential."

Where Executive discretion is not limited, there is no
need for a hearing. In the latter event, where the statute has provided that employment was conditioned on
" 'maintain[ing] the respect due to courts of justice and
judicial officers,' " *Ex parte Secombe,* 19 How. 9, 14
(1857) (attorney and counsellor of court), or was subject to no conditions at all, *Ex parte Hennen,* 13 Pet.
225 (1839) (clerk of the court), no hearing is required.
See also *Crenshaw* v. *United States,* 134 U. S. 99 (1890)
(Navy officer could be removed at will); *Parsons* v.
United States, 167 U. S. 324 (1897) (district attorney
could be terminated by the President at his pleasure);
Keim v. *United States,* 177 U. S. 290 (1900) (post office

clerks removable at pleasure). To like effect is *Cafeteria Workers* v. *McElroy*, 367 U. S. 886 (1961), where the Court held that no hearing need be provided to a cook employed by a private concessionaire of the Navy before the Government revoked her security clearance. The revocation of security clearances was within the "unfettered control" of the Navy in order "to manage the internal operation of an important federal military establishment." *Id.*, at 896. The Court there assumed that "Rachel Brawner could not constitutionally have been excluded from the Gun Factory if the announced grounds for her exclusion had been patently arbitrary or discriminatory . . . ." *Id.*, at 898.

Where the Congress has confined Executive discretion, notice and hearing have been required. In *Anti-Fascist Committee* v. *McGrath*, 341 U. S. 123 (1951), an organization was put on the Attorney General's list, as disloyal to the United States, without a hearing before the Attorney General. The Executive Order, as defined by implementing regulations, required the Executive to make an "appropriate determination" of disloyalty. It was apparent that members of organizations employed by the Government who belonged to an organization on the Attorney General's list would be in danger of losing their jobs. The Court held, assuming the facts as alleged by the complaints were true, that it would be arbitrary, and not consistent with an "appropriate determination," to deny a hearing on the matter to the affected organizations. As Mr. Justice Frankfurter observed in his concurring opinion, "[t]he heart of the matter is that democracy implies respect for the elementary rights of men, however suspect or unworthy; a democratic government must therefore practice fairness; and fairness can rarely be obtained by secret, one-sided determination of facts decisive of rights." *Id.*, at 170.

To some extent, *McGrath,* and like cases, see *Greene* v. *McElroy,* 360 U. S. 474 (1959), depended on statutory construction—the intent of Congress to require that procedural fairness be observed in making decisions on security clearances or status, which affected employment—but it is obvious that the constitutional requirements of fairness were a guiding hand to the Court's statutory interpretation. "Where administrative action has raised serious constitutional problems, the Court has assumed that Congress or the President intended to afford those affected by the action the traditional safeguards of due process," and it has been "the Court's concern that traditional forms of fair procedure not be restricted by implication or without the most explicit action by the Nation's lawmakers . . . ." *Id.,* at 507–508.

The concern of the Court that fundamental fairness be observed when the State deals with its employees has not been limited to action which is discriminatory and infringes on constitutionally protected rights, as in *Wieman* v. *Updegraff,* 344 U. S. 183 (1952); *Slochower* v. *Board of Education,* 350 U. S. 551 (1956); *Speiser* v. *Randall,* 357 U. S. 513 (1958); *Sherbert* v. *Verner,* 374 U. S. 398 (1963). See also *Connell* v. *Higginbotham,* 403 U. S. 207 (1971). It has been observed that "constitutional protection does extend to the public servant whose exclusion pursuant to a statute is *patently arbitrary or discriminatory.*" *Wieman* v. *Updegraff, supra,* at 192; *Slochower* v. *Board of Education, supra,* at 556. (Emphasis added.) In *Slochower, supra,* New York law provided that a tenured employee taking the Fifth Amendment before a legislative committee inquiring into his official conduct could be fired. Quite apart from the Fifth Amendment "penalty" assessed by the State, the Court was concerned with the arbitrariness of drawing a conclusion, without a hearing, that any employee who took the Fifth Amendment was guilty or unfit for employment. The Court stated:

> "This is not to say that Slochower has a constitutional right to be an associate professor of German at Brooklyn College. The State has broad powers in the selection and discharge of its employees, and it may be that proper inquiry would show Slochower's continued employment to be inconsistent with a real interest of the State. But there has been no such inquiry here." *Id.*, at 559.

The Court's decisions in *Board of Regents* v. *Roth,* 408 U. S. 564 (1972), and *Perry* v. *Sindermann,* 408 U. S. 593 (1972), reiterate the notion that the Executive Branch cannot be arbitrary in depriving a person of his job, when the Legislative Branch has provided that a person cannot be fired except for cause, and, if anything, extend the principles beyond the facts of this case.

In *Sindermann,* a teacher who had held his position for a number of years but was not tenured under contract, alleged that he had *de facto* tenure under contract law due to "the existence of rules or understandings" with the college which employed him, *id.*, at 602. The Court held that if the professor could prove the existence of a property interest it would "obligate college officials to grant a hearing at his request, where he could be informed of the grounds for his nonretention and challenge their sufficiency." *Id.*, at 603. In *Roth,* an assistant professor was hired for a fixed term of one academic year, and had no tenure. The Court held that the teacher had no property interest in the job, since the terms of employment allowed that his contract not be renewed. The critical consideration was that the terms "did not provide for contract renewal absent 'sufficient cause.'" 408 U. S., at 578. The rights to continued employment were determined by state law. The Court took great pains, however, to point out that a tenured appointment, providing for entitlement to a job, absent cause, would be a far different case.

These cases only serve to emphasize that where there is a legitimate entitlement to a job, as when a person is given employment subject to his meeting certain specific conditions, due process requires, in order to insure against arbitrariness by the State in the administration of its law, that a person be given notice and a hearing before he is finally discharged. As the Court stated in *Dismuke* v. *United States,* 297 U. S. 167, 172 (1936):

> "If [the administrative officer] is authorized to determine questions of fact his decision must be accepted unless he exceeds his authority . . . by failing to follow a procedure which satisfies elementary standards of fairness and reasonableness essential to the due conduct of the proceeding which Congress has authorized."

To be sure, to determine the existence of the property interest, as for example, whether a teacher is tenured or not, one looks to the controlling law, in this case federal statutory law, the Lloyd-La Follette Act, which provides that a person can only be fired for cause. The fact that the origins of the property right are with the State makes no difference for the nature of the procedures required. While the State may define what is and what is not property, once having defined those rights the Constitution defines due process, and as I understand it six members of the Court are in agreement on this fundamental proposition.

I conclude, therefore, that as a matter of due process, a hearing must be held at some time before a competitive civil service employee may be finally terminated for misconduct. Here, the Constitution and the Lloyd-La Follette Act converge, because a full trial-type hearing is provided by statute before termination from the service becomes final, by way of appeal either through OEO, the Civil Service Commission, or both.[7]

A different case might be put, of course, if the termination were for reasons of pure inefficiency, assuming such a general reason could be given, in which case it would be at least arguable that a hearing would serve no useful purpose and that judgments of this kind are best left to the discretion of administrative officials. This is not such a case, however, since Kennedy was terminated on specific charges of misconduct.

III

The second question which must be addressed is whether a hearing of some sort must be held *before* any "taking" of the employee's property interest in his job occurs, even if a full hearing is available before that taking becomes final. I must resolve this question because in my view a full hearing must be afforded at some juncture and the claim is that it must occur prior to termination. If the right to any hearing itself is a pure matter of property definition, as the plurality opinion suggests, then that question need not be faced, for any kind of hearing, or no hearing at all, would suffice. As I have suggested, the State may not dispense with the minimum procedures defined by due process, but different considerations come into play when deciding whether a pretermination hearing is required and, if it is, what kind of hearing must be had.

---

[7] *Bailey* v. *Richardson,* 86 U. S. App. D. C. 248, 182 F. 2d 46 (1950), aff'd by an equally divided court, 341 U. S. 918 (1951), is not controlling. "The basis of this holding has been thoroughly undermined in the ensuing years" with the rejection of the "right-privilege" distinction. *Board of Regents* v. *Roth,* 408 U. S. 564, 571 n. 9 (1972).

In passing upon claims to a hearing before preliminary but nonfinal deprivations, the usual rule of this Court has been that a full hearing at some time suffices. "We have repeatedly held that no hearing at the preliminary stage is required by due process so long as the requisite hearing is held before the final administrative order becomes effective." "It is sufficient, where only property rights are concerned, that there is at some stage an opportunity for a hearing and a judicial determination." *Ewing* v. *Mytinger & Casselberry,* 339 U. S., at 598, 599. See also *Phillips* v. *Commissioner,* 283 U. S. 589, 596–597 (1931); *Scottish Union & National Insurance Co.* v. *Bowland,* 196 U. S. 611, 631–632 (1905); *Springer* v. *United States,* 102 U. S. 586, 593–594 (1881). This has seemingly been the rule whether the State was taking property from the person, as in the above-cited cases, or whether one person was taking it from another through the process of state courts. See *Ownbey* v. *Morgan,* 256 U. S. 94 (1921); *Coffin Brothers* v. *Bennett,* 277 U. S. 29 (1928); *McKay* v. *McInnes,* 279 U. S. 820 (1929).

In recent years, however, in a limited number of cases, the Court has held that a hearing must be furnished at the first stage of taking, even where a later hearing was provided. This has been true in the revocation of a state-granted license, *Bell* v. *Burson,* 402 U. S. 535 (1971), and in suits between private parties, where summary replevin procedures, *Fuentes* v. *Shevin,* 407 U. S. 67 (1972), or garnishment procedures, *Sniadach* v. *Family Finance Corp.,* 395 U. S. 337 (1969), were attacked, and when the State has sought to terminate welfare benefits, *Goldberg* v. *Kelly,* 397 U. S. 254 (1970).[8]

---

[8] *Wisconsin* v. *Constantineau,* 400 U. S. 433 (1971), is not properly part of this quartet of cases, since no hearing was apparently ever provided to challenge the posting of one's name as an excessive drinker.

These conflicting lines of cases demonstrate, as the Court stated in *Cafeteria & Restaurant Workers v. McElroy,* 367 U. S., at 895, that "consideration of what procedures due process may require under any given set of circumstances must begin with a determination of the precise nature of the government function involved as well as of the private interest that has been affected by governmental action." See also *Hannah* v. *Larche,* 363 U. S. 420, 440, 442 (1960); *Goldberg* v. *Kelly, supra,* at 263. In assessing whether a prior hearing is required, the Court has looked to how the legitimate interests asserted by the party asserting the need for a hearing, and the party opposing it, would be furthered or hindered.

In many cases, where the claim to a pretermination hearing has been rejected, it appears that the legitimate interest of the party opposing the hearing might be defeated outright if such hearing were to be held.[9] For example, when the Government or a private party lays claim to property there is often the danger that the person in possession of the property may alienate or waste it, and the Government or private party may be without recourse. Thus, the Court has held that there is no need for a prior hearing where the Government has taken preliminary custody of alleged enemy property before actual title to the property is determined, *Central Trust Co.* v. *Garvan,* 254 U. S. 554 (1921); *Stoehr* v. *Wallace,* 255 U. S. 239 (1921), or where a private creditor has sought to attach property of a debtor. See *Ownbey* v. *Morgan, supra; Coffin Brothers* v. *Bennett, supra; McKay* v. *McInnes, supra.* Of course, such summary action must be authorized in such a manner as to minimize the possibilities of a mistaken deprivation, by a

---

[9] See generally Freedman. Summary Action by Administrative Agencies, 40 U. Chi. L. Rev. 1 (1972).

public official in the case of administrative action, or a judge where the processes of the court are used. *Fuentes v. Shevin, supra.*

The danger that the purpose of the action may be defeated, or made exceedingly difficult, by requiring a prior hearing, is illustrated by *North American Cold Storage Co.* v. *Chicago,* 211 U. S. 306 (1908), where the Court sustained the constitutionality of an Illinois statute permitting health inspectors to enter cold-storage houses and "forthwith seize, condemn and destroy" unfit food. The defendants in the action claimed that while it may be necessary to seize the food pending a hearing, surely destruction of that food could not be justified. Nonetheless, the Court observed:

> "If a hearing were to be always necessary, even under the circumstances of this case, the question at once arises as to what is to be done with the food in the meantime. Is it to remain with the cold storage company, and if so under what security that it will not be removed? To be sure that it will not be removed during the time necessary for the hearing, which might frequently be indefinitely prolonged, some guard would probably have to be placed over the subject-matter of the investigation, which would involve expense, and might not even then prove effectual." *Id.,* at 320.

Similar inabilities of the party claiming a right to a prior hearing, to make the moving party in the suit whole, have appeared where incompetence and malfeasance in the administration of a bank could precipitate a financial collapse in the community, which would go uncompensated, see *Fahey* v. *Mallonee,* 332 U. S., at 250, or where, in the absence of a jeopardy assessment by the Tax Commissioner, a taxpayer might waste or conceal his assets, see *Phillips* v. *Commissioner, supra.* In all

such cases it is also significant that the party advancing
the claim to a summary procedure stands ready to make
whole the party who has been deprived of his property,
if the initial taking proves to be wrongful, either by the
credit of the public fisc or by posting a bond.

Of course, this principle cannot be applied with success
to explain the Court's decisions in cases holding that a
pretermination hearing is required; it is not true that the
party entitled to the hearing stands ready to compensate
the adversary for what may be the wrongful possession of
the property in question during the pendency of the
litigation.   This is vividly illustrated in *Goldberg* v.
Kelly where the Court observed that "the benefits paid to
ineligible recipients pending decision at the hearing probably cannot be recouped, since these recipients are likely
to be judgment proof."   397 U. S., at 266.   However,
other considerations have proved decisive, such as: the
risk that the initial deprivation may be wrongful; the
impact on the claimant to a hearing of not having the
property while he waits for a full hearing; the interest
of the party opposing the prior hearing and asserting the
need for immediate possession in not alerting the current possessor to the lawsuit; and the risk of leaving the
property in possession of the current possessor between
the time notice is supplied and the time of the preliminary
hearing.

In *Goldberg* and *Sniadach*, the Court observed that
there was a substantial chance that the claimant to the
property, be it the State or garnishor, would lose in the
ultimate resolution of the controversy.   In *Goldberg*, the
Court took note of the "welfare bureaucracy's difficulties
in reaching correct decisions on eligibility."   397 U. S.,
at 264 n. 12.   Since the time of the decision in *Goldberg*,
at least one study has shown that decisions to terminate
benefits have been reversed with a fair degree of fre-

quency.[10] Concern was also expressed with the use of garnishment in a vast number of cases where the debt was fraudulent. *Sniadach*, 395 U. S., at 341. In *Fuentes*, although no such empirical evidence was available, the risk of wrongful deprivations was unnecessarily increased by allowing a clerk, rather than a judge, to pass on the creditor's claim for summary replevin. In *Bell*, the Court held unconstitutional a state statute requiring summary suspension of a driver's license of any uninsured motorist who was unable after an accident to post security for the amount of the damages claimed against him. The only hearing held by the State on the issue of suspension excluded *any* consideration of fault, the standard on which the validity would ultimately turn. Without some kind of probable-cause determination of fault, it was obvious that many suspensions would prove to be unwarranted.

As for the impact on the current property possessor of not having an early pretermination hearing, the Court has held that without possession of the property a person may be unable to exist at even a minimum standard of decency. In *Goldberg*, where the person would have lost the last source of support available, aside from charity, the Court observed that "termination of aid pending resolution of a controversy over eligibility may deprive an *eligible* recipient of the very means by which to live while he waits. Since he lacks independent resources, his situation becomes immediately desperate." 397 U. S., at 264. In fact, the magnitude of deprivation may be such as to prevent the welfare recipient from pursuing his right to a later full hearing. *Ibid.* In *Sniadach*, the seizure of an individual's wages could "as a practical

---

[10] See Handler, Justice for the Welfare Recipient: Fair Hearings in AFDC—The Wisconsin Experience, 43 Soc. Serv. Rev. 12, 22 (1969).

matter drive a wage-earning family to the wall." 395
U. S., at 341–342 (footnote omitted). In *Bell*, the petitioner was a clergyman whose ministry required him to
travel by car to cover three rural Georgia communities,
and he was "severely handicapped in the performance of
his ministerial duties by a suspension of his licenses."
402 U. S., at 537. The impact of deprivation increases,
of course, the longer the time period between the initial
deprivation and the opportunity to have a full hearing.
In *Goldberg*, the Court noted that although pertinent
New York regulations provided that a "fair hearing" be
held within 10 working days of the request, with decision
within 12 working days thereafter, "[i]t was conceded in
oral argument that these time limits are not in fact observed." 397 U. S., at 260 n. 5. In *Sniadach* and
Fuentes, there was no indication of the speed with which
a court ruling on garnishment and possession would be
rendered, and of course the ultimate issues on the merits
in such cases must wait for a still later determination.
In *Bell*, the issue of liability might not be determined
until full trial proceedings in court.

The last factor to be weighed in the balance is the
danger to the party claiming possession occasioned by
alerting the current possessor to the lawsuit, and then
leaving the property in his hands pending the holding
of the preliminary hearing. In *Goldberg* and *Sniadach*,
the property right seized was a flow of income, in one
case from the government, and in the other from the
private employer, pending the preliminary hearing. The
government ran no special risk by supplying notice in
advance of the cutoff, since the government was in possession of the flow of income until it was turned over
piecemeal to the welfare recipient. Further, though the
government could assert in the welfare case that it would
incur an uncompensated loss, that risk would only be

incurred from the time the last check is delivered until the pretermination hearing is held and the administrative agency certainly has the power to offer a speedy hearing before that time is reached. See *Goldberg* v. *Kelly, supra,* at 266. In *Sniadach,* while it was true that the inability to garnish wages could leave the creditor uncompensated, if the debtor proved judgment proof, this was a risk the creditor assumed at the outset by being unsecured. Further, notice to the debtor of the pendency of the lawsuit is not likely to increase the risk that the debtor will prove to be judgment proof, since the debtor is not likely to leave his job due to the pendency of the suit. Likewise, the risk to the creditor of the debtor's drawing on his wages between the time of notice and the availability of a court hearing on the claim in no way interferes with the creditor's claim to the future flow of earnings after the hearing has been held. The garnishor, therefore, asserts not only the right to take the debtor's wages, but to take them before the controversy has been resolved. In *Bell,* the risk to the State of supplying notice to the licensee and of leaving the person in possession of the license until the hearing, was not at issue, since the state statute provided for notice and a presuspension hearing. There were few costs attached to expanding the scope of that hearing to include a probable-cause determination of fault.

With the above principles in hand, is the tenured civil-service employee entitled to a pretermination hearing, such as that provided by the Lloyd-La Follette Act?

There would be a problem of uncompensated loss to the Government, if the employee were to draw wages without working for the period between notice of a discharge and a preliminary hearing. Yet, if the charge against the employee did not indicate that the employee should be excluded from the workplace pending this hearing, some work could be exacted by the Government in exchange for its payment of salary. One must also consider another type of cost to the Government if preseparation hearings were provided—the necessity of keeping a person on the scene who might injure the public interest through poor service or might create an uproar at the workplace. However, suspension with pay would obviate this problem.

On the employee's side of the ledger, there is the danger of mistaken termination. Discharge decisions, made *ex parte,* may be reversed after full hearing. One study reveals that in fiscal year 1970, in agencies where full pretermination hearings were routine, employees contesting removal were successful almost 20% of the time. Merrill, Procedures for Adverse Actions Against Federal Employees, 59 Va. L. Rev. 196, 204 n. 35 (1973).

The impact on the employee of being without a job pending a full hearing is likely to be considerable because "[m]ore than 75 percent of actions contested within employing agencies require longer to decide than the 60 days prescribed by [Civil Service] Commission regulations. Over 50 percent take more than three months, and five percent are in process for longer than a year." *Id.,* at 206. Of course, the discharged civil servant, deprived of his source of income, can seek employment in the private sector and so cut or minimize his losses, opportunities largely unavailable to the welfare recipient in *Goldberg* or the debtor in *Sniadach.* Nonetheless, the employee may not be able to get a satisfactory position in the private sector, particularly a tenured one, and his marketability may be under a cloud due to the circumstances of his dismissal. See *Lefkowitz* v. *Turley,* 414 U. S. 70, 83–84 (1973). Cf. *Board of Regents* v. *Roth,* 408 U. S., at 574 n. 13. It should be stressed that if such employment is unavailable the Government may truly be pursuing a partially counter-productive policy by forcing the employee onto the welfare rolls.

Finally, by providing a pretermination hearing, the Government runs no risk through providing notice, since the employee cannot run away with his job, and can surely minimize its risk of uncompensated loss by eliminating the provision for personal appearances and setting early dates for filing written objections. Altogether different considerations as to notice might be applicable, if the employee would be likely to do damage to the Government if provided with such notice. See 5 CFR § 752.202 (c)(2) (1972), providing that an agency may dispense with the 30-day notice requirement "[w]hen there is reasonable cause to believe an employee is guilty of a crime for which a sentence of imprisonment can be imposed."

Perhaps partly on the basis of some of these constitutional considerations, Congress has provided for pretermination hearings. Certainly the debate on the Lloyd-La Follette Act indicates that constitutional considerations were present in the minds of Congressmen speaking in favor of the legislation.[11] In any event, I conclude that the statute and regulations, to the extent they require 30 days' advance notice and a right to make

---

[11] Congressman Calder stated that the Act would "give assurance and confidence to the employees that they will at least get a square deal and will not permit of supervisory or executive officers filing charges of one kind against an employee and having him removed from the service or reduced in salary on evidence submitted on matters entirely foreign to the original charges that the employee has answered in writing." 48 Cong. Rec. 4654 (1912).

Congressman Konop stated:

"Any man in public service should have a right as a citizen to know why he is discharged from public duty, and as a citizen should certainly have a chance to be heard." *Id.,* at 5207.

a written presentation, satisfy minimum constitutional requirements.

IV

Appellee in this case not only asserts that he is entitled to a hearing at some time before his property interest is finally terminated, and to a pretermination hearing of some kind before his wages are provisionally cut off, which are currently provided to him, but also argues that he must be furnished certain procedures at this preliminary hearing not provided by Congress: an impartial hearing examiner, an opportunity to present witnesses, and the right to engage in cross-examination. In other words, his claim is not only to a pretermination hearing, but one in which full trial-type procedures are available.

A

The facts in this case show that the Regional Director, Verduin, who charged appellee Kennedy with making slanderous statements about him as to an alleged bribe offer, also ruled in the preliminary hearing that Kennedy should be terminated.

The "Notification of Proposed Adverse Action," signed by Verduin, charged that appellee had "made statements knowingly against officials of this agency which could harm or destroy their authority, official standing or reputation" and that appellee had engaged "in a course of conduct intended to produce public notoriety and conclusions on the part of the public, without any proof whatsover and in reckless disregard of the actual facts known to you [appellee], or reasonably discoverable by you [appellee], that officials of this agency had committed or attempted to commit acts of misfeasance, nonfeasance and malfeasance." Facts were marshaled to support the charges that appellee had spoken at a union meeting "to the effect that [Verduin and his assistant] had attempted to bribe Mr. James White Eagle Stewart by offering him a $100,000 grant of OEO funds if he would sign a statement against you [appellee] and another employee," and that appellee had spoken of the bribe to a newspaper reporter and to a radio station.

After appellee had received this notice, he made no response to the merits of the charges, but instead wrote to Verduin requesting that he was entitled to certain procedural rights at the hearing, one of which was to have "a genuinely impartial hearing officer," thus furnishing Verduin with the opportunity to recuse himself and provide an alternative hearing examiner. This was not done.

In considering appellee's claim to have an impartial hearing examiner, we might start with a first principle: "[N]o man shall be a judge in his own cause." *Bonham's Case*, 8 Co. 114a, 118a, 77 Eng. Rep. 646, 652 (1610). Verduin's reputation was certainly at stake in the charges brought against Kennedy. Indeed, the heart of the charge was that Kennedy had spoken of Verduin in reckless disregard of the truth. That Verduin almost seemed to be stating a libel complaint against Kennedy under *New York Times Co.* v. *Sullivan*, 376 U. S. 254 (1964), dramatizes the personal conflict which precipitated the proposed termination.

Our decisions have stressed, in situations analogous to the one faced here, that the right to an impartial decision-maker is required by due process. The Court has held that those with a substantial pecuniary interest in legal proceedings should not adjudicate these disputes. *Tumey* v. *Ohio*, 273 U. S. 510 (1927); *Ward* v. *Village of Monroeville*, 409 U. S. 57 (1972). The Court has observed that disqualification because of interest has been extended with equal force to administrative adjudications. *Gibson* v. *Berryhill*, 411 U. S. 564, 579 (1973).

In the context of contempt before a judge, where a judge trying a defendant is the object of "efforts to denounce, insult, and slander the court," and "marked personal feelings were present on both sides," the Court has held that criminal contempt proceedings should be held before a judge other than the one reviled by the contemnor. *Mayberry* v. *Pennsylvania*, 400 U. S. 455, 462, 464 (1971). See *In re Oliver*, 333 U. S. 257 (1948); cf. *In re Murchison*, 349 U. S. 133 (1955).

We have also stressed the need for impartiality in administrative proceedings, stating in *Goldberg* v. *Kelly, supra,* that an "impartial decision maker is essential," 397 U. S., at 271. (Citations omitted.) To the same effect was *Morrissey* v. *Brewer*, 408 U. S. 471, 485–486 (1972), involving revocation of parole. In both *Goldberg* and *Morrissey*, this requirement was held to apply to pretermination hearings.[12]

It may be true that any hearing without an impartial hearing officer will reflect the bias of the adjudicator. The interest of the Government in not so providing would appear slim. Given the pretermination hearing, it would seem in the Government's interest to avoid lengthy appeals occasioned by biased initial judgments, and it would be reasonable to expect more correct decisions at the initial stage at little cost if the hearing officer is impartial.

---

[12] In *Pickering* v. *Board of Education*, 391 U. S. 563, 579 n. 2 (1968), where the Court set aside a discharge by a Board of Education of a teacher for writing a letter to a newspaper attacking the Board, the trier of fact, the Board, was the same body that was the object of accusations in the letter. Although the Court did not rule on the due process question, since it was first raised here, it observed that "we do not propose to blind ourselves to the obvious defects in the fact-finding process occasioned by the Board's multiple functioning *vis-à-vis* appellant," citing *Tumey* v. *Ohio*, 273 U. S. 510 (1927), and *In re Murchison*, 349 U. S. 133 (1955).

My view is a narrower one, however. Fairness and accuracy are not always threatened simply because the hearing examiner is the supervisor of an employee, or, as in this case, the Regional Director over many employees, including appellee. But here the hearing official was the object of slander that was the basis for the employee's proposed discharge. See *Mayberry* v. *Pennsylvania, supra.* In ruling that the employee was to be terminated, the hearing examiner's own reputation, as well as the efficiency of the service, was at stake; and although Mr. Verduin may have succeeded, in fact, in disassociating his own personal feelings from his decision as to the interests of OEO, the risk and the appearance that this was not the case were too great to tolerate. In such situations the official normally charged with the discharge decision need only recuse and transfer the file to a person qualified to make the initial decision. We need not hold that the Lloyd-La Follette Act is unconstitutional for its lack of provision for an impartial hearing examiner. Congress is silent on the matter. We would rather assume, because of the constitutional problems in not so providing, that, if faced with the question (at least on the facts of this case) Congress would have so provided. *Volkswagenwerk* v. *FMC,* 390 U. S. 261, 272 (1968). "Where administrative action has raised serious constitutional problems, the Court has assumed that Congress or the President intended to afford those affected by the action the traditional safeguards of due process." *Greene* v. *McElroy,* 360 U. S., at 507 (citations omitted).[13]

---

[13] We further note that appellants suggest that "the Act and regulations, fairly construed, require the determination of cause to be made without bias." Brief for Appellants 24 n. 12.

B

Appellee also claims a right to a full trial-type hearing at the pretermination stage, particularly asserting that he is denied due process, if not given the opportunity to present and cross-examine witnesses.

While fully realizing the value of a full trial-type hearing as a method for ultimate resolution of the facts, see *id.*, at 496–497, the pretermination hearing is not held for the purpose of making such an ultimate determination. This is provided for through the appeal procedure where the employee is afforded the procedural rights he now seeks at an earlier stage of the proceedings. The function of the pretermination hearing is, and no more is required by due process, to make a probable-cause determination as to whether the charges brought against the employee are or are not true. Where the Court has held that pretermination hearings are required, in past decisions, it has spoken sparingly of the procedures to be required. *Sniadach* was silent on the matter, and *Fuentes* merely required something more than an *ex parte* proceeding before a court clerk. In *Bell,* the Court held that the hearing must involve a probable-cause determination as to the fault of the licensee, and "need not take the form of a full adjudication of the question of liability," realizing that "[a] procedural rule that may satisfy due process in one context may not necessarily satisfy due process in every case." 402 U. S., at 540. Thus, "procedural due process [was to] be satisfied by an inquiry limited to the determination whether there is a reasonable possibility of judgments in the amounts claimed being rendered against the licensee." *Ibid.* We think the clear implication of *Bell* to be that "full adjudication," including presentation of witnesses and cross-examination, need not be provided in every case where a pretermination hearing of some kind is required by due process or provided by the statute.

In *Goldberg* v. *Kelly,* the Court struck a different note on procedures. Although stating that the only function of the pretermination hearing was "to produce an initial determination of the validity of the welfare department's grounds for discontinuance of payments," and seemingly adopting a probable-cause standard, the Court required cross-examination of witnesses relied upon by the department. The Court was careful to observe, however, that these procedural rules were "tailored to the capacities and circumstances of those who are to be heard." 397 U. S., at 267, 268–269. The decision to cut off AFDC welfare payments leaves the recipient literally without any means to survive or support a family. While this level of deprivation may not be insisted upon as a necessary condition for requiring some kind of pretermination hearing, it may well be decisive in requiring the Government to provide specific procedures at the pretermination stage. The greater the level of deprivation which may flow from a decision, the less one may tolerate the risk of a mistaken decision, cf. *Morrissey* v. *Brewer, supra,* and thus the Court in *Goldberg,* while maintaining that the pretermination hearing was in the nature of a probable-cause determination, was less willing to allow a margin of error as to probable cause. Rules of procedure are often shaped by the risk of making an erroneous determination. See *In re Winship,* 397 U. S. 358, 368 (1970) (Harlan, J., concurring). Indeed, all that was specifically not required in *Goldberg* was a complete record and a comprehensive opinion. 397 U. S., at 267.

In this case, the employee is not totally without prospect for some form of support during the period between the pretermination and final hearing on appeal, though it may not be equivalent in earnings or tenure to his prior competitive service position. Although the employee may not be entitled to unemployment compensation, see *Christian v. New York Dept. of Labor*, 414 U. S. 614 (1974), since he has been terminated for cause he may get some form of employment in the private sector, and, if necessary, may draw on the welfare system in the interim. Given this basic floor of need, which the system provides, we should not hold that procedural due process is so inflexible as to require the Court to hold that the procedural protections, of a written statement and oral presentation to an impartial hearing examiner provided by regulation, are insufficient. The Court stated in *Richardson v. Wright*, 405 U. S. 208 (1972), that new regulations of the Department of Health, Education, and Welfare required that Social Security disability payments were not to be suspended in a pretermination hearing without "notice of a proposed suspension and the reasons therefor, plus an opportunity to submit rebuttal evidence," but could be without an oral presentation, since "[i]n the context of a comprehensive complex administrative program, the administrative process must have a reasonable opportunity to evolve procedures to meet needs as they arise." Cf. *Torres v. New York State Department of Labor*, 333 F. Supp. 341 (SDNY 1971), aff'd, 405 U. S. 949 (1972). Necessarily, to some extent, the Court must share with Congress, in an area where one is called upon to judge the efficacy of particular procedures, a role in defining constitutional requirements, and Congress explicitly left it to the discretion of the agency as to whether such procedures were required. I would not upset that judgment in this case.

In accord with these views, I would affirm the judgment of the three-judge court, ordering reinstatement and backpay, due to the failure to provide an impartial hearing officer at the pretermination hearing. I would reverse that part of the court's order enjoining the application of the statute on First Amendment vagueness and overbreadth grounds.

MR. JUSTICE DOUGLAS, dissenting.

The federal bureaucracy controls a vast conglomerate of people who walk more and more submissively to the dictates of their superiors. Our federal employees have lost many important political rights. *CSC* v. *Letter Carriers*, 413 U. S. 548, held that they could be barred from taking "an active part in political management or in political campaigns," a restriction that some of us thought to be unconstitutional, *id.*, at 595 *et seq.* (DOUGLAS, J., dissenting). Today's decision deprives them of other important First Amendment rights.

Heretofore, as my Brother MARSHALL has shown, we have insisted that before a vital stake of the individual in society is destroyed by government he be given a hearing on the merits of the government's claim. Among these personal and vital stakes are welfare benefits, *Goldberg* v. *Kelly*, 397 U. S. 254; the weekly wage of a worker, *Sniadach* v. *Family Finance Corp.*, 395 U. S. 337; a person's driver's license, *Bell* v. *Burson*, 402 U. S. 535; repossession of household goods, *Fuentes* v. *Shevin*, 407 U. S. 67; the position of a tenured professor in a state educational institution, *Board of Regents* v. *Roth*, 408 U. S. 564; revocation of parole, *Morrissey* v. *Brewer*, 408 U. S. 471.

There is more than employment and a job at issue in this case. The stake of the federal employee is not only in a livelihood, but in his right to speak guaranteed by the First Amendment. He is charged with having stated that his superior and the superior's assistant had attempted to bribe a representative of a community action organization with whom the agency (OEO) had

dealings. He is charged with having stated that those
men offered a bribe of $100,000 in OEO funds to that
organization if its representative would sign a statement against appellee and another OEO employee.
This statement in my view was on a subject in the
public domain. We all know merely by living in Washington, D. C., the storms that have swept through that
agency and its branches. It has dealt with inflammatory problems in the solution of which inflammatory
utterances are often made. I realize that it is the tradition of the Court to "balance" the right of free speech
against other governmental interests and to sustain the
First Amendment right only when the Court deems that
in a given situation its importance outweighs competing interests. That was the approach in *Pickering* v.
Board of Education, 391 U. S. 563, where the Court
deemed what a teacher said against the school board
was more important than the board's sensibilities. The
Court, however, reserved decision where the comments
of an employee involved "either discipline by immediate
superiors or harmony among coworkers," *id.*, at 570.
That is one reason why Mr. Justice Black and I concurred
in the result citing, *inter alia*, our opinion in *Time, Inc.*
v. *Hill*, 385 U. S. 374. Mr. Justice Black said that the
"balancing" or "weighing" doctrine "plainly encourages
and actually invites judges to choose for themselves between conflicting values, even where, as in the First
Amendment, the Founders made a choice of values, one
of which is a free press. Though the Constitution requires that judges swear to obey and enforce it, it is
not altogether strange that all judges are not always
dead set against constitutional interpretations that expand their powers, and that when power is once claimed
by some, others are loath to give it up," *id.*, at 399–400.

The fact that appellee in the present case inveighed

against his superior is irrelevant. The matter on which
he spoke was in the public domain. His speaking may
well have aroused such animosity in his superior
as to disqualify him from being in charge of disciplinary
proceedings;[1] and conceivably it could cause disharmony
among workers. And these consequences are quite
antagonistic to the image which agencies have built.
Their dominant characteristic is the application of
Peter's Inversion. See L. Peter & R. Hull, The Peter
Principle 24–26 (Bantam ed. 1970). In a few words
Peter's Inversion marks the incompetent cadre's interest
in an employee's *input,* not his *output.*[2]

His *input* reflects his attitude toward the cadre, and
toward his work. A pleasant manner, promotion of staff
harmony, servility to the cadre, and promptness, civility,
and submissiveness are what count. The result is a

---

[1] A judge so reviled is normally not the one to sit in judgment
in a criminal contempt proceeding. *Mayberry* v. *Pennsylvania,* 400
U. S. 455. Cf. *Goldberg* v. *Kelly,* 397 U. S. 254, 271.

[2] "The competence of an employee is determined *not by outsiders
but by his superior in the hierarchy.* If the superior is still at a
level of competence, he may evaluate his subordinates in terms of
the performance of useful work—for example, the applying of medical services or information, the production of sausages or table legs
or achieving whatever are the stated aims of the .hierarchy. That
is to say, *he evaluates output.*

"But if the superior has reached his level of incompetence, he
will probably rate his subordinates in terms of institutional values;
he will see competence as the behavior that supports the rules,
rituals and forms of the status quo. Promptness, neatness, courtesy
to superiors, internal paperwork, will be highly regarded. In short,
such an official *evaluates input* . . .

"In such instances, *internal consistency is valued more highly
than efficient service:* this is *Peter's Inversion.* A professional
automaton may also be termed a 'Peter's Invert.' He has inverted
the means-end relationship." L. Peter & R. Hull, The Peter Principle 25 (Bantam ed. 1970).

great leveling of employees. They hear the beat of only one drum and march to it. These days employers have psychological tests by which they can separate the ingenious, offbeat character who may make trouble from the more subservient type. It is, of course, none of a court's problem what the employment policies may be.[3] But once an employee speaks out on a public issue and is punished for it, we have a justiciable issue. Appellee is in my view being penalized by the Federal Government for exercising his right to speak out. The excuse or pretense is an Act of Congress and an agency's regulations promulgated under it in the teeth of the First Amendment: "Congress shall make no law . . . abridging the freedom of speech, or of the press . . . ." Losing one's job with the Federal Government because of one's discussion of an issue in the public domain is certainly an abridgment of speech.

MR. JUSTICE MARSHALL, with whom MR. JUSTICE DOUGLAS and MR. JUSTICE BRENNAN concur, dissenting.

I would affirm the judgment of the District Court, both in its holding that a tenured Government employee must be afforded an evidentiary hearing prior to a dismissal for cause and in its decision that 5 U. S. C. § 7501 is unconstitutionally vague and overbroad as a regulation of employees' speech.

I

The first issue in this case is a relatively narrow one— whether a federal employee in the competitive service, entitled by statute to serve in his job without fear of

---

[3] Apart from discrimination based on race, *Griggs* v. *Duke Power Co.*, 401 U. S. 424, or on other suspect classifications such as sex. See *id.*, at 436; 42 U. S. C. § 2000e–2; *Frontiero* v. *Richardson*, 411 U. S. 677, 682 *et seq.*

dismissal except for cause,[1] must be given an evidentiary hearing before he is discharged. We are hardly writing on a clean slate in this area. In just the last five years, the Court has held that such a hearing must be afforded before wages can be garnished, *Sniadach* v. *Family Finance Corp.,* 395 U. S. 337 (1969); welfare benefits terminated, *Goldberg* v. *Kelly,* 397 U. S. 254 (1970); a driver's license revoked, *Bell* v. *Burson,* 402 U. S. 535 (1971); consumer goods repossessed, *Fuentes* v. *Shevin,* 407 U. S. 67 (1972); parole revoked, *Morrissey* v. *Brewer,* 408 U. S. 471 (1972); or a tenured college professor fired by a public educational institution, *Board of Regents* v. *Roth,* 408 U. S. 564 (1972); *Perry* v. *Sindermann,* 408 U. S. 593 (1972).

A

In the *Roth* and *Sindermann* cases, MR. JUSTICE STEWART established the framework for analysis to determine in what circumstances the Due Process Clause demands a hearing. He observed that although due process is a flexible concept, it is not unlimited in application. "The requirements of procedural due process apply only to the deprivation of interests encompassed by the Fourteenth Amendment's protection of liberty and property." *Roth, supra,* at 569. Thus the first issue to be decided is whether appellee had an interest in his tenured Government employment such that his discharge amounts to a deprivation of liberty or property.

The decisions of this Court have given constitutional recognition to the fact that in our complex modern society, wealth and property take many forms.[2] We

---

[1] 5 U. S. C. § 7501 (a).

[2] One noted commentator has observed:

"Changes in the forms of wealth are not remarkable in themselves; the forms are constantly changing and differ in every culture. But today more and more of our wealth takes the form

have said that property interests requiring constitutional protection "extend well beyond actual ownership of real estate, chattels, or money." *Roth, supra,* at 572. They extend as well to "safeguard . . . the security of interests that a person has already acquired in specific benefits." *Id.,* at 576. The test for whether a protected interest has been infringed reflects this broad concept of "property":

> "To have a property interest in a benefit, a person . . . must . . . have a legitimate claim of entitlement to it. It is a purpose of the ancient institution of property to protect those claims upon which people rely in their daily lives, reliance that must not be arbitrarily undermined." *Id.,* at 577.

Accordingly, in *Goldberg* v. *Kelly, supra,* the Court found that public assistance recipients had such a claim of entitlement to welfare benefits grounded in the statute defining eligibility. In *Bell* v. *Burson, supra,* the Court held that a driver's license, once issued, becomes an important property interest because its "continued possession may become essential in the pursuit of a livelihood." 402 U. S., at 539. More to the point, in *Roth* the Court

---

of rights or status rather than of tangible goods. An individual's profession or occupation is a prime example. To many others, a job with a particular employer is the principal form of wealth. A profession or job is frequently far more valuable than a house or bank account, for a new house can be bought, and a new bank account created, once a profession or job is secure." Reich, The New Property, 73 Yale L. J. 733, 738 (1964).

"Society today is built around entitlement [and m]any of the most important of these entitlements now flow from government . . . . Such sources of security . . . are no longer regarded as luxuries or gratuities; to the recipients they are essentials, fully deserved, and in no sense a form of charity." Reich, Individual Rights and Social Welfare: The Emerging Legal Issues, 74 Yale L. J. 1245, 1255 (1965).

surveyed the constitutional restraints applicable in the area of public employment:

> "[T]he Court has held that a public [...] professor dismissed from an office held under tenure provisions, *Slochower* v. *Board of Education,* 350 U. S. 551, and college professors and staff members dismissed during the terms of their contracts, *Wieman* v. *Updegraff,* 344 U. S. 183, have interests in continued employment that are safeguarded by due process." 408 U. S., at 576–577.

See also *Connell* v. *Higginbotham,* 403 U. S. 207 (1971). In *Perry* v. *Sindermann, supra,* we found a property interest in the implied tenure policy of a state university.

We have already determined that a legitimate claim of entitlement to continued employment absent "sufficient cause" is a property interest requiring the protections of procedural due process.[3] Thus, there can be little doubt that appellee's tenured Government employment, from which he could not legally be dismissed except for cause, must also be a "property" interest for the purposes of the Fifth Amendment. The job security appellee enjoyed is clearly one of "those claims upon which people rely in their daily lives." *Roth, supra,* at 577. And appellee's interest in continued public employment encompassed more than just the periodic accrual of wages. His dismissal also affects his valuable statutory entitlements to retirement credits and benefits, 5 U. S. C. §§ 8301, 8311–8322, 8331–8348; periodic salary increases, 5 U. S. C. § 5335; and life and health insurance, 5 U. S. C. §§ 8701–8716, 8901–8913 (1970 ed. and Supp II).

We are in agreement that appellee does have a claim of entitlement to his Government job, absent proof of

---

[3] *Board of Regents* v. *Roth,* 408 U. S. 564, 576–578 (1972); *Perry* v. *Sindermann,* 408 U. S. 593, 599–603 (1972).

specified misconduct. MR. JUSTICE REHNQUIST explains, however, that this claim is founded only in statute, and that the statute which guarantees tenure also provides that a hearing is not required before discharge. He concludes that "the property interest which appellee had in his employment was itself conditioned by the procedural limitations which had accompanied the grant of that interest," *ante*, at 155, wryly observing that "a litigant in the position of appellee must take the bitter with the sweet," *ante*, at 154.

Courts once considered procedural due process protections inapplicable to welfare on much the same theory—that "in accepting charity, the appellant has consented to the provisions of the law under which charity is bestowed." [4] Obviously, this Court rejected that reasoning in *Goldberg, supra,* where we held that conditions under which public assistance was afforded, which did not include a pretermination hearing, were violative of due process. [5] In *Sindermann, supra,* the Court held that the Constitution required a hearing before dismissal even where the implicit grant of tenure did not encompass the right to such a hearing. In *Morrissey* v. *Brewer,* 408 U. S. 471 (1972), the Court held that although the limited grant of liberty afforded by parole was conditioned by statute on the possibility of revocation without a prior evidentiary hearing, such a hearing was constitutionally required. In *Bell* v. *Burson, supra,* the

---

[4] *Wilkie* v. *O'Connor,* 261 App. Div. 373, 375, 25 N. Y. S. 2d 617, 620 (1941).

[5] The mechanism for welfare terminations is described in *Goldberg* v. *Kelly,* 397 U. S. 254, 258–260 (1970). In short, the procedure involved prior notice and an opportunity to respond in writing before termination as well as a full trial-type hearing before an independent state official after the termination had been effected. If the recipient prevailed at the later hearing he would be entitled to recover any funds wrongfully withheld.

state statute under which drivers' licenses were issued provided for the suspension of an uninsured
motorist's license without a prior hearing. The Court
nonetheless held that a hearing was required before the
suspension could be effected. In none of these cases
did the Court consider a statutory procedure to be an
inherent limitation on the statutorily created liberty or
property interest.[6] Rather, once such an interest was
found, the Court determined whether greater procedural
protections were required by the Due Process Clause
than were accorded by the statute.

Applying that analysis here requires us to find that
although appellee's property interest arose from statute,
the deprivation of his claim of entitlement to continued
employment would have to meet minimum standards of
procedural due process regardless of the discharge
procedures provided by the statute. Accordingly, a
majority of the Court rejects MR. JUSTICE REHNQUIST's
argument that because appellee's entitlement arose from
statute, it could be conditioned on a statutory limitation
of procedural due process protections, an approach which
would render such protection inapplicable to the deprivation of any statutory benefit—any "privilege" extended
by Government—where a statute prescribed a termination procedure, no matter how arbitrary or unfair. It
would amount to nothing less than a return, albeit in
somewhat different verbal garb, to the thoroughly discredited distinction between rights and privileges which
once seemed to govern the applicability of procedural
due process.[7]

---

[6] Although *Perry* v. *Sindermann, supra,* did not involve a
statutorily created interest, it is plainly analogous in that the *de facto*
tenure program on which Sindermann's claim of entitlement was
grounded did not explicitly include the right to a hearing.

[7] In a leading case decided many years ago, the Court of Appeals
for the District of Columbia Circuit held that procedural due

B

We have repeatedly observed that due process requires
that a hearing be held "at a meaningful time and in a
meaningful manner," *Armstrong* v. *Manzo,* 380 U. S. 545,
552 (1965), but it remains for us to give content to that
general principle in this case by balancing the Government's asserted interests against those of the discharged employee. *Goldberg* v. *Kelly,* 397 U. S., at 263;
see *Cafeteria Workers* v. *McElroy,* 367 U. S. 886, 895
(1961).

The interests of a public employee in a secure Government job are as weighty as other interests which we
have found to require at least the rudimentary protection of an evidentiary hearing as a precondition to
termination.

> "This Court has often had occasion to note that the
> denial of public employment is a serious blow to any
> citizen. . . . Employment is one of the greatest, if
> not the greatest, benefits that governments offer in
> modern-day life." *Roth,* 408 U. S., at 589 (MAR-
> SHALL, J., dissenting).

See *Perry* v. *Sindermann, supra; Connell* v. *Higginbotham,* 403 U. S. 207 (1971); *Keyishian* v. *Board of*

---

process protections did not apply to Government employment because it was merely a privilege and not a right. *Bailey* v. *Richardson,* 86 U. S. App. D. C. 248, 182 F. 2d 46 (1950), aff'd by an equally
divided Court, 341 U. S. 918 (1951). As we have previously observed, "[t]he basis of this holding has been thoroughly undermined
in the ensuing years." *Board of Regents* v. *Roth,* 408 U. S., at 571
n. 9. "[T]he Court has fully and finally rejected the wooden distinction between 'rights' and 'privileges' . . . ." *Id.,* at 571. For example,
the Court has found constitutional restraints applicable to disqualification for unemployment compensation, *Sherbert* v. *Verner,* 374 U. S.
398 (1963); denial of a tax exemption, *Speiser* v. *Randall,* 357 U. S.
513 (1958); termination of welfare benefits, *Goldberg* v. *Kelly, supra;*
and dismissal from public employment, *e. g., Slochower* v. *Board of
Higher Education,* 350 U. S. 551 (1956).

Regents, 385 U. S. 589 (1967); *Cramp* v. *Board of Public Instruction*, 368 U. S. 278, 288 (1961); *Anti-Fascist Committee* v. *McGrath*, 341 U. S. 123, 185 (1951) (Jackson, J., concurring); *United States* v. *Lovett*, 328 U. S. 303, 316–317 (1946). The Court has recognized the vital importance of employment in related contexts. In *Sniadach* v. *Family Finance Corp.*, the Court expressed its particular concern that "garnishment [of wages] often meant the loss of a job," 395 U. S., at 340, and in *Bell* v. *Burson, supra,* we relied heavily on the fact that a driver's license may be "essential in the pursuit of a livelihood," 402 U. S., at 539. In *Greene* v. *McElroy,* 360 U. S. 474, 508 (1959), the Court construed federal security clearance regulations to avoid the constitutional issues that would be presented if the petitioner were deprived "of his job in a proceeding in which he was not afforded the safeguards of [procedural due process]." See *id.,* at 506–507; *Willner* v. *Committee on Character,* 373 U. S. 96, 103–104 (1963).

An exhaustive study by the United States Administrative Conference of the problem of agency dismissals led the author of the Conference's report to observe:

> "One cannot escape the conclusion, however, that the government employee who is removed from his job loses something of tremendous value that in a market of declining demand for skills may not be replaceable." [8]

And the report also observes:

> "[O]ne must acknowledge what seems to be an accepted, if regrettable, fact of life: Removal from government employment for cause carries a stigma

---

[8] Merrill, Report in Support of Recommendation 72–8, Procedures for Adverse Actions Against Federal Employees, in 2 Recommendations and Reports of the Administrative Conference of the United States 1007, 1015 (1972) (hereinafter Merrill).

that is probably impossible to outlive.   Agency personnel officers are generally prepared to concede . . . that it is difficult for the fired government worker to find employment in the private sector." [9]

Dismissal from public employment for cause may also, therefore, implicate liberty interests in imposing on the discharged employee a stigma of incompetence or wrongdoing that forecloses "his freedom to take advantage of other employment opportunities."   *Roth, supra,* at 573; see *Wisconsin* v. *Constantineau,* 400 U. S. 433, 437 (1971).

Given the importance of the interest at stake, the discharged employee should be afforded an opportunity to test the strength of the evidence of his misconduct by confronting and cross-examining adverse witnesses and by presenting witnesses in his own behalf, whenever there are substantial disputes in testimonial evidence.   See *Morrissey* v. *Brewer,* 408 U. S., at 487. A dismissal for cause often involves disputed questions of fact raised by accusations of misconduct.   Mistakes of identity, distortions caused by the failure of information sources, faulty perceptions or cloudy memories, as well as fabrications born of personal antagonisms are among the factors which may undermine the accuracy of the factual determinations upon which dismissals are based.   The possibility of error is not insignificant. Almost a fourth of all appeals from adverse agency actions result in reversal.[10]

In our system of justice, the right of confrontation

---

[9] *Ibid.* The report of the Administrative Conference seems to bear out my Brother DOUGLAS' recent observation:

"Once there is a discharge from a . . . federal agency, dismissal may be a badge that bars the employee from other federal employment. The shadow of that discharge is cast over the area where private employment may be available." *Sampson* v. *Murray,* 415 U. S. 61, 95 (1974) (dissenting).

[10] Merrill 1014 n. 33.

provides the crucible for testing the truth of accusations such as those leveled by appellee's superior and strenuously denied by appellee. "In almost every setting where important decisions turn on questions of fact, due process requires an opportunity to confront and cross-examine adverse witnesses." *Goldberg* v. *Kelly,* 397 U. S., at 269 (citations omitted).[11] The *Goldberg* Court's citation to a well-known passage from *Greene* v. *McElroy,* 360 U. S. 474 (1959), is equally applicable to a dismissal from public employment for cause as to a termination of welfare benefits.

" 'Certain principles have remained immutable in our jurisprudence. One of these is that where government action seriously injures an individual, and the reasonableness of the action depends on fact findings, the evidence used to prove the Government's case must be disclosed to the individual so that he has an opportunity to show that it is untrue. While this is important in the case of documentary evidence, it is even more important where the evidence consists of the testimony of individuals whose memory might be faulty or who, in fact, might be perjurers or persons motivated by malice, vindictiveness, intolerance, prejudice or jealousy. We have formalized these protections in the requirements of confrontation and cross-examination.' " *Id.,* at 496–497, quoted in *Goldberg* v. *Kelly, supra,* at 270.

See also *Chambers* v. *Mississippi,* 410 U. S. 284, 295–298 (1973); *Pointer* v. *Texas,* 380 U. S. 400 (1965).

---

[11] This case presents no question as to the requirements of due process "where there are no factual issues in dispute or where the application of the rule of law is not intertwined with factual issues." *Goldberg* v. *Kelly,* 397 U. S., at 268 n. 15; see *Mills* v. *Richardson,* 464 F. 2d 995, 1001 (CA2 1972); cf. *FCC* v. *WJR,* 337 U. S. 265, 275–277 (1949); 1 K. Davis, Administrative Law Treatise 412 (1958).

This case and *Goldberg* involve the termination of income, whether in salary or public assistance payments, upon which the recipient may depend for basic sustenance. A person should not be deprived of his livelihood "in a proceeding in which he was not afforded the safeguards of confrontation and cross-examination." *Greene, supra,* at 508; see *Jenkins* v. *McKeithen,* 395 U. S. 411, 423–429 (1969); *Willner* v. *Committee on Character,* 373 U. S., at 103. The stakes are just too high and the possibility of misjudgment too great to allow dismissal without giving the tenured public employee an opportunity to contest its basis and produce evidence in rebuttal. See *Goldberg, supra,* at 266.

It also seems clear that for the hearing to be meaningful, the hearing officer must be independent and unbiased and his decision be entitled to some weight. We addressed the importance of this element of due process in *Goldberg, supra,* where we found the requirements of due process were not met by the review of a welfare termination decision by the caseworker who was, in effect, also the complainant. 397 U. S., at 271. In *Morrissey* v. *Brewer, supra,* we held that an independent decisionmaker must determine whether reasonable grounds exist for parole revocation because an "officer directly involved in making recommendations cannot always have complete objectivity in evaluating them." 408 U. S., at 486. The need for an independent decisionmaker is particularly crucial in the public employment context, where the reason for the challenged dismissal may well be related to some personal antagonism between the employee and his superior, as appears to be the case here.[12] See *Pickering* v. *Board of Education,* 391 U. S. 563, 578–579, Appendix n. 2 (1968).

---

[12] See *ante,* at 137–138. Cf. T. Arnold, Fair Fights and Foul 151 (1965) (describing the potential abuse in a situation where the head

C

A discharged federal worker in the competitive service is, in fact, guaranteed a full evidentiary hearing before an impartial decisionmaker whose report is entitled to considerable weight.[13] But the timing of the hearing is discretionary with the employing agency, see 5 CFR § 771.208 (a) (1972), and in many agencies, such as the OEO, the hearing comes long after the employee has been removed from the Government service and payroll. In a sense, then, the real issue is not whether appellee must be accorded an evidentiary hearing, but only whether that hearing should have been afforded *before* his discharge became effective. Although the nature of the hearing required by due process is determined by a balancing process, that hearing must be held at a meaningful time. Accordingly, the Court has embraced a general presumption that one who is constitutionally entitled to a hearing should be heard before the deprivation of his liberty or property takes place. Thus, in *Boddie* v. *Connecticut,* 401 U. S. 371 (1971), the Court observed that the fact that "the hearing . . . is not fixed in form does not affect its root require-

---

of a department is the decisionmaker in a public employee discharge proceeding).

[13] The discharged employee is entitled to a full trial-type proceeding before a single examiner who may not occupy a position directly or indirectly under the jurisdiction of the official who proposed the dismissal or who bears ultimate responsibility for that decision. The examiner's decision is afforded substantial weight; if it is rejected, the rejection must be accompanied by a full statement of reasons that is subject to review. Both the employee and the agency may produce, examine, and cross-examine witnesses under oath or affirmation, and documentary evidence may also be introduced. Rigorous trial formality is avoided and care taken not to place an uncounseled employee at a disadvantage. See Merrill 1038–1040; 5 CFR §§ 771.209–771.211 (1972).

ment that an individual be given an opportunity for a hearing *before* he is deprived of any significant property interest, except for extraordinary situations where some valid governmental interest is at stake that justifies postponing the hearing until after the event." *Id.,* at 378–379. (Emphasis in orginal.) In *Bell* v. *Burson, supra,* we held that "except in emergency situations . . . due process requires that when a State seeks to terminate an [important property] interest . . . it must afford 'notice and opportunity for hearing . . .' *before* the termination becomes effective." 402 U. S., at 542 (emphasis in original) (footnote omitted). In *Goldberg* v. *Kelly, supra,* the Court found that an evidentiary hearing held after the termination of welfare benefits was inadequate to satisfy constitutional requirements.[14]

Even if we accept appellants' assertion that a subsequent hearing affords the discharged employee an opportunity to clear his name,[15] the worker still has a significant interest in retaining his job pending a full hearing.[16]   Almost a fourth of all appeals from agency

---

[14] The procedure in *Goldberg* also involved a pretermination right of reply and a full trial-type hearing after termination, see n. 5, *supra,* but the scheme was nonetheless found not to satisfy due process requirements and a full pretermination hearing was required. See O'Neil, Of Justice Delayed and Justice Denied; The Welfare Prior Hearing Cases, 1970 Sup. Ct. Rev. 161, 169.

[15] See n. 9, *supra,* and n. 19, *infra.*

[16] Both MR. JUSTICE REHNQUIST and MR. JUSTICE WHITE dismiss the need for a full prior hearing partially by reference to the Court's decision in *Cafeteria Workers* v. *McElroy,* 367 U. S. 886 (1961). That case is entirely inapposite. First, it involved not the dismissal for cause of a tenured civil service employee, but rather the withdrawal of the security clearance of the employee of a private contractor, which, in effect, barred the worker from her job in the commissary at a military base. The employer was prepared to employ the worker at another of his restaurants, so the withdrawal of her security clearance was not

dismissals result in a finding that the termination was illegal.[17]   And, the delay from discharge to ultimate vindication at a hearing on appeal is far from insubstantial.   More than 75% of adverse personnel actions take more than two months to process; over half take more than three months and a not insignificant number take more than a year.[18]   The longer the period between the discharge and the hearing, the more devastating will be the impact of the loss of employment.

During the period of delay, the employee is off the Government payroll.   His ability to secure other employment to tide himself over may be significantly hindered by the outstanding charges against him.[19]   Even aside from the stigma that attends a dismissal for cause, few employers will be willing to hire and train a new employee knowing that he will return to a former Government position as soon as an appeal is successful.[20]

---

apt to cause the serious financial hardship that appellee's dismissal from public employment might entail. See *Board of Regents* v. *Roth,* 408 U. S., at 584–585 (DOUGLAS, J., dissenting).   Moreover, the Court has since read *Cafeteria Workers* to be a case where the Government's "exceptional" interest in national security justified an abridgment of the right to a hearing. *Fuentes* v. *Shevin,* 407 U. S. 67, 91 n. 23 (1972); see *Boddie* v. *Connecticut,* 401 U. S. 371, 379 (1971).

[17] Merrill 1014 n. 33.

[18] *Id.,* at 1016.

[19] My Brother REHNQUIST argues that the stigma imposed by dismissal is only temporary in that the discharged employee can clear his name at the *post-hoc* hearing, hence does not "foreclose his freedom to take advantage of other employment opportunities." *Board of Regents* v. *Roth,* 408 U. S., at 573; see n. 9, *supra.*   But the stigma of outstanding charges would nonetheless be borne by the employee in the interim period while he waits for his hearing and seeks alternative employment to tide himself over.

[20] See, *e. g.,* Hearings on Postal Labor Relations and Employee Morale before the Subcommittee on Postal Operations of the House

And in many States, including Illinois, where appellee
resides, a worker discharged for cause is not even eligible
for unemployment compensation.[21]

Many workers, particularly those at the bottom of the
pay scale, will suffer severe and painful economic dislocations from even a temporary loss of wages. Few
public employees earn more than enough to pay their
expenses from month to month. See *Sampson* v. *Murray,* 415 U. S. 61, 97 (1974) (MARSHALL, J., dissenting).
Like many of us, they may be required to meet substantial fixed costs on a regular basis and lack substantial
savings to meet those expenses while not receiving a
salary. The loss of income for even a few weeks may well
impair their ability to provide the essentials of life—to
buy food, meet mortgage or rent payments, or procure
medical services. *Ricucci* v. *United States,* 192 Ct. Cl. 1,
9–11, 425 F. 2d 1252, 1256–1257 (1970) (Skelton, J., concurring). The plight of a discharged employee may not be
far different from that of the welfare recipient in *Goldberg*
who, "pending resolution of a controversy . . . may [be]
deprive[d] . . . of the very means by which to live while
he waits." 397 U. S., at 264. Appellee, although earning
an annual salary of $16,000 before his dismissal, far above
the mean salary for federal employees,[22] was nonetheless
driven to the brink of financial ruin while he waited.
He had to borrow money to support his family, his debts
went unpaid, his family lost the protection of his health
insurance and, finally, he was forced to apply for public

Committee on Post Office and Civil Service, 91st Cong., 1st Sess.
(1969); Kennedy, Adverse Actions in the Agencies—Words and
Deeds—Postal Adverse Action Procedures, 19 Am. U. L. Rev. 398,
412 (1970).

[21] See, e. g., Ill. Rev. Stat., c. 48, § 432 (1973); see *Christian* v.
New York Dept. of Labor, 414 U. S. 614 (1974).

[22] See Mandate for Merit: 1972 Annual Report of the United
States Civil Service Commission 64–65.

assistance. App. 128 *et seq.* In this context justice delayed may well be justice denied.

To argue that a dismissal from tenured Government employment is not a serious enough deprivation to require a prior hearing because the discharged employee may draw on the welfare system in the interim, is to exhibit a gross insensitivity to the plight of these employees. First, it assumes that the discharged employee will be eligible for welfare. Often welfare applicants must be all but stripped of their worldly goods before being admitted to the welfare roles, hence it is likely that the employee will suffer considerable hardship before becoming eligible. He may be required not only to exhaust his savings but also to convert many of his assets into cash for support before being able to fall back on public assistance. He may have to give up his home or cherished personal possessions in order to become eligible. The argument also assumes all but instant eligibility which is, sadly, far from likely even when all the employee's other sources of support have been depleted. Moreover, rightly or wrongly, many people consider welfare degrading and would decline public assistance even when eligible. Finally, the level of subsistence provided by welfare is minimal, certainly less than one is apt to expect from steady employment. The substitution of a meager welfare grant for a regular paycheck may bring with it painful and irremediable personal as well as financial dislocations. A child's education may be interrupted, a family's home lost, a person's relationship with his friends and even his family may be irrevocably affected. The costs of being forced, even temporarily, onto the welfare rolls because of a wrongful discharge from tenured Government employment cannot be so easily discounted.

Nor does the availability of backpay upon an ultimate

finding that the dismissal was improper alleviate the compelling nature of the employee's plight. Cf. *Sampson* v. *Murray*, 415 U. S., at 97 (MARSHALL, J., dissenting). In *Sniadach* v. *Family Finance Corp., supra,* the Court recognized that the employee had an interest in the enjoyment of his wages as they accrued and noted that even a temporary loss of salary could put a wage earner below the poverty level or "drive a wage-earning family to the wall." 395 U. S., at 341–342. Thus, we held that a wage earner is entitled to a hearing prior to the garnishment of his wages even though he would ultimately get his frozen earnings back when and if he prevailed in a suit on the merits. See also, *id.,* at 343 (Harlan, J., concurring). And, in *Fuentes* v. *Shevin,* 407 U. S. 67 (1972), the Court held that due process required a hearing before a seizure of property by writ of replevin, observing:

> "If the right to notice and a hearing is to serve its full purpose, then, it is clear that it must be granted at a time when the deprivation can still be prevented. At a later hearing, an individual's possessions can be returned to him if they were unfairly or mistakenly taken in the first place. Damages may even be awarded to him for wrongful deprivation. But no later hearing and no damage award can undo the fact that the arbitrary taking that was subject to the right of procedural due process had already occurred. 'This Court has not . . . embraced the general proposition that a wrong may be done if it can be undone.'" *Id.,* at 81–82.

The *Fuentes* Court, applying these considerations, albeit in dicta, observed that, "[i]n cases involving deprivations of other interests, such as government employment, the Court similarly has required an unusually important governmental need to outweigh the right to a prior hearing." *Id.,* at 91 n. 23.

The Court has recognized a number of instances where a vital governmental interest may outweigh the right to a prior hearing, including the need to seize property to "collect the internal revenue of the United States, to meet the needs of a national war effort, to protect against the economic disaster of a bank failure, and to protect the public from misbranded drugs and contaminated foods." *Id.,* at 92 (footnotes omitted).[23] Such a vital interest is clearly lacking here.

The Government's asserted interests in not affording a predismissal hearing are twofold. First, appellants argue that the delay in holding the hearing makes the functioning of the agency more efficient. We rejected a similar rationale in *Goldberg,* 397 U. S., at 266, and observed in *Fuentes, supra:*

> "A prior hearing always imposes some costs in time, effort, and expense, and it is often more efficient to dispense with the opportunity for such a hearing. But these rather ordinary costs cannot outweigh the constitutional right. Procedural due process is not intended to promote efficiency or accommodate all possible interests: it is intended to protect the particular interests of the person whose possessions [or property] are about to be taken.
>
> " ' . . . [T]he Constitution recognizes higher values than speed and efficiency. Indeed, one might fairly say of the Bill of Rights in general, and the Due Process Clause in particular, that they were designed to protect the fragile values of a vulnerable citizenry from the overbearing concern for efficiency and efficacy that may characterize praiseworthy government officials no less, and perhaps more, than mediocre

---

[23] See, *e. g., Central Union Trust Co.* v. *Garvan,* 254 U. S. 554, 566 (1921); *Phillips* v. *Commissioner,* 283 U. S. 589, 597 (1931); *Ewing* v. *Mytinger & Casselberry,* 339 U. S. 594 (1950).

ones.' "   407 U. S., at 90–91, n. 22 (citations omitted).

Moreover, the Government's interest in efficiency in this case is entirely unconvincing. The applicable statute does not prohibit prior hearings but rather makes them discretionary with the agency. Nine federal agencies, including the FCC, NLRB, HUD, HEW, the Department of Justice, and the Civil Service Commission itself, regularly accord evidentiary hearings prior to the dismissal of a tenured employee.[24] The Administrative Conference of the United States, on the basis of its exhaustive study of federal agency proceedings for the dismissal of employees in the competitive service, strongly recommended that evidentiary hearings be held prior to discharge.[25]

The Administrative Conference found that the evidence, although inconclusive, indicates that the agencies that provided pretermination hearings closed adverse action proceedings more quickly than those which did not hold an evidentiary hearing until after the dismissal had been effected. It also found that the delays in closing cases involving hearings are typically caused not by the length of the hearings—almost all are completed within a day—but rather by scheduling difficulties. And those agencies which take three months or more to hold post-termination hearings have little incentive to decide dismissal cases more promptly, since the employee has already been discharged and he bears most of the costs of delay. If the hearing were required before termination, agencies would have a far greater incentive to decide

---

[24] Merrill 1056.

[25] Recommendation 72–8, Adverse Actions Against Federal Employees, in 2 Recommendations and Reports of the Administrative Conference of the United States 73–75 (1972).

these cases expeditiously.[26]   Finally, providing an evidentiary hearing before the discharge might well obviate the
practical and constitutional need for a full post-termination proceeding.[27]

The Government also argues that if a supervisor were
unable to effect an immediate removal of a troublesome
employee from his agency, the discipline and efficiency
of the whole office might be disrupted.   Under the pre-
vailing practice, an agency may not dismiss an employee
until 30 days after he has received notice of the charges
against him and has had an opportunity to reply.   Thus,
fellow workers and supervisors must now function with
the threatened employee in their midst for at least a
month, and there seems little reason why a hearing could
not be held during that 30-day period.[28]   If the
employee actually threatens to disrupt the operation of
the office, he could be put on administrative leave or
temporarily assigned to a less sensitive position pending
his hearing, as currently provided for by regulation.
5 CFR § 752.202 (d).

------

[26] Merrill 1017, 1056–1057, 1060. Scheduling problems might be
largely overcome by more skillful use of personnel. See *Goldberg* v.
Kelly, 397 U. S., at 266.

[27] As we observed, *id.,* at 267 n. 14, due process does not, of course,
require two hearings. Under current procedures, an employee is
afforded one and sometimes two *post-hoc* evidentiary hearings (one
before the agency and the other before the Civil Service Commission). See Merrill 1013, 1043. If an adequate review mechanism is
maintained, a single pretermination hearing might obviate the need
for these later proceedings.

[28] See, *e. g.,* U. S. Dept. of Justice, Adverse Action Hearings, Appeals and Grievance Policies and Regulations, c. 2 (Sept. 28, 1972);
Recommendation 72–8, n. 25, *supra,* at ¶ B, 74. The notice requirement need not be any impediment to holding the hearing within
the 30-day period. In *Goldberg* v. *Kelly, supra,* at 268, for
example, the Court found a seven-day period between notice and
termination hearing constitutionally permissible.

The only pretermination proceeding accorded appellee was a "right of reply," see 5 CFR § 752.202 (b), but the "right of reply" falls far short of being the meaningful hearing which, in my view, is constitutionally required. As the author of the Administrative Conference Report observed:

> "In most agencies . . . an employee's right to reply simply means that he may meet informally with a representative of the agency and advance oral representations that he hopes will sway the final decision. He has no right at this stage to present witnesses or to confront and cross-examine the agency's witnesses." [29]   (Footnotes omitted.)

The agency official before whom the employee appears need not be the decisionmaker; he need only be able to recommend a decision.   Moreover, the hearing examiner or the person responsible for the decision to discharge the employee may well be the complainant or his direct subordinate.   In the case before us, for example, the decision as to whether appellee should be discharged was made by the OEO Regional Director whom appellee had accused of misconduct.   The Regional Director assembled the evidence against appellee, proposed the dismissal, then decided it should be effected; he acted as complaining witness, prosecutor, and judge.   The meaningless bureaucratic paper shuffling afforded appellee before his discharge would surely not alone satisfy the stringent demands of due process when such an important interest is at stake.

The decisions of this Court compel the conclusion that a worker with a claim of entitlement to public employment absent specified cause has a property interest protected by the Due Process Clause and there-

---

[29] Merrill 1033.

fore the right to an evidentiary hearing before an impartial decisionmaker prior to dismissal.   Accordingly,
I would affirm the decision of the court below that
appellee had been discharged in violation of his procedural due process rights.

II

The court below also held that the provision of the
Lloyd-La Follette Act which authorizes dismissal of tenured Government employees for "such cause as will promote the efficiency of the service" is unconstitutionally
vague and overbroad.[30]

There is no dispute that the phrase " 'such cause as
will promote the efficiency of the service as a standard of employee job protection is without doubt intended
to authorize dismissal for speech," *ante,* at 160.   The majority finds this permissible because in *Pickering* v. *Board
of Education,* 391 U. S. 563, 568 (1968), we observed that
"the State has interests as an employer in regulating the
speech of its employees that differ significantly from
those it possesses in connection with the regulation of
the speech of the citizenry in general."   But, the majority seems to have ignored the passage in *Pickering*
that directly precedes the quoted material:

"[T]o suggest that teachers may constitutionally be
compelled to relinquish the First Amendment rights

---

[30] Other cases in this area hardly provide substantial guidance
as to what speech is or is not protected. See, *e. g., Pickering* v.
Board of Education, 391 U. S. 563, 570 n. 3 (1968).   Nor do the ex-
tant regulations provide substantial guidance; they merely repeat the
language of the statute and provide examples as unelucidating
as the particular regulation relevant to this case which proscribed "any action . . . which might result in, or create the appearance of . . . (e) [i]mpeding Government efficiency or economy ... [or] (f) [a]ffecting adversely the confidence of the public in
the integrity of the Government."   5 CFR § 735.201a; see 45 CFR
§ 1015.735–1.

they would otherwise enjoy as citizens to comment
on matters of public interest in connection with the
operation of the public schools in which they
work, . . . proceeds on a premise that has been un-
equivocally rejected in numerous prior decisions of
this Court. *E. g., Wieman* v. *Updegraff,* 344 U. S.
183 (1952); *Shelton* v. *Tucker,* 364 U. S. 479 (1960);
Keyishian v. *Board of Regents,* 385 U. S. 589 (1967)."
391 U. S., at 568.

The importance of Government employees' being assured of their right to freely comment on the conduct
of Government, to inform the public of abuses of power
and of the misconduct of their superiors, must be self-
evident in these times. In *Pickering,* this Court specifically upheld the right of a public employee to criticize
the conduct of his superiors. *Id.,* at 573–574. In
fact, it appears that one of the primary purposes of
the Lloyd-La Follette Act was to protect such criticism
from official retribution. Senator La Follette gave the
following example of an abuse sought to be cured by the
bill:

> "The cause for [the employee's] dismissal was that
> he gave publicity to the insanitary conditions ex-
> isting in some part of the post-office building in Chi-
> cago where the clerks were required to perform their
> services. . . . [H]e furnished some facts to the press of
> Chicago, and the publication was made of the condi-
> tions. They were simply horrible . . . . The public
> health officers of Chicago, as soon as their attention
> was called to the conditions, condemned the situation
> as they found it; and yet this young man, one of
> the brightest fellows I have met, was removed from
> the service because, he had given publicity to these
> outrageous conditions." 48 Cong. Rec. 10731 (1912).

The "efficiency of the service" standard would appear to bring within its reach, as permissible grounds for dismissal, even truthful criticism of an agency that in any way tends to disrupt its operation. One can be sure, for example, that the young man's criticism in Senator La Follette's example disrupted the operation of the Chicago Post Office. It seems clear that the standard could be construed to punish such protected speech.

The majority purports to solve this potential overbreadth problem merely by announcing that the standard in the Act "excludes protected speech." Nonetheless, it leaves the statutory standard intact and offers no guidance other than general observation as to what conduct is or is not punishable.[31] The Court's answer is no answer at all. To accept this response is functionally to eliminate overbreadth from the First Amendment lexicon. No statute can reach and punish constitutionally protected speech. The majority has not given the statute a limiting construction but merely repeated the obvious.

The majority misunderstands the overbreadth principle which concerns the potential deterrent effect on constitutionally protected speech of a statute that is overbroad or vague on its face. The focus of the doctrine is not on the individual actor before the court but on others who may forgo protected activity rather than run afoul of the statute's proscriptions. Hence, the Court has reversed convictions where the subject speech could have been punished under a more narrowly drawn statute because the statute as drawn purported to cover, and

---

[31] The Administrative Conference Report reserved particularly harsh criticism for the "efficiency of the service" standard, terming it "deficient both as a guide to agency management and as a warning to employees of the sorts of behavior that will get them in trouble," warning that it is "an invitation to arbitrary action by government agencies." Merrill 1054; see *id.*, at 1053.

might deter others from engaging in, protected speech.
The Court explained this vagueness-overbreadth relationship in *Keyishian* v. *Board of Regents*, 385 U. S., at 603–
604:

> "We emphasize once again that '[p]recision of reg-
> ulation must be the touchstone in an area so closely
> touching our most precious freedoms,' *N. A. A. C. P.*
> v. *Button*, 371 U. S. 415, 438; '[f]or standards of per-
> missible statutory vagueness are strict in the area
> of free expression. . . . Because First Amend-
> ment freedoms need breathing space to survive, gov-
> ernment may regulate in the area only with narrow
> specificity.' *Id.*, at 432–433. . . . When one must
> guess what conduct or utterances may lose him his
> position, one necessarily will 'steer far wider of the
> unlawful zone . . . .' *Speiser* v. *Randall*, 357 U. S.
> 513, 526. For '[t]he threat of sanctions may de-
> ter . . . almost as potently as the actual application
> of sanctions.' *N. A. A. C. P.* v. *Button, supra*, at 433.
> The danger of that chilling effect upon the exercise
> of vital First Amendment rights must be guarded
> against by sensitive tools which clearly inform [pub-
> lic employees] what is being proscribed."

By the uncertainty of its scope, the standard here
creates the very danger of a chilling effect that concerned
the Court in *Keyishian*.[32] Employees are likely to limit

---

[32] Further refinement of the statutory "efficiency of the service"
standard, is not, as the majority implies, impossible. The Administrative Conference points out that the agencies and the Civil Service
Commission "have developed a large, still essentially secret body
of law on the meaning of 'efficiency.' " Merrill 1054. Reference
to this body of precedent might well serve as a basis for the amplification of the statutory standard. Relevant guidelines might, for
example, distinguish between statements made in an official as
opposed to a private capacity, see *Pickering* v. *Board of Education*,
391 U. S. 563 (1968); between knowingly false statements and those

their behavior to that which is unquestionably safe, for
"the threat of dismissal from public employment is . . . a
potent means of inhibiting speech." *Pickering*, 391 U. S.,
at 574. The dismissal standard hangs over their heads
like a sword of Damocles, threatening them with dismissal for any speech that might impair the "efficiency
of the service." That this Court will ultimately vindicate an employee if his speech is constitutionally protected is of little consequence—for the value of a sword
of Damocles is that it hangs—not that it drops. For
every employee who risks his job by testing the limits
of the statute, many more will choose the cautious path
and not speak at all.

The District Court found that "[b]ecause employees
faced with the standard of 'such cause as will promote
the efficiency of the service' can only guess as to what
utterances may cost them their jobs, there can be little
question that they will be deterred from exercising their
First Amendment rights to the fullest extent." I agree
with that characterization of the effect of the standard
and would, therefore, uphold the conclusion of the
District Court that the statute is unconstitutionally
vague and overbroad.

I respectfully dissent.

---

which are reasonably believed to be true, see, *e. g.*, *Pickering, supra,*
at 569; *New York Times Co.* v. *Sullivan*, 376 U. S. 254, 280 (1964);
cf. *Garrison* v. *Louisiana*, 379 U. S. 64 (1964); *Rosenbloom* v.
Metromedia, Inc., 403 U. S. 29 (1971); and between statements
which pertain to a legitimate subject of public comment and those
which disclose confidential Government information, see *Pickering,
supra*, at 570 n. 3 and 571–572; cf. *Time, Inc.* v. *Hill*, 385 U. S. 374
(1967).

The Academic Profession

An Arno Press Collection

Annan, Noel Gilroy. **Leslie Stephen:** His Thought and Character in Relation to His Time. 1952

Armytage, W. H. G. **Civic Universities:** Aspects of a British Tradition. 1955

Berdahl, Robert O. **British Universities and the State.** 1959

Bleuel, Hans Peter. **Deutschlands Bekenner** (German Men of Knowledge). 1968

Bowman, Claude Charleton. **The College Professor in America.** 1938

Busch, Alexander. **Die Geschichte des Privatdozenten** (History of Privat-Docentens). 1959

Caplow, Theodore and Reece J. McGee. **The Academic Marketplace.** 1958

Carnegie Foundation for the Advancement of Teaching. **The Financial Status of the Professor in America and in Germany.** 1908

Cattell, J. McKeen. **University Control.** 1913

Cheyney, Edward Potts. **History of the University of Pennsylvania:** 1740-1940. 1940

Elliott, Orrin Leslie. **Stanford University:** The First Twenty-Five Years. 1937

Ely, Richard T. **Ground Under Our Feet:** An Autobiography. 1938

Flach, Johannes. **Der Deutsche Professor der Gegenwart** (The German Professor Today). 1886

Hall, G. Stanley. **Life and Confessions of a Psychologist.** 1924

Hardy, G[odfrey] H[arold]. **Bertrand Russell & Trinity:** A College Controversy of the Last War. 1942

Kluge, Alexander. **Die Universitäts-Selbstverwaltung** (University Self-Government). 1958

Kotschnig, Walter M. **Unemployment in the Learned Professions.** 1937

Lazarsfeld, Paul F. and Wagner Thielens, Jr. **The Academic Mind:** Social Scientists in a Time of Crisis. 1958

McLaughlin, Mary Martin. **Intellectual Freedom and Its Limitations in the University of Paris in the Thirteenth and Fourteenth Centuries.** 1977

Metzger, Walter P., editor. **The American Concept of Academic Freedom in Formation:** A Collection of Essays and Reports. 1977

Metzger, Walter P., editor. **The Constitutional Status of Academic Freedom.** 1977

Metzger, Walter P., editor. **The Constitutional Status of Academic Tenure.** 1977

Metzger, Walter P., editor. **Professors on Guard:** The First AAUP Investigations. 1977

Metzger, Walter P., editor. **Reader on the Sociology of the Academic Profession.** 1977

Mims, Edwin. **History of Vanderbilt University.** 1946

Neumann, Franz L., et al. **The Cultural Migration:** The European Scholar in America. 1953

Nitsch, Wolfgang, et al. **Hochschule in der Demokratie** (The University in a Democracy). 1965

Pattison, Mark. **Suggestions on Academical Organization with Especial Reference to Oxford.** 1868

Pollard, Lucille Addison. **Women on College and University Faculties:** A Historical Survey and a Study of Their Present Academic Status. 1977

Proctor, Mortimer R. **The English University Novel.** 1957

Quincy, Josiah. **The History of Harvard University.** Two vols. 1840

Ross, Edward Alsworth. **Seventy Years of It:** An Autobiography. 1936

Rudy, S. Willis. **The College of the City of New York:** A History, 1847-1947. 1949

Slosson, Edwin E. **Great American Universities.** 1910

Smith, Goldwin. **A Plea for the Abolition of Tests in the University of Oxford.** 1864

Willey, Malcolm W. **Depression, Recovery and Higher Education:** A Report by Committee Y of the American Association of University Professors. 1937

Winstanley, D. A. **Early Victorian Cambridge.** 1940

Winstanley, D. A. **Later Victorian Cambridge.** 1947

Winstanley, D. A. **Unreformed Cambridge.** 1935

Yeomans, Henry Aaron. **Abbott Lawrence Lowell:** 1856-1943. 1948